THE COMPLETE
CHESAPEAKE BAY RETRIEVER

Probably the best-known Chesapeake picture ever taken. Ch. Sasnakra Sassy, CD, owned by Eloise Heller. "Sas" produced 2 Field Trial Champions and an Amateur Field Champion, sired by FC & AFC Nelgard's King Tut. — *Shafer*

The Complete
CHESAPEAKE BAY RETRIEVER

by ELOISE HELLER CHERRY

FIRST EDITION

HOWELL BOOK HOUSE

Howell Book House
Macmillan Publishing Company
866 Third Avenue, New York, NY 10022
Collier Macmillan Canada, Inc.

Library of Congress Cataloging in Publication Data

Cherry, Eloise Heller.
    The complete Chesapeake Bay retriever.

    Bibliography: p.288
    1. Chesapeake Bay retrievers. I. Title.
SF429.C4C47   636.7′52   80-25037
ISBN 0-87605-074-7

Macmillan books are available at special discounts for bulk purchases for sales promotions, premiums, fund-raising, or educational use. For details, contact:

                Special Sales Director
                Macmillan Publishing Company
                866 Third Avenue
                New York, NY 10022

10 9 8 7

Printed in the United States of America

Dedicated to
my husband Guy Cherry.
His infinite patience with me
while I worked on this book,
helped tremendously.

Chesapeake puppy
(8 weeks old). — *Carver*

Ch. Bernard retrieving at the famous Carroll's Island Gun Club. Painting by J. M. Tracy, in the late 1890s.

Contents

Foreword

By August Belmont

ELOISE CHERRY has been a highly successful breeder of Chesapeake Bay Retrievers for many years. She has finished Chesapeakes to dual championships, bench and field, and to Obedience titles. She has served as president of the American Chesapeake Club, and is the author of a number of reference books and pamphlets on the breed. No one is as ideally fitted to write the comprehensive work on this truly American breed — and she has done it here.

Chesapeakes are marvelous dogs. Like most of us, they have their extremely strong points, and like most of us they have their share of weak ones, too. And they come by both naturally.

Although the Chesapeake springs from the same origins as the Labrador, its evolvement has been through different paths.

The Labrador was developed in Great Britain by the landed gentry. He had to get along in large kennels, be mannered and easily controlled, and generally conform to the rather specialized grouse and pheasant drives developed to a high degree in that land.

Conversely, the Chesapeake was designed to prosper in a very different world. Although many early dogs of the breed belonged to land-owning American families, scores of Chesapeakes were the property of the lonely, professional market hunters along the Atlantic seaboard in the eighteenth and early nineteenth centuries. This dog's abode was no well ordered kennel. His nest was a pile of sacking outside his owner's shack on the marsh. Typically, he was a dog that didn't get to associate with other dogs, or with humans other than his owner. His primary job was to retrieve, in whatever fashion appealed to him, many tens—even hundreds—of waterfowl crippled and killed by the enormous "punt gun." His second job, perhaps no less important, was to guard his owner's hut and equipment during absences involved in marketing the game. There were no sheriffs or game wardens in those areas then, and the hunters were not above easing their lot by appropriating necessities from others.

9

August Belmont with AFC Bomarc of South Bay CD, whom he owned, trained and handled. Bomarc would only do his best work for "Augie".

It is easy to see how then, along with the desire and ability to retrieve preserved from his original ancestors, this dog became furnished with a thick, oily coat so necessary to protect him in his work and his rest. Also, the one-man nature, the protective attitude and the need to stay home and not wander, were all obvious necessities.

The efforts of today's fanciers to breed Chesapeakes which can fit into the average modern household—with a family of kids, next door neighbors, numbers of strangers coming into the house as guests, delivery men, meter readers, postmen and others—have been entirely successful with some dogs, partially so with others, and not at all with still others.

I like to remember a big woolly Chesapeake I used to know, who lived with a family boasting six children near the beach at a Long Island resort. "Gunner" was his name—not a too unusual one for a Chesapeake—and he would accompany the children on their daily visits to the town beach to play and swim in the surf. Gunner was everybody's friend, visiting and greeting all. When it was too rough to seem safe to him, he would herd the smaller children back to the beach. After some years, because of sanitary considerations, the Town Council issued an order banning all dogs from the beach during summer months. The whole community rose up in wrath and actually presented a petition to the powers that be, which resulted in a special dispensation exempting Gunner for the rest of his life. As a postscript to this story, I should add that one of the children, when he got into his late teens, went into the business of guiding duck and hunting parties. Gunner was one of the best advertisements he had, and successfully retrieved for the customers over a period of years.

I like to remember, too, my Bomarc of South Bay, my devoted and able friend, who achieved an Obedience degree, his bench championship, and his amateur field championship for me. Bo was reserved though friendly enough with others, but at every turn clearly showed his faith in me. He was high strung but afraid of almost nothing except going to the vet. In the end, I would have to go with him. In spite of having been quite demonstrative in his objection to the procedure in my absence, when I was there he would stand shaking but quiet while being treated. You can't be the recipient of that kind of love without returning it.

It is my hope that this book, through the broad distribution it is bound to have, and through the substance contained in it, will not only make new friends for the Chesapeake, but will be helpful to Chesapeake fanciers everywhere in their efforts to enhance the truly remarkable qualities of this fine animal and to select away from those qualities not fully compatible with modern society.

It is with progress in these directions that the popularity of the Chesapeake as a breed will continue to increase.

A charming sixteenth century Chinese painting of a puppy carrying pheasant feathers. — *Philadelphia Museum of Art*

Introduction

THERE IS no denying I am in love with Chesapeakes. I am, and have been since I met my first one at Walter Heller's duck club. Following the progress of those wavy, wiggly, little Chesapeake pups that look like lion cubs, is fascinating to me, and, I suppose it always will be.

I like Chesapeakes because they have good dispositions, as well as natural retrieving ability on land and water. They have keen noses, are birdy, and it is the exception who does not like to hunt. They have great courage and endurance, and a willingness to please. They are wonderful children's playmates, companions, and guardians.

This does not mean that I think they are perfect, for no man or dog can be that. They have their good points, and like the rest of us, their faults. But, in my estimation, their few breed faults are more than outweighed by their many virtues.

I consider their main fault their possessiveness. *Please* do not permit your dog to become too possessive. It will only be a nuisance to you in the long run.

Remember, also, that Chesapeakes are very personal dogs, and that they will never respond to a trainer as they do to their owner. Trainers often consider them stubborn, for they are hard to force to do something. But if you will *teach* your dog what you want, and he knows it will please you, he usually is quite cheerful about it.

There is no better hunting dog or, to my mind, no more devoted companion.

— ELOISE HELLER CHERRY

I WISH TO THANK the many friends who assisted with this book.

First of all, August Belmont, who wrote the Foreword. Mr. Belmont is not only an important figure in the Chesapeake field trial scene, as you will discover in the text of this book, but has served all dogdom strongly as a long-time member of the Board of Directors of the American Kennel Club. He has held office as Treasurer, and more recently as Chairman of the Board, of the AKC.

Then, the six ladies who were kind enough to contribute chapters:

Anne Rogers Clark, the well-known and well-liked judge, whose commentary on the standard is so interesting and valid. I know it will be appreciated by all serious Chesapeake owners and breeders.

Eve Keeler, who is an authority on Obedience training, has presented the newest ideas in starting puppies, as well as her methods of teaching formal Obedience.

Nancy Lowenthal, who, besides writing an extremely interesting chapter on character of the Chesapeake, lent me her father's helpful collection of memorabilia of the 1920s.

Ellen Loftsgaard, whose chapter on Showing Your Chesapeake is written with expertise. Ellen is a most knowledgeable professional handler.

Mildred Buchholz, who is nationally known for her success in Tracking, has prepared an excellent chapter on the subject.

Janet Horn, who describes the situation of Chesapeakes in European countries, is the acknowledged expert on this subject, and I am grateful for her fine report.

In addition to these guest authors, I am indebted to Charles Sambrailo, who lent me his splendid photo collection, and to Dorothy Carter, who copied many of these pictures for me.

Kathleen Miller, who is assembling a terrific book of all available Chesapeake pedigrees, was of inestimable assistance.

I frequently called on Elizabeth Humer and Lorraine Berg for help, which was cheerfully and quickly given.

Susan Cone and her husband, Christopher, were kind enough to take a series of good pictures that I felt were needed.

William Reid, the American Chesapeake Club trophy chairman, was most prompt and accommodating in making all his records available.

There are too many people to properly salute all. But I cannot overlook my secretary, Lynne Ingraham, who was most patient with me, and extremely conscientious about finding errors in the text.

And last, but not least, my daughter Jill, who proofread, again and again.

I am truly grateful to all.

Glossary of Terms and Abbreviations

AFC	Amateur Field Champion
AKC	The American Kennel Club, 51 Madison Avenue, New York, New York 10010.
CAFC	Canadian Amateur Field Champion
CD	Companion Dog—Obedience Title
CDX	Companion Dog Excellent—Obedience Title
CERF	The Canine Eye Registration Foundation, Inc. PO Box 15095, San Francisco CA 94114—a non-profit organization which issues a certificate to clear-eyed dogs, after examination by a veterinary ophthalmologist.
CFC or **Can. FC**	Canadian Field Champion
Ch.	Bench Show Champion
Dual Ch.	A dog who is both a bench and field champion
FC	Field Champion
OFA	The Orthopedic Foundation for Animals, 817 Virginia Avenue, Columbia, MO 65201. OFA has three veterinarians (each a radiologist, located in a different area of the country) examine the x-rays of a dog's hips. A consensus report is issued, and if it is favorable the owner will receive a numbered certificate attesting that the dog has sound hips.
OT Ch.	Obedience Trial Champion
TD	Tracking Dog
TDX	Tracking Dog Excellent
UD	Utility dog - the highest Obedience title
UDT	Utility and Tracking Dog.
WD	A title earned under the American Chesapeake Club regulations in which a dog retrieves game on both land and water.
WDX	Similar to WD except that the dog must be steady to shot and must retrieve doubles on land and water.

15

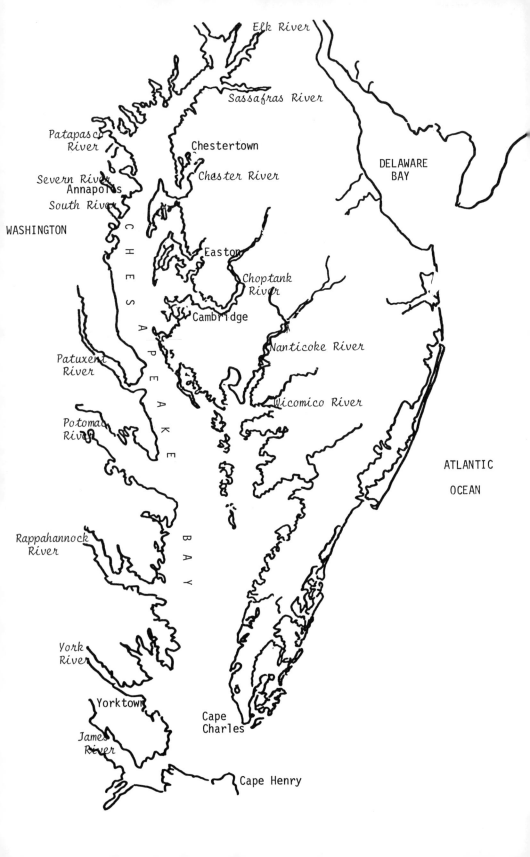

1

Origin and Early History

$\mathbf{F}$EW BREEDS, if any, have had as interesting a history as the Chesapeake Bay Retriever—one of the two sporting breeds (the other being the American Water Spaniel) born in America.

It all started in 1807 when an English Brig went aground on the Maryland shore. The passengers, crew, and two puppies were saved by the American ship, Canton.

George Law, a member of a well-known Maryland family, gives a first-hand account of this shipwreck in the following letter, written to J. S. Skinner and published in *The Dog and the Sportsman* in 1845. Law's letter has been widely quoted, but only recently did I see the entire letter which is printed here:

Baltimore, Maryland, Jan. 7, 1845.

My Dear Sir:

In the fall of 1807 I was on board of the ship Canton, belonging to my uncle, the late Hugh Thompson, of Baltimore, when we fell in, at sea, near the termination of a very equinoctial gale, with an English brig in a sinking condition, and took off the crew. The brig was loaded with cod-fish and was bound to Poole, in England, from Newfoundland.

I boarded her, in command of a boat from the Canton, which was sent to take off the English crew, the brig's own boats having all been swept away, and her crew in a state of intoxication.

I found on board of her two Newfoundland pups, male and female, which I saved, and subsequently on landing the English crew at Norfolk, our own destination being Baltimore, I purchased these two pups of the English captain for a guinea apiece. (Worth about five U.S dollars in those days.—*Author)*

Being bound again to sea, I gave the dog-pup, which was called Sailor, to Mr. John Mercer, of West River, and the slut pup, which was called Canton, to Dr. James Stewart, of Sparrows Point.

17

A Newfoundland. Indubitably, Newfoundlands were the main ancestors of Sailor and Canton, who were brought to this country in 1807.

Bluebelle, picture taken in the 1890s, showing the longer and thicker fur of the old Newfoundland type of early Chesapeakes.

Representations of Sailor and Canton (cast in iron in 1850) flank the doorway of the Koppers Company plant in Baltimore, Maryland. The owners of this business, Edward Bartlett, Dwight Mallory and Thomas Hayward, were all duck hunting enthusiasts.

The history which the English captain gave me of these pups was that the owner of his brig was extensively engaged in the Newfoundland trade, and had directed his correspondent to select and send him a pair of pups of the most approved Newfoundland breed, but of different families, and that the pair I purchased of him were selected under this order.

The dog was of a dingy red color, and the slut, black. They were not large. Their hair was short, but very thick-coated; they had dew-claws.

Both attained great reputation as water dogs. They were most sagacious in everything, particularly in all duties connected with duck shooting.

Governor Lloyd exchanged a merino ram for the dog, at the time of the merino fever, when such rams were selling for many hundred dollars, and took him over to his estate on the eastern shore of Maryland, where his progeny were well known for many years after, and may still be known there and on the western shore as the Sailor breed.

The slut remained at Sparrows Point till her death, and her progeny were and are still well-known through Patapsco Neck, on the Gunpowder, and up the bay, amongst the duck-shooters, as unsurpassed for their purposes.

I have heard both Dr. Stewart and Mr. Mercer relate most extraordinary instances of the sagacity and performance of both dog and slut, and would refer you to their friends for such particulars as I am unable at this distance of time to recollect with sufficient accuracy to repeat.

Yours, in haste,

GEORGE LAW

J. S. Skinner also gives us, in the same publication, John Mercer's own description of Sailor which tells us he was "of fine size and figure—lofty in his carriage, built for strength and activity, muscular and broad across the hips and chest, head large, muzzle rather longer than is common, coulour a dingy red with some white in the face and chest, coat short and smooth, but uncommonly thick, more like a coarse fur than hair, full tail with long hair—always carried high. His eyes were very peculiar; they were so very light as to have an almost uhnnatural appearance, something which is termed wall-eye in a horse. I saw that many of his descendants were marked with this peculiarity." Mr. Mercer also expressed the opinion that their light colored eye probably gave Chesapeakes their superior vision, as it does the eagle, owl, lion, and cat.

Mr. Mercer also gives a description of Canton about whom he says, she was "Not large, had short hair, very thick-coated and had dew claws." And he continues, "Were Dr. Stewart still alive he could relate many most extraordinary feats performed by Canton at Sparrows Point. Her patience and endurance of fatigue seemed almost incredible—and her performances with wounded swans—pursuing them in the water for miles. Also her extraordinary pursuits of wounded ducks, amongst rotten and floating ice, and sometimes in fog and darkness.'' Her progeny were well-known "Amongst the duck hunters as unsurpassed for their purposes.''

The unusual retrieving ability that both Sailor and Canton possessed was not surprising since Newfoundland dogs for generations had been bred for this quality. They were the working companions of the cod fisherman and were kept on their boats for retrieving fish which broke from their hooks when they came to the surface of the water. They were also used as shooting dogs and were expected to jump from considerable heights into cold, rough water, to retrieve fallen birds.

In addition, these intelligent Newfoundland dogs were taught to carry ropes in their mouths and swim to ships in distress; the ropes were given to the people aboard so that they could be pulled to shore. The dogs were then expected to swim back several times and get another, and yet another, rope. They often perished in their strenuous efforts.

Evidently these dogs had been the constant companions of the people of Newfoundland for untold centuries. Daniel Harmon's diary, kept from 1800 to 1819, tells us that the Indians of Newfoundland had "a large breed of dog, 60 to 100 pounds, that they used as a beast of burden. In the winter they drew sledges; in the summer they carried loads on their backs. They were well domesticated and they also hunted with them.''

Bones of dogs, dating back to 3000 B.C., have been found buried alongside their masters, the Maritime Indians of Newfoundland. We are also told that the Newfoundland dogs had the closest possible association with their Indian masters, and in addition to being beasts of burden were also co-hunters, guards, and trusted companions. These Indians had an almost reverent attitude towards their dogs, whom they felt were a gift of the Gods.

The American Indian word, *Chesepiook*, gave the Chesapeake Bay, as well as our dogs, the name. It is composed of three Indian Words:

Che, *meaning* Big
Sepi, *meaning* River
Ook, *meaning* Many

Because of its countless rivers and its many bays with hundreds of square miles of marshes. the Chesapeake Bay area had attracted, from time immemorial, tremendous populations of waterfowl. Ducks were there by the thousands, while geese came in the hundreds of thousands. It was said that their numbers darkened the sky.

Originally there were many Indian tribes that counted these waterfowl as a staple of their winter diet, and they hunted them by carving crude decoys of oak or pine, which they colored with herbs and roots. By placing the decoys near the shore they could lure the birds close enough to shoot them with their arrows. They also trapped them in nets.

The first English settlers came to Maryland in a square rigger in

1634. To the people of those early days the supply of wildlife seemed inexhaustible. There was no hunting season, nor was there any bag limit. And as waterfowling was the favorite sport, there was much rivalry among the gentlemen as to who had, and could produce, the best dogs. It was reported in 1739 that "the shooting of waterfowl is performed with a spaniel on the shores of the Chesapeake Bay."

The gentlemen landowners were intensely interested in all the livestock on their farms and worked to improve the strains of the dogs as well as of the farm animals. They were ruthless in discarding, for breeding purposes, any poor specimens.

The Chesapeakes of those days spent much time with their owners and the children of the family—in fact they were *part* of the family and highly valued.

On both the Eastern and Western shores of the Chesapeake Bay a very definite type of dog was developed. They might have varied in coat—curly like an Irish Water Spaniel, wavy like a Newfoundland, or straight like a Pointer or Hound—variances which came from the outcrosses made. Or they might have varied in their shade of brown, or in their height and weight. But their temperaments and great abilities were fixed and earned them the name—Chesapeakes.

They were bred for their superior courage, strength and endurance. They often made mile-long swims. And as ducks and geese were so plentiful, and there were no bag limits, they often brought in over 200 fowl in a single day. Their marking ability was phenomenal, and they did not forget the location of a duck, even if five or six were shot. They also knew, naturally, the importance of getting cripples first, and then going after the dead birds. They were, without doubt, a peerless water retrieving dog in snow, ice, and heavy seas, as cold water did not bother them.

Sailor and Canton became famous, but there is no record of their ever being bred to each other. At first they probably were bred to the Indian dogs. But as Maryland grew in population, and more white settlers came to the Cheapeske Bay area, they brought their dogs with them from England.

Water Spaniels were one of the crosses. Written word tells us that Columbus brought a pair of Spaniels with him when he first visited America. Later Ray B. Holland wrote, "They all looked alike, a small, curly-coated liver colored Spaniel that brought in ducks from lake and river. Small when compared with a Chesapeake, but a big solid dog alongside a Cocker."

Pointers, Setters, Flat-coats, and Irish Water Spaniels were some of the other outcrosses. General Latrobe, of the Carrolls Island Duck Club said he used "Yellow and Tan coon hounds, getting from them their great nose and stamina." Unfortunately, the Carrolls Island Duck Club house burned down so that their breeding records are forever lost.

Woodcut of early retrievers, when breeds were often mixed. Left, Water Spaniel-Setter cross. Right, Setter-Newfoundland cross. Rear dog, Water Spaniel-Newfoundland cross. — *Retriever International*.

The poor worker was discarded, and the unsound and weak broke down under the relentless work, so that only the sound and strong survived. Right from the start, the Chesapeake was subject to rigid selection, based on his efficiency.

Early Identifications of the Chesapeake

Since they were bred in such a wide area, at first many local names were given to Chesapeakes. The first written reference to any American retriever appeared in 1827 in *The American Shooting Manual* in an article written by a "Gentlemen from Philadelphia" who called what must have been a Chesapeake, THE NEWFOUNDLAND BREED OF DUCK DOG and who says, "The Newfoundland breed makes the best water dogs and will plunge into the most rapid stream, or break through ice in the coldest weather, to bring out the ducks."

THE CHESAPEAKE BAY DUCK DOG, or the Sailor strain, was developed on the Eastern shore and described as a large, reddish, long-haired dog, heavy headed and with many other Newfoundland characteristics.

THE BAY DUCK DOG was yet another name for them, these being bred to be more compact and smaller, bright red or sedge in color, lighter boned but with short hair.

THE GUNPOWDER RIVER DOG, or OTTER DOG, was bred on the Western shore of Chesapeake Bay by Dr. James Stewart and the sportsmen of that side. Stemming from Canton, this strain had a coarse heavy coat, closely resembling fur. The webbed paws and head were similar to those of an otter. The legend was often told of their imagined origin: a gyp, as a female was called in those days, was tied to a tree and left overnight near an otter den, and subsequently mated by an otter. Obviously this is nonsense, but it is a story widely believed in some areas.

THE RED WINCHESTER DUCKING DOG was another appellation, supposedly originating from crossing the Newfoundland with English Water Poodles. O. D. Foulks, who wrote for *The American Sportsman,* in the last quarter of the 19th century also called those dogs the BROWN WINCHESTER, or the RED CHESTER, and says, "He does not shiver like a setter, or raise and drop his fore-feet like a wet spaniel; the shaking he has given his wet, oily coat, has freed it entirely from ice and water; he cannot be enticed into a kennel, but must sit out on the frozen shore, rain or shine, and watch as well as the gunner.

"If one of the fallen birds chance to be only crippled, he swims past dead ones, keeping the wounded in sight; when it dives he swims to the spot, and there continues turning round and round, now and then throwing himself high in the water, especially if the waves are heavy. If the duck falls too far out for the dog to see, he takes his direction from the motion of the hand."

Foulks also describes the Winchester as "a low, heavy set, densely coated dog, of a dark reddish brown color on the back, shading lighter on the sides, and running into a very light yellow or white on the belly and inside of the legs; the throat and breast are also frequently marked with white."

In character, this dog was "kind and gentle, a child can handle him; his heart knows no fear; he will stand to the death in defense of his master's person and property; on the bleakest shore, the coldest night, if a coat or gun or other property is accidentally left, he will faithfully guard it."

Chesapeakes were shown in a bench show for the first time in Baltimore in 1876, under the classification of CHESAPEAKE BAY DUCK DOGS. There were two strains competing—quite unlike each other. The gentlemen present decided to have a meeting to discuss the possibility of improving the breed, as well as to standardize the names of the types. It was decided three classifications were acceptable: the otter dog (by Mr. Stewart's Sailor strain); the straight-haired dog; and the curly haired dog.

The First Standard

The formation of the Baltimore Chesapeake Bay Dog Club in the last part of the nineteenth century also helped to develop uniformity of type. Three of its members—James F. Pearson, Isaac T. Norris and H. Malcolm—drew up the first real standard of the breed. It was quite comprehensive and exceedingly well done, and was adopted by the Club on April 17, 1890.

In 1878 the first American Kennel Club registration of a Chesapeake was recorded—"Sunday", a male, bred by O. D. Foulks, and owned by G. W. Kierstead of La Porte, Indiana.

"By 1885, a very definite type of dog had developed and this type was known far and wide for the prowess it exhibited in the rough cold waters of the Chesapeake Bay." This observation is from the very first book on Chesapeakes, a paperback published in 1935 by Anthony Bliss. He continues: "There were several differences between this dog and the present-day type, the most noteworthy being the fact that the breed could be found in one color only—dark brown, shading into a sort of reddish sedge. The dead-grass color was unknown. The head was inclined to be of a more wedge-shaped type, and the coats were longer and thicker than the best that can be found today."

The watermen of Chesapeake Bay have sometimes erroneously been given the credit for developing the Chesapeake breed. These watermen

Earl Henry and one of his first dogs, from a cut printed in the *New York Herald Tribune* in 1914.

Anthony Bliss and his Dual Ch. Sodak's Gypsy Prince, whose name can be found in all the best pedigrees of early and modern field trial dogs.

were described by an early American Chesapeake Club president as, "A rugged lot, and most of them were market hunters from the time the flights arrived in the fall until early spring. In fact, almost everyone who lived along the coast gunned either for market or the pot. These gunners found a perfect retriever was almost as important as their gun and ammunition, for ammunition was mostly hand loaded and hard to come by, and the retriever saved ammunition and increased the bag."

The long hours on the bays and waterfronts required a dog of great stamina and courage. Also, when the big guns were developed in the last decade of the nineteenth century, it was necessary to have a super dog to gather up the dozens of birds killed by one shot into a raft of hundreds of birds that were sleeping.

The watermen were too busy making their living shooting in the fall and spring, and gathering oysters and soft-shelled crabs in the summer, to spend much time ashore. They were not well situated financially and could not afford to raise litters of pups. Nor did they have the knowledge of pedigrees and planned breedings necessary to develop a good line of dogs. It was the gentlemen farmers and the sportsmen who accomplished this goal.

Jay F. Towner of the Bush River area, at Locust Grove, Maryland, bred Chesapeakes from 1860 to 1904 and his records are still intact. Mr. Towner advertised and his brochure was sent to hunters all over the United States. It stated, "I guarantee every pup I sell to be delivered in good order. I also guarantee every pup to make a good retriever if properly trained, or party can kill him, send me the certificate of his death, and I will send another pup free, as I do not want anyone to own a worthless pup from my kennel."

Many famous Chesapeake lines were developed in the late 1880s and were well-known throughout the country: the aforementioned Carrolls Island Gun Club strain; the great dogs of Earl Henry, who was the founder of the Western Chesapeake; and the early dogs of the Chesacroft Kennels of Baltimore, Maryland.

The Chesacroft Kennels belonged to the Hurst family, whose ducking shore was located where the Bush and Gunpowder rivers entered the Chesapeake Bay, at a place known as Legos Point. The first brochure printed by the Hursts advertised their dogs as coming from "Maryland — the original Home of the Chesapeake."

Chesapeakes had also been imported to Canada, and David Rankin of Saskatchewan tells us that records indicate that many Chesapeakes were used in Canada before the railroads were completed in 1885.

The apparently inexhaustible supply of wildfowl started to diminish everywhere in the early 1900s, so that the demand for shooting dogs grew less. There still were countless privately owned Chesapeake hunting and family dogs around the Chesapeake Bay. Many of these owners, including the watermen, did not bother to register them. Unfortunately, in this locality, this is also true today.

Earl Henry of Albert Lea, Minnesota, claimed to have started breeding Chesapeakes in 1888. By 1901, he had developed his own dead-grass strain. He was deeply concerned with the welfare of the breed and was such a colorful figure that in 1906 he was dubbed the "Chesapeake King", a title he readily accepted.

It was Earl Henry who, in 1918, organized the present American Chesapeake Club, with a beginning membership of only 14. The purpose of the Club was to improve the breed, to make it more uniform, and especially to emphasize the working ability of the dogs.

A new standard was drawn up by W. H. Orr, Earl Henry and F. E. Richmond. This was submitted to over fifty breeders in the United States and Canada, and approved by them. On August 14, 1918 this standard was officially adopted by the American Chesapeake Club. It was sent on to the American Kennel Club, who approved it and, also at this time accepted the American Chesapeake Club as a member.

Other early Midwestern breeders were Barron and Orr, of Mason City, Iowa, and Father Joseph Schuster of Onaka, South Dakota, who registered his dogs with the prefix of Sioux Mission.

One of the earliest West Coast breeders was William Wallace Dougall of San Francisco. He started with two good bitches, Jane Cowl, whom he purchased in Oregon, and Puff O' Smoke, whom he bought in 1920 from Barron and Orr. Both made their bench championships. Dougall's kennel was called Berteleda, and being an enthusiastic hunter, he specialized in fine gun dogs. As early as 1923, his ads constantly appeared in the sporting sections of the San Francisco newspapers.

Writing of this era, Anthony Bliss noted:

"Shortly before World War I the Chesapeake began to take a great hold in the Middle West and here the dead-grass color was developed, a development which has been a source of much argument and misunderstanding. Whether the addition of the lighter colored coat really benefited the breed and made it suitable for a wider variety of conditions is a debatable point. But certainly it is acknowledged that the coats of the Chesapeake suffered in this innovation. At the same time, the size of the dog was decreased to cover the needs of shooting conditions in the Midwest. Meantime, the East, while not tampering with color, did seem to increase the size of its dog."

A very well done booklet on the breed was put out in 1926 by the American Chesapeake Club. The advertising shows the geographical distribution of our dogs. Four breeders from Iowa took ads: M. S. Barron of Barron and Orr; Goodspeed Kennels; Harry Carney; and D. W. Dawson. From South Dakota there were ads from J. L. Schmidt and

One of Earl Henry's earliest dogs. Picture taken in 1875.

Earl Henry's famous Mose.

Chestmere Babe, one of Earl Henry's greatest brood bitches.

Two early Chesapeakes owned by Charles Berg. Headstudy above, is of Bud Parker's Prince. At right, Lake Como Sprig.

Charles Morgan. Earl Henry and the Land O' Lakes Kennels of Albert Lea, Minnesota, each took a page, as did the Clift Farm of Nebraska and Dr. J. Johnson of the state of Washington. Two Canadian ads appeared — those of L. Caldecott of Steveston, British Columbia and Harry Felt of Findlater of Saskatchewan.

Some of the advertisements are most amusing. Harry Felt's ad reads:

> Why not purchase your young stock from the north country where game is plentiful and where puppies are taught to retrieve early, when they should be? Every puppy shipped by me is guaranteed to retrieve from land and water upon receipt. I have had 25 years experience with the breed, and know what the intender purchaser reasonably expects—young stock ready for business. Every one guaranteed a gilt-edge specimen. Correct color, and registered, of course. I cater especially to the skeptical purchaser. Price of males and females exactly the same—$50, here.

Goodspeed's Kennels of Waverly, Iowa, claimed they were the breeders of "Standard Bred, Otter Coated, Chesapeake Bay Retrievers." One breeder proudly said his stud dog "Never lost a fight or a duck."

Shipping puppies, or even grown dogs, presented a real problem in those days as there was no preventive distemper serum or distemper shots. Puppies were purposely exposed to distemper, naturally with a high loss. If they survived to the age of five months, they were thought to have overcome the disease. Also, shipping by rail with a train ride of several days was very hazardous for young puppies. Even if food and water were sent along with them, the breeder could not be sure that the baggage car attendant would give it to them.

1930 to 1940

A new era dawned when the American Chesapeake Club's headquarters were moved East in 1934, with the election of young Tony Bliss as president. He was enthusiastic and innovative and he stimulated great activity among the Chesapeake owners. He encouraged attendance at the bench shows and field trials and obtained excellent publicity for the breed.

In the East, many new kennels were started:

The *Native Shore Kennels*, belonging to Mrs. Royce R. Spring, was established in the early 1930s near Easton, Maryland.

Dilwyne was the name of Robert Carpenter's place in Montchanin, Delaware, and Dilwyne dogs were prominent in field trials and on the bench.

Marvadel Kennels, belonging to J. Gould Remick, who had both Labradors and Chesapeakes, was located near Easton, Maryland.

Chesdel Kennels was started in 1935 by Alex Spear, who was interested principally in field trials. He remembers that, "In those days Chesapeakes were so popular that on Sunday mornings we would have 25 lined up in a field near Dover, each taking his or her turn to retrieve." Alex Spear is still a very active breeder.

Chesacroft Kennels carried on. Due to the war the government had taken over their original farm and the kennels was relocated in Lutherville, 17 miles from Baltimore, Maryland. They claimed "All our dogs are registered in both the American Kennel Club and the Field Dog stud book. We are very particular about this, as it protects both ourselves and our customers. In order to improve the breed we have adopted two all-important policies. The first is that we never permit our stud dogs to be bred to any bitch without papers, nor to one of poor type or bad bloodlines. Thus we elevate the breed by judicious selection. Secondly, the dogs of true type and bloodlines which we keep in the kennels for breeding must be first trained before we permit them to be used as breeding stock, thus keeping the full hunting qualities while improving the show points." The Chesacroft name is still carried on by Anthony A. Bliss.

In the Midwest, *Cocoa King Kennels* was established in the early '30s by Ferdinand Bunte at his Springcrest Farm at Genoa City, Wisconsin, in the heart of great hunting country. Mr. Bunte himself was an inveterate hunter and both he and Arthur Storz followed the ducks from the early fall opening of the Canadian season, through the American season, and later down on into Mexico—almost half a year of hunting! Bunte wrote, "I have shot over just about every type of gun dog in North America, Central America, and the Philippines, but the Chesapeake is the best all-round retriever a sportsman can have. His prowess is by no means limited to the water. For, as a non-slip retriever of upland game, he is exceptionally intelligent, endowed with an excellent nose, and is so persevering that a lost bird is a rarity. His stamina serves him well and it is no novelty to find a Chessy still tireless at the end of a tough shoot!"

He continues, "One of my first outstanding Chesapeake dogs was Cocoa King, a big 90 pound duck dog, a sturdy hunter and a staunch pal, whose bloodlines are preserved in my Cocoa King Kennels, where his descendants carry on his superior heritage." Cocoa King was followed by Champion The Second Cocoa, whom sportman and author William J. Brown described as among the "Retriever Immortals." Charles Morgan trained and successfully ran The Second Cocoa in field trials, and Cocoa also had a great record on the bench. He produced husky, robust pups with great natural ability. Cocoa King Kennels is no longer active.

Ducklore was the name of Arthur Storz's outstanding kennel which also specialized in producing a super hunting strain. Storz had a hunting lodge in Nebraska by the name of Ducklore, where his dogs were kept.

He was an excellent amateur chef, and his feasts of wild game, which he cooked for his guests, were an annual treat to which many of the country's celebrities looked forward each year. Ducklore has discontinued breeding dogs.

In the West, *Grizzley Island Kennels*, belonging to Louis Traung, was kept on the Suisun marshes near San Francisco, and became very well-known. Grizzley Island advertised that they "combined the finest Champion Field Trial and Bench show lines. Our kennel is headed by Champion Nippy Bob, a beautiful specimen who has a fine nature. His mate is Champion Dotty, who is also affectionate and easy to handle. Their pedigrees contain 21 Champions of Record." Louis Traung purchased a great many dogs, and bred extensively. He has since passed away and the kennel no longer exists, but even today, in Northern California, his bloodlines are in most of the shooting dog pedigrees.

Bench championships in the breed were scarce in the decade 1930 to 1940, as only 47 Chesapeakes made their titles. Of these, eight were owned by Anthony Bliss, who had in 1932 purchased the Chesacroft Kennels and moved them to his residence at Westbury, Long Island, New York. Five championships belonged to R. R. M. Carpenter, four to Phillip Dater, and two each to Mrs. Royce Spring and Charles Berg.

Forty-seven bench championships may seem a small number, but we must remember that a Chesapeake is not primarily a pretty and stylish dog. He is a working dog, still able to do that for which he was originally bred. Lorraine Berg, says, "Many of the sporting breeds have been allowed to split into two lines, one for show and one for the field. This, fortunately, has not happened to the Chesapeake. The breeders and fanciers, even of the early days, were careful to preserve the breed's integrity and to produce animals that not only looked like Chesapeakes, but were also able to do the work originally intended for Chesapeakes. We hope our breed will never have to suffer the insult of divergent lines."

Obedience, as officially recognized by the American Kennel Club, got its start in America in June, 1936. The first two Chesapeakes to attain the Companion Dog title were: Bay Rum (in 1937), owned by Allein Owens, Jr. and Daybreak (in 1938), owned by Mrs. Owens.

The first AKC-licensed field trial for retrievers in this country was held by the Labrador Club on December 31, 1931—for Labradors only. The American Chesapeake Club put on their first trial November 27, 1932, which was a Specialty Trial—for Chesapeakes only. The club continued the event every year until 1941, when the war interfered. In the early retriever trials only Labradors, Curly Coats, Irish Water Spaniels and Chesapeakes competed, and the Chesapeakes more than held their own. It was not until 1938 that a Golden Retriever placed.

Skipper Bob, the first Chesapeake Field Trial Champion. Bob was whelped March 12, 1931.

King of Montauk, owned by J. C. Hadder of East Hampton, N. Y. Winner of the All-Age Stake at the first Chesapeake retriever trial.

Trials became more and more popular, and by 1940 the number per year had increased to 17, including a few being held in the Midwest.

1940 to 1950

The 1940s were not good for our breed due to World War II. However, several new kennels sprang up.

In the East Eugene Weems showed his first dog, Native Shore Brandt, to a championship in 1943. In 1947 he made this title with his Wings. Although Mr. Weems did not maintain a kennel, he was very active in the American Chesapeake Club and in breed activities and he was greatly respected by all. He passed away in 1978.

In the Midwest, *Mount Joy Kennels*, owned by Robert and Jessie Brown of Davenport, Iowa, started in the early 1940s. A picture of their installation appears in this book. At first they produced show dogs, but in the 1950s Bob became interested in field trials and had the famous Charles Morgan train Bob's Field Champion and Amateur Field Champion Nelgard's King Tut. A large dead-grass male, Tut was a good marker and willing to handle, although not too stylish, and a little distrustful of people. Tut's son, Chuck's Rip Joy, had an excellent potential. He was sold to Ralph Mock of Dayton, Ohio, who had little time to train. Consequently, Rip Joy made his Amateur Field Championship, but never his Open. Bob Brown died in the late 1950s, and in 1960 the Mount Joy name was acquired from his estate, by Helen and Ed Fleischmann. Both the Fleischmanns are now dead and the Mount Joy name is inactive.

Wisconong Kennels, registered in 1947 by William Hoard of Fort Atkinson, Wisconsin, is a kennel name that often appears in field trial pedigrees. Actually Wisconong is a combination of two Indian names—Wisconsin and Koshkonong, the big lake where Bill often hunted. Mary Hoard tells us that Bill got his first Chesapeake in 1946, because he wanted a dog to use in the freezing waters of Canada. He was so pleased with this dog that he arranged to buy Deerwood Trigger from Phil Gagnon. Trigger, also, was sent to Charles Morgan, the foremost trainer of his day. Trigger suited Bill perfectly, and Bill made him both an Amateur and Open Field Trial Champion.

The Wisconong dogs were vibrant, very light, dead-grass color and were quite handsome. As bench shows bored Bill, his dogs were seldom shown. But all of Trigger's get were excellent shooting dogs and were famous throughout Wisconsin. Trigger's pup, Wisconong Jodri, owned and trained by Mrs. W. H. Drisko, became a bench champion and was, as well, the first Chesapeake to make the Utility title in 1954. William Hoard's kennels were discontinued with his death.

Deerwood was the kennel name of Phillip Gagnon of Robbinsdale, Minnesota, who bred some outstanding dogs. His bitch, Field Champion and Amateur Field Champion Raindrop of Deerwood, whom he bred and trained himself, was an exceptional performer, with a fine point-record. Deerwood Kennels have been inactive since Phillip Gagnon died.

Kamiakin was one of our first Northwestern kennel names, used by D. R. Iorns of Seattle, Washington. He bred and showed Parker's Airline Peggy to her bench championship in 1940. Peggy was an unusually handsome female, tracing back to the Chesacroft line. In the late '40s, Russ Iorns became active in West Coast field trials. One of the best field trial dogs I have ever seen, of any breed, was his Duke of Kamiakin, who was handsome, fast, stylish and a peerless marker. The Kamiakin name was abandoned when Mr. Iorns died.

Fifty-three bench championships were made by Chesapeakes in the years 1940 to 1950, 45 of them by Eastern dogs. The decade started well but then the war came along and put many breeders out of business. It was 1948 before shows got back to normal. The leading exhibitors in this period were Mrs. Royce Spring, Mrs. Allein Owens, Jr., and Eugene Weems in the East, Mount Joy Kennels and Ferdinand Bunte in the Midwest, and D. R. Iorns and Louis Traung in the West.

Obedience exhibitors were scarce in the years 1940 to 1950. Only 17 Chesapeakes made their Companion Dog title, and only three their Companion Dog Excellent. The majority of their owners lived in the East. Midwestern fanciers were not active and practically no Chesapeakes were shown in Obedience in the Far West. When I competed with my Grizzley in San Francisco in 1945 , and made CD, the comments I received were extremely annoying. People just didn't realize that a Chesapeake could be handled by a woman—because they thought that the breed was so tough! Ridiculous!

Interest in running field trials seemed to lag, to the point where after the Chesapeake Specialty Field Trial of 1941 this event was discontinued until 1950. There were probably several reasons for this. Until the 1940s, most of the field trial Chesapeake owners had been located in the East at Long Island and Maryland. Most of these men had become too old to participate any longer, and after the war years had not resumed their breeding programs, or any dog activities. Also, Labradors had become the stylish and popular breed to run in trials, and many of the new, young field trial handlers purchased a Labrador. In Maryland, Chesapeakes continued to be the leading retriever, but few Maryland owners attended field trials.

From 1940 to 1950, only five Field Championships were attained with Chesapeakes: E. K. Ward with Sodak Rip; E. Monroe Osborne with Guess of Shagwong; R. N. Crawford with Chesacroft Baron; Vance

Ch. Bud Parker's Ripple, an outstanding bench show Chesapeake of the 1930s, owned by Anthony Bliss.

Ch. Water Devil, owned by R. R. M. Carpenter. This dog had a great bench show record.

Ch. Chesacroft Newt. owned by Anthony Bliss. Newt was one of the leading show winners of 1935-36.

Morris and his Bayle; and Dr. George Gardner with the snappy little female, Tiger of Clipper City. All of these competed in the National Championship Stakes which started in 1942.

Despite the fact that Club activities were nil in the period, and that very few dogs were shown on the bench or in Obedience, or entered in field trials, American Kennel Club registrations increased each year. In 1938 there were only 178 Chesapeake individual registrations. By 1945, the total had risen to 427, and in 1950 there were 543. Chesapeakes had "caught on" and were here to stay.

There was, and always will be, a loyal and dedicated group of Chesapeake owners. For, without a doubt, the Chesapeake is an all-round dog. They are both playmates and guardians for children. They protect family property. They have intense personalities, and each is an individual. They seem to have an inherent sense of self-respect. Although very affectionate, they do not fawn on you; often they are a little standoffish with strangers. They are extremely intelligent, and seem to be able to reason things out for themselves in everyday life, as well as in the hunting field. Almost all of their owners feel that they possess many wonderful qualities not easily found in other breeds. For many of us, there is no other dog.

Judge Henry and Chief Justice, a handsome pair owned a long time ago by Anna Frank of Madison, New Jersey.

2

The Modern Chesapeake

W E SHALL, for practical purposes, consider the modern Chesapeakes to be the dogs that were prominent and important from 1950 until the present. For we know that time diminishes the importance of both breeders and bloodlines, especially if the bloodlines have not been kept up and there are no direct descendants that can be used for breeding today.

When, in 1951, William Hoard, Jr., became the president of the American Chesapeake Club, his boundless energy and skillful leadership resulted in a great stimulus for the breed. He carried on an extensive correspondence with almost all of the good Chesapeake kennels and he encouraged their owners to try to better their breeding programs. An avid hunter himself, Hoard really understood the attributes that were important in a good shooting dog. He also tried to encourage new owners to participate in field trials, where the qualities of *super* shooting dogs are demonstrated. Here Chesapeakes compete against the Labradors and Goldens, and generally give a good account of themselves.

Of course, the good hunting dogs really are the backbone of our breed, even though the vast majority of them never compete in any organized activity. They are family dogs, whose big moment comes in the fall when the birds begin to fly. The public never sees them, except at home, or at duck clubs, or on the marshes and prairies, where they are used for upland game—pheasant, quail, sagehen, or dove.

I am quite familiar with breed history from the 1950s on, as it was about this time that I owned my first Chesapeakes, and began to hunt over them instead of the Pointers and German Shorthaired Pointers which had previously been my shooting dogs. I also began to show a few Chesapeakes on the bench, compete with them in Obedience, and bring

The good-looking George Carmoney family, with their litter of equally good-looking pups. Mr. Carmoney owned and ran Native Shore Pink Lady in field trials of the early days.

The Mount Joy kennels in the 1940s, then owned by Robert Brown of Davenport, Iowa.

some pups to the early West Coast field trials. And as I traveled a great deal, I also was able to see many bench shows and field trials in many different areas, and to become acquainted with quite a few exhibitors of that time.

In this chapter, I have aimed at providing a decade-by-decade overall survey of the years since 1950. A more detailed report of the individual dogs, with their records, is to be found in the separate chapters devoted to each phase of Chesapeake activity: Bench, Field Trials, Obedience and Tracking.

1950 to 1960

The number of Chesapeake owners who entered into American Kennel Club activities increased tremendously in all parts of the country during the years 1950 to 1960. In bench competition, 76 champions were made and they were geographically well distributed. In Obedience, 56 Companion Dog, 14 Companion Dog Excellent and 3 Utility Dog titles were won—again by owners distributed throughout the United States. In the field, 11 Amateur Field championships and 5 Field Trial championships were awarded.

In the East, the now famous *Eastern Waters'* Kennels, owned by Dan and Janet Horn, became established. Janet tells us that her first Chesapeake was Glorianna the Second, whose CD title was won in 1949. Tempest of Eastern Waters became a bench champion in 1951, first of three bench champions finished by the Horns in the decade.

Chesachobee Kennels was started in 1954 by Mildred Buchholz of Florida. Her best known dog of this time was Ch. Eastern Waters' Nugget, with whom she made the CD, CDX and UD titles. Quite a feat for a first dog! Altogether, "Millie"was knowledgeable, competent, a hard worker—and her dogs enjoyed a fine reputation. Nugget was the first of the long line of Chesachobee Chesapeake champions and Obedience and Tracking title-holders.

Lake Como Kennels, owned by Phillip Berg of Philadelphia, started to show in 1955, making its first championships with Lake Como's Donald Jay and Lake Como's Lady Mallard.

Eugene Weems in 1956 made a champion of his Wing's Drake, and in 1957 of West River Ripple.

Chesdel Kennels continued to produce fine field trial dogs. Alex Spear's dogs of the early years were Chesdel Joe, who ran in the Chesapeake Club Specialty of 1938, taking first in the novice class and Judges' Award of Merit in the Open. In 1950 his Chesdel Texas took first in sanctioned trials and places in the licensed trials. Chesdel Potlatch Charley was on the national Derby list, while his Chesdel's Bebe of Kennett and Potlatch Sandy both placed in licensed Derby stakes.

Chesarab Kennels, belonging to the Richard DiVaccaros of New Jersey, was started in 1957 and they are still showing today. Their best known dog of the period was Ch. Chesarab's Little Acorn.

In the Midwest, Ferdinand Bunte's *Cocoa King Kennels* in Illinois established an exceptionally good line of hunting dogs, as well as some fine bench champions. All of his dogs stemmed from Ch. Cocoa King and Ch. The Second Cocoa.

Mock's Kennels of Dayton, Ohio, was established by Ralph Mock who secured his foundation stock from Mr. Bunte. Seven of Mock's dogs made their bench championships in the decade, tops for the period, but he really specialized in a good shooting dog strain.

Alpine Kennels, belonging to Fred Woodall of Tinley, Illinois, started in 1956 and produced very large hunting dogs. Several of their breeding did well on the bench, particularly their Ch. Alpine's Big Butch, a handsome 90-pound specimen, who also won his share of field trial ribbons.

In the West, *Tesque Kennels,* belonging to Winnabelle Beasley of Sante Fe, New Mexico, was started in 1945 with the purchase of her first dogs from Mrs. A. W. Owens of Maryland. Mrs. Beasley has sent many of her dogs to France and to Mexico. She writes: "I never advertise and still sell for $150. because we need more people to own and know the value of a Chesapeake. I now breed a fine, big, tall, dark brown bitch to Margi Willis' champion stud."

Chesnoma's Kennels, belonging to the E. C. Fleischmanns of Sebastapol, California, bred quite a few dogs, mainly for hunters. In 1955, they started showing on the bench, making a bench champion of their Bayberry Pete, and then of Mount Joy's Mallard in 1957. Both of these dogs were also good field trial contenders.

Heller's Kennels, kept at the Irvington, California duck club of my late husband, Walter Heller, had registered litters as early as 1923. Walter concentrated on producing good gundogs, most of whom were given to his hunting pals. When I married him, I started showing some of these duck dogs and made three bench championships with them in the mid-50s. Although Walter did not own him, Buddy Brown was the foundation sire of this strain.

Jack Clifford of Boise, Idaho, was at that time practically the only Chesapeake bench exhibitor in that state. His Nelgard's Riptide was an excellent specimen and quickly won his bench championship. Riptide was a full brother to my Nelgard's Baron, and was as handsome as Baron was ugly.

Of the 56 Companion Dog titles made in the years 1950 to 1960, 5 were made by the Eugene Pantzers, 5 by Mrs. W.H. Drisko, 4 by the Horns, 3 by Millie Buchholz and 2 by myself. The other 37 all had different owners.

The lovely painting by W. Crowe of the Second Moko.

Ch. The Second Cocoa, owned by Ferdinand Bunte, one of the best known dogs of his era. He participated in field trials, won consistently on the bench and was a super hunting dog.

In 1954, Mrs. Drisko made the breed's first Utility title with her Ch. Wisconong Jodri. Only two more dogs were able to pass these difficult exercises during the decade: Ch. Jodri's Catamaran, owned by Mrs. Carl Underwood, and Mildred Buchholz's Ch. Eastern Waters' Nugget.

The first Tracking title in the breed was acquired by Ch. Wisconong Jodri in 1955. In 1958 and 1959, Eugene and Mary Pantzer passed with three of their Tengri line, and in 1959 Bernadette Foster's Wings Tertius accomplished it.

The field trial situation in the East was not a happy one in the period. No field trial championships were made by an Eastern Chesapeake from 1946 to 1970—a long, dry stretch of time.

As already observed, many of the Eastern gentlemen who had run their Chesapeakes in the trials did not resume after the war. Perhaps they were becoming too old, or their dogs were, or both. Labradors had become the stylish dogs to own. Furthermore, the Labradors and Goldens of that day were trained and almost always handled by the professionals. Chesapeakes just do not do as well in any professional situation—true then and true now.

Vincent O'Shea of Long Island made an AFC with his Gypsy, who was sired by the great Buddy Brown. No other Eastern dog was to do this for 13 years, the next being Bomarc of South Bay, owned by August Belmont.

But though we lost ground in the East, a tremendous new interest in Midwestern and Western field trials was shown from 1950 to 1960, as 8 Chesapeakes made their Field Championships, and 12 their Amateur Field Championships. We have not done that well in any decade since.

In the Midwest, five dogs did very well: William Hoard with his FC & AFC Deerwood Trigger, and Robert Brown with his FC & AFC Nelgard's King Tut did well in the trials. There was a tremendous amount of friendly rivalry between these two men, each of whom usually ran his own dogs, although both dogs were trained by the famous Charlie Morgan.

Phil Gagnon trained and owned FC & AFC Raindrop of Deerwood, who was fast and stylish, as well as being an excellent performer.

Ralph Mock's handsome Ch. Chuck's Rip Joy, also trained by Charlie Morgan, made his Amateur Field Championship in 1955. Mock gave a party that won't be forgotten.

Star King of Mount Joy, a full brother to Chuck's Rip Joy and to Mallard, was trained by owner Harold Johnson, who made King's Amateur Field Championship in 1958.

Zippy little dead-grass Rip, owned and trained by Frank Holliday, was the fifth Midwest dog to make his Amateur Field Championship in 1957.

Robert Brown, of Davenport, Iowa, with AFC Chuck's Rip Joy on his right and AFC King Tut on his left. Both were well-known early field trial contestants.

FC & AFC Star King of Mount Joy, with his owner-trainer-handler Harold Johnson of Nebraska.

William Hoard of Wisconsin, with his FC & AFC Deerwood Trigger, a serious competitor in the field trials of the 1950s.

The famous Meg's Pattie O'Rourke, flashy little female, pictured with Dr. F. A. Dashnaw. "Missy" was the National Derby Champion of 1958, with a record never equaled.

In the Far West, we had a new and dedicated group of handlers. Among these was L. P. (Pat) Montgomery, a professional from Klamath Falls, Oregon. Pat made his female Montgomery Sal, a Field champion in 1952. Sal was a fabulous triple marker, and the crowd often turned out to watch her scoop up all three birds, when many previous dogs had failed.

The first Western Amateur Field Championship was made by Sal's son, Odessa Creek Spunky, owned and handled by Sandy MacKay of Newport Beach, California.

Four more Western Field Championships were quickly made. In 1956 the E. C. Fleischmanns succeeded with their Mount Joy's Mallard, who had been given them by Bob Brown. Mallard was a large, dark, dead-grass dog. Rex Carr trained him, and he ran the long diagonal "Carr" line on blind retrieves. He also was an excellent triple marker. Originally, both Helen and Ed took turns running him, but due to a serious hip operation, Ed was unable to continue his handling.

Dr. John Lundy of Boise, Idaho, owned and trained his excellent Atom Bob, and made Bob's Amateur Field Championship in 1957. Dr. Lundy has been an important influence in the field trial world. He is an excellent field trial judge, popular throughout the country. He was an avid hunter and was able to interest many of his hunting friends in becoming active in field trials. These included Winston Moore, Dr. Miles Thomas, Dr. Jack Clifford, Jake Nance and several others.

John Lundy writes: "Our first Chesapeake was obtained in 1929 from a country doctor who had a sled team near McCall, Idaho. He was truly an all-round hunting dog and companion.

"In the 1940s, during World War II, while in service in the Aleutian Islands, I used to think how nice it would have been to have a Chesapeake for hunting in the cold, miserable country. So I planned to raise Chessies when the war was over, and to call my dogs by the Aleutian prefix.

"My foundation dogs were: Aleutian Water Chief—sired by Westminister Best of Breed Ch. Felt's Chesty; and then, Aleutian Water Spray, who was my first serious field trial dog. Spray placed in several Qualifying stakes in the early '50s and won third in the Open and first in the Amateur at the Klamath Falls trial in 1953."

Dr. Lundy has bred many fine Chesapeakes since those days, his most recent success being FC & AFC Aleutian Surf Breaker.

Cliff Brignall, in 1958, made his CFC Nelgard's Baron an American Amateur Field Champion. I had always been a Baron fan, and I know I was much more excited than Brignall was. Baron was a good marker and a terrific handling dog, but as a team he and Brignall did not click. I bought Baron (then seven years old) from Brignall in 1958. He was still a fabulous and consistent contender, and he really gave me his all.

Helen Fleischmann, in 1959, made an Amateur Field Champion of

her Chesnoma's Louis, a Mallard son. The Fleischmanns had bred
Louis, and Helen had trained him herself.

Undoubtedly the best field trial year our breed ever had in the West
was 1959, in which Mallard, Bob, and Baron all made their Field Trial
Championships. All three were extensively bred and their bloodlines are
the foundation of today's successful field trial contenders.

1960 to 1970

An enormously increased activity in our breed characterizes the
1960s. In this period, 160 bench championships, 108 Companion Dog
titles and 14 Companion Dog Excellent titles, were made. A new interest
in Tracking was shown as 10 dogs acquired this title. We also did well
field trial-wise, as 8 dogs became Field Champions and 7 Amateur Field
Champions.

Over twenty new kennels were started. None of these were commer-
cial kennels in the sense of being "puppy mills" that produce a great
number of dogs each year. Individuals or families who had some excellent dogs bred a few litters each year, and these matings were carefully
selected.

In the East, *Chesdel Kennels* continued to produce good field trial
dogs for Alex Spear.

Eastern Waters' made 17 champions in these years. The Horns have
real family togetherness and all competently show their own dogs: Janet
and Dan; their daughter, Marguerite Willis; their daughter, Elizabeth
Humer and her husband, Rupert; their son, Roger Horn; another son,
Nathaniel Horn and his wife, Susan; and a granddaughter, Laura
Humer.

Janet Horn writes: "We have never thought of ourselves as a kennel; we have just been breeding Chesapeakes, trying to maintain and improve quality."

When I inquired which she considered her most important dog, the
response was, "My Ch. Eastern Waters' Baronessa, CD, TD, was the
'once in a lifetime dog.' She was a nearly perfect specimen of the breed
and as lovely in character as she was in looks. I cannot write about her
without tears."

I saw Baronessa in the field when she was about a year old, and in
my opinion she definitely had field trial potential, had she been properly trained.

Janet handled Baronessa to 55 Bests of Breed, while Baronessa's full
brother, Ch. Eastern Waters' Dark Knight took 54 Bests of Breed,
handled by Dan. These dogs were sired by my FC, CFC & AFC
Nelgard's Baron, CD, and their dam was Ch. Eastern Waters' Silver
Star.

In 1966 Dan came up with another good one, his Ch. Eastern Waters' Brown Charger, who was a joy to watch in the ring. Charger gathered up 126 Bests of Breed and 40 Group placements.

Betsy Horn's husband, Rupert Humer, made a champion of his Eastern Waters' Oak, CD, TD & WD, who won 8 Bests of Breed. He proved to be a fine stud and has sired 24 champions.

Nathaniel and Susan Horn's Ch. Eastern Waters' Chargn Knight is splendidly carrying on the grand tradition. Even as we go to print, he has climaxed a fine record with win of an all-breeds Best in Show at Newcastle Kennel Club (Pennsylvania) in September 1979.

Quite a family, the Horns!

Chesachobee Kennels and Mildred Buchholz continued their winning ways in the 1960s. In 1960 Millie put a championship on her Random Lake Bill's Darky. In 1966 she not only made a champion of her Eastern Waters' Bronze Rex, CD, but also took a fourth in the Sporting Group with him. Darky was a full brother to Baronessa and Dark Knight. Single-handedly, Millie made 10 bench championships in this period.

Longcove Kennels, owned by the Alfred Kinneys of Buena, New Jersey, started in 1965. They have produced 6 champions, of whom they consider Ch. Longcove's Golden Gemini, CD, WD the finest dog they have ever had. By the end of 1978, Gemini had won 49 Bests of Breed and 2 Groups, with 9 Group placements.

Koolwater's Kennels of New Jersey was started by the Kenneth Kruegers and made 5 bench championships in the years 1966 to 1968. Their best known dog was Ch. Koolwater's Kolt of Tricrown. He went on to make his Amateur Field Championship, and when he made his Field Championship he became one of our Dual Champions. Also, their Ch. Native Shore Jumbo Belle, CD took 44 Bests of Breed. She was a handsome and sturdy specimen.

Burning Tree Kennels, operated by Dr. Marston and Judy Jones of Salisbury, Maryland, was started in 1968. They made their first bench championship in 1969, but their best known show dog was Ch. Salty of Bomarc, WD, who won his title in 1974 and gathered up 12 Bests of Breed. Today they are concentrating on field trials with their Chemin De Fer of Chesdel, WD. Chemin De Fer won the Maryland Retriever Clubs's sanctioned Derby Trophy in 1975, and in 1978 won the American Chesapeake Club's annual Dashnaw Derby Trophy.

Chestnut Hill Kennels, owned by the Ronald Andersons and located in Monrovia, Maryland, started in 1969. Two really fine specimens formed their foundation stock: Ch. Tuffy Anderson, CD and WD, and Ch. Cub's Lady Belle, CD & TD (OFA C B-383).

Karen Anderson writes: "Tuffy's breeding is Native Shore. He is a dead-grass dog of 100 pounds, and is 26 inches tall. He is an enthusiastic, outgoing Chesapeake, fast and stylish, a very good marker with an impressive water entry. He is bullish yet gentle, and will open doors, gates—anything not padlocked. He is our house dog, and at 10½ years he is still rambunctious and eager, and I suppose he will be until the end.

"Lady Belle, our brood bitch, was large—23 inches high and 75 pounds. She produced three bench champions. She was protective of her family and home, but was always eager to please."

In the Midwest, *Cherokee Kennels,* owned by the John Urbens of Oregon, Wisconsin, commenced in 1960. Ch. Cherokee Tanya, CD, was their first to win a title, and they consider her their most important dog. She took 31 Bests of Breed and won 3 Group placements. The Urbens made five other champions from 1960 to 1970, and the Cherokee name can still be found in the list of today's winners.

Cur-San Kennels was established in 1965 in Hancock, Wisconsin by Curt and Sandy Dollar. They consider their Timbers Shadow, CD & WD, their best dog. Their son, Kurt, Jr., owns him and has trained him for shows. The Dollars also train their Chesapeakes for sled work—and Cur-San's Super Pop of Marpa is their lead sled dog.

Rigby's Kennels, started in 1961, was owned by Clyde Rigby. His Ch. Rigby's Rosemount Dancer was the first dog of our breed to really roll up a terrific record. Dancer won 90 Bests of Breed and took 2 Sporting Group Firsts, as well as 16 Group placements. Rigby finished six bench champions in the 1960s.

Webfoot Kennels was started in 1962 by the William Boysons, then in North Carolina but now of Champaign, Illinois. Their first dog to achieve a bench championship (in 1964) was Conroy's Bird, CDX. But their best known dog was Ch. Eastern Waters' Big Gunpowder, who won 51 Bests of Breed and 2 Group placements.

Crosswinds Kennels was started in 1969 by Kent and Fran Lowman, outside of Rockford, Illinois. They show on the bench and in Obedience, and more recently, in field trials. Their dogs have won 17 show championships, 13 Working Dog certificates, 4 Working Dog Excellent titles and a Utility title. They also have placed in licensed and sanctioned Derby stakes.

Chesapine Kennels, belonging to Ray and Lorraine Berg of Fremont, Wisconsin, also started in 1969. Their most outstanding dog has been Ch. Ray's Drake of the Pines, WD (OFA-CB-57), who scored 43 Bests of Breed and 3 Group placements and has sired 9 champions.

In the West, more and more people became interested in breeding and raising Chesapeakes.

Chesareid Kennels, owned by William and Sybil Reid of Bellingham, Washington, has produced a fine group of dogs for almost twenty years. Best known has been their Am-Can Ch. Chesareid Amber

Ch. West River Ripple, owned and shown by Eugene Weems,
was one of the outstanding bench winners of the early days. She
represents a classic example of the breed.

Ch. Rigby's Rosemount Dancer, with owner Clyde Rigby, winning a Sporting Group under judge Alva Rosenberg. Dancer was the first Chesapeake
to win a lot in bench show competition.

Hue, sired by Russ Iorn's fine Duke of Kamiakin, out of a Baron female. Amber was a handsome, dead-grass dog, who made the record of 25 Bests of Breed and 2 Group placements. Sybil trains and shows her own dogs on the bench, in Obedience, and in field trials, and does a good job.

Von Nassau Kennels, belonging to A. Mesdag of Seattle, Washington, had some nice bench specimens in the late '60s, but is no longer active.

Baptist Corner Kennels, located at Olathe, Colorado, was started in 1969. Mrs. Rosenbaum writes: "Most of our puppies have gone as pets and gundogs. We consider our best dog to have been Ch. Chesaford Yankee Phoebe, winner of 4 Bests of Breed. But we are equally proud of another dog we bred, who got 67 pheasants last year for his owner and his owner's friends. We have two very good bitches we can't show—one had a poorly set broken leg and, unfortunately, the other had a leg shot off."

Hi-Ho Kennels, owned by the Stephen Loftsgaards and located in Hayward, California, was also started in 1969. Their Ch. Hi-Ho Guns of Canton, WDX, (OFA-231 and CERF for fourth year), is a large, handsome and completely sound male. He has accumulated over 100 Bests of Breed as well as a Group First and 12 Group placements. In addition, he has placed in several licensed field trials in the United States and has won a Canadian Amateur stake. He sired 9 champions in 1978, bringing his overall total to 16.

Dunnell's Ranch Kennels, owned by Adey Mae Dunnell, is in Fairfield, California. Miss Dunnell specializes in quality shooting dogs, but in addition to this, her Ch. Skipper Big John and several other of her fine specimens have done well on the bench. Big John has both his OFA and CERF certifications.

Miss Dunnell is conducting an interesting experiment. She keeps all of her pups until they are six months old—then has them all x-rayed. She discards any unsound specimens and only breeds brood matrons—*all* of whose puppies are sound. Bravo to her! It is unfortunate that more of us are not located, as she is, in the countryside, so that we could do the same thing.

Snocree Kennels, started by Dr. and Mrs. John Schmidt of Snowmass, Colorado, began to breed Chesapeakes in 1969. At first, their interest was confined to show dogs, but today they are also training some of their dogs for field trials. Their Ch. Kaste's Christie of Snocree, CD, winner of 4 Bests of Breed, has become one of our top producing brood matrons. Certified OFA-Excellent, at the end of 1978 she had 10 bench champions to her credit. The Schmidts are real Chesapeake enthusiasts.

Smart's Kennels, first in California and now in Klamath Falls, Oregon, also started in 1969. John Smart is interested in hunting and running his dogs in field trials. His wife and three daughters decided to make it a family project, so they learned to show on the bench and in Obedience. Their Ch. Kobi's California Quail, CD, (OFA CB-436 and CERF 122-77-64), has placed in several Derby and Qualifying stakes. Dark brown in color, he is 26 inches high and weighs 90 pounds. He was handled to his championship by the Smarts' teenage daughter, Teena. Quail got his CD title in only four shows.

Mount Joy Kennels, previously owned by Robert Brown of Davenport, Iowa, was sold to the Fleischmanns in California when Mr. Brown died in the late 1950s. The Fleischmanns used this kennel identification from 1960 on. They concentrated on their field trial dogs and discontinued showing on the bench. However, they continued to breed five or six litters a year, most of whom were sold to hunters.

Baronland was the name I adopted when I was fortunate enough to buy Nelgard's Baron from Cliff Brignall. Baron had a great temperament and was a first class field trial contender. Despite the fact that he was not good looking, many of his pups were, and they were all mentally and physically sound, for Baron himself was eminently sound. I easily made a champion of his handsome son, Baron's Tule Tiger, and of two more dogs in the 1960s.

Larson's Kennels started in the mid-60s in Manti, Utah, belongs to Lyle Larson. His work keeps him from participating in field trials, but he is a real enthusiast and attends them whenever possible. He has procured dogs of all of the best field bloodlines and keeps up on what is going on at the trials today. His dogs are good, sound, working specimens and Lyle is deadly serious about his program.

Wildwood Kennels is located in Tok, Alaska, and is owned by the John Martiniuks. Despite the geographical handicap of their great distance to any bench shows, they made several bench championships. Their best known dog is Ch. Wildwood's Midnight Sundance, WD, (OFA CB-479 and CERF 103-76-74), who has 7 Bests of Breed and a Group placement in the United States, as well as 2 Bests of Breed and 2 Group placements in Canada. Born in 1966, Sundance is dark dead-grass in color, 25 inches tall, and weighs 75 pounds. Wildwood Kennels teach their Chesapeakes to compete in sled races and they are very well known for their ability in this field.

In tune with the encouraging number of 160 bench championships made in the years from 1960 to 1970, Obedience also flourished. Of the 108 Companion Dog titles attained, Millie Buchholz made 14 with her dogs, and Eastern Waters' 11. I made 4 with my field trial dogs (Baron, Echo, Tiger and Cub). Sybil Reid made 3 and so did Margaret Long.

Fourteen CDX titles were made, with 3 going to the Ray Bergs and their Chesapine dogs, 2 going to Millie Buchholz and all the rest to individual owners.

Twelve Tracking titles were made, of which 5 went to Millie, 2 to Eugene and Mary Pantzer and 5 to individual owners.

The field trial picture for this decade was encouraging in the West and Midwest, but there were practically no top field trial Chesapeakes in the East.

When we think of the small percentage of the Chesapeakes that ran, we can be happy with the large percentage of those that won and placed, for our breed is greatly outnumbered by Labradors and Goldens. Unfortunately, not too many Chesapeake owners wish to compete in trials because it takes several years to properly school a dog, once he is out of the Derby. Few people have enough interest or patience to go on with their young dog, for it will mean lots of hard work before your dog can start to win or place in licensed trials' All-Age stakes.

Eight field trial championships were made from 1960 to 1970:

One lone Midwesterner, Harold Johnson of Nebraska, made a Field Champion of his Star King of Mount Joy.

Dr. L. E. Reppert of San Antonio, Texas, did the same with his Slow Gin, and Dr. W. E. Peltzer of Salt Lake City, Utah, gained this honor with his snappy little Chesnoma's Kodiak.

The other five titles went to Californians:

Dr. F. A. Dashnaw ran his fabulous Meg's Pattie O'Rourke, commonly known as "Missie." She had been the National Derby Champion of 1958, with the amazing record of 67 points during her second year. A spectacular marker, Missie took well to her handling, taught her by Rex Carr. Missie's full brother, Meg's O'Timothy, also trained by Rex Carr, became a Field Champion. Bud Dashnaw was a fine handler, and got the most out of his dogs.

The E. C. Fleischmanns won a Field Trial Champion title for their Mount Joy's Louistoo, a Mallard son they had bred. In 1968 they also made a Field Champion of their Mount Joy's Bit O'Ginger, a Timothy daughter.

Baronland succeeded with my Tule Tiger, who won three All-Breed Open firsts in '65, and three Double Headers in the Chesapeake Specialty field trials of '64, '65, and '66. Tiger established the Chesapeake all-time High Point record, which still stands today. He had a total of 208 licensed trial points, of which 112 were Amateur and 96 Open.

Seven Amateur Field Championships were made in the decade—with only one dog coming from the East. August Belmont, from Long Island, New York, was successful with his Bomarc of South Bay, CD. The other six were the dogs listed above: the Fleischmann's Louistoo and Ginger, Dashnaw's Missie and O'Timothy, Dr. Peltzer's Chesnoma's Kodiak, and my Tule Tiger.

1970 to 1979

Again I would like to stress that all of the breeders of the modern Chesapeake are individual fanciers who only raise one or two litters a year, from carefully selected matings.

Little money is to be made from raising dogs, if it is done in the proper manner. Kennel costs have almost doubled. Distemper shots have tripled in price. Dog food is now sky high. Cod liver oil, vitamins and calcium, today are very expensive. If a Caesarian or other operation is needed, you will find that these veterinarian charges have also skyrocketed. The salary of a kennel man, when you can get one, is at least twice what it used to be.

Moreover, not too many people live in areas where a kennel full of dogs is permitted. And most people do not have the time to spend on properly caring for a group of dogs. A litter of puppies requires two months of constant attention and supervision if you are going to produce strong and healthy specimens. The average Chesapeake breeder only schedules one or two litters a year, and then makes it a rule to stay home with the puppies and do very little else at the time.

There is only one Chesapeake kennel that I know of where six brood bitches are kept. This belongs to Ernest Wermerskirchen of New Prague, Minnesota. He started it in 1957 and has produced a large number of puppies each year. Since his dogs are not entered in any phase of competition, it is hard to evaluate his stock. Most of his puppies are sold to hunters.

Several new kennels were started in the East in the 1970s and are doing well.

Chesrite Kennels of Sharon, Massachusetts, owned by Jan and Jody Thomas, has produced 6 bench champions. Their best-known dog, Am-Can Ch. Chesrite's Justin Tyme, CD, WD, in August 1979 became the sixth dog of the breed to win an all-breeds Best in Show. He has both his OFA and CERF certification.

I had often wondered how he got his name, but then so many dog names are odd. Mrs. Thomas wrote me this explanation: "When our daughter Jan was handling Justin in his Working Dog test, he swam out and retrieved the duck. But as he came in, he stopped on the bank and just looked at Jan for what seemed hours. Finally, Justin came on in and presented the duck to her. The judge announced to the crowd, "Just in time, just in time.""

Chesaford Kennels, owned by the Charles Cranfords of Greenboro, North Carolina, was started in 1973. Ch. Chesaford Chestnut Newfy, TD, has at this writing already won 22 Bests of Breed and is also their favorite hunting dog. All seven of the current dogs at Chesaford have both CFA and CERF certification.

Montauk Waters is the kennel name adopted by Christopher and Susan Cone of Livingston, New Jersey. Susan has put CDXs on two of her Chesapeakes, and has entered them in many racing events. Their Ch. Eastern Waters' Betsy Ross, CDX, has taken top scores in Obedience and is a strong competitor in the scent hurdle relay races. Son David shows Betsy in Junior Showmanship, and the Cones' daughter, Jenny, shows their Montauk Waters' Genie, CDX, in the breed and Junior Showmanship. Susan writes, "Betsy is what we call a housekeeping dog—delivering messages, tools, anything a dog can carry around the house and out into the yard."

Northcreek Kennels, in Kennett Square, Pennsylvania, was established by the Hoaglands in 1972. Their Ch. Northcreek Tule Tunk (born 1975, by FC, AFC, CFC & CAFC Chesdel Chippewa Chief ex Shore Water's Tule Kel, WD) was shown to his championship and several Bests of Breed by Peggy Long. Tunk is also Maggie Hoagland's field trial dog and performed very well in Qualifying stakes in 1978. A dead-grass male, he stands at 24 inches and weighs about 85 pounds. His OFA number is 619.

Rockrun Kennels, belonging to Diana Hankin of Castle Creek, New York, started in 1976. Their Ch. Big Ben of Westminister has 7 Bests of Breed. Rockrun Chesapeakes have accounted for 11 bench championships, and are now being worked in Obedience and trained for their Working Dog certificates.

Mitsu-Kuma Kennels was started in Thurmont, Maryland by Barbara Mullen. Their foundation dam is Eastern Waters' Mitsu-Kuma Cub, CD, who has been handled by Barbara's daughter Sharron, only eleven years old at the time. "Kuma", whelped in 1970, is about 22 inches high and, Mrs. Mullen says, "always weighs too much." The Mitsu-Kuma prefix is becoming especially prominent in Obedience.

Oak 'N Thistle is the prefix adopted by James and Brenda Stewart, both veterinarians, of Woodbine, Maryland. Their handsome dogs are shown in bench and Obedience. Their first representative on the list of bench champions of the breed was Ches' True Grit in 1974. He has since become one of the top best of Breed winners and has added Obedience, Tracking and Bermudian Championship titles.

Chesavieda Kennels, owned by young Dianna Blakey of Maitland, Florida, only started in 1974, but has had whirlwind success over the last few years. Her foundation bitch was Ch. Melody's Spun Smoke of Blabro, CDX, TD & WD, who won 21 Bests of Breed and a Group placement. Spun Smoke is the dam of Ch. Chesavieda's Ornamental Buoy, UDT & WDX, who has gone as high as any dog can go in the Obedience ring.

In the Midwest, Ferdinand Bunte's Cocoa King Kennels and Ralph Mock's strain were discontinued. Alpine Kennels bred some Chesapeakes for shooting dogs, but went into Labradors as well.

Briarmoor Kennels, formerly in Indiana but now located in Horton-ville, Wisconsin, was started by Patricia and Nancy Leakey in 1971, and has since finished 8 bench champions. Patricia Leakey handles the dogs herself and her record of 65 Bests of Breed on Ch. Briarmoor's Bearpaw is most impressive. Mrs. Leakey also competes her dogs in Obedience and is training them for Working Dog certificates.

Blustrywood Kennels, owned by Karen and John Wood, Jr., was established in 1972 in Princeton, Indiana. Their foundation bitch is Chapel Jene, CD, who has produced 5 bench champions. The most famous of these is their Am-Can Ch. Crispin Roderick, CD, who is their hunting dog. "Chris" has the enviable record of 115 Bests of Breed, 9 Group Firsts, 31 Group placements and a Best in Show.

Cogley's Klamath Kennels, owned by the Lloyd Cogley family in Klamath Falls, Oregon, was started in 1971. Their homebred Ch. Ben-jamin Franklin, whelped in April of 1976, has won 9 Bests of Breed. He has both OFA CB-648 and CERF CB-174-78-28 certification. He has a busy hunting season as he is Lloyd's shooting pal.

Willowpond Kennels in Concord, California, was started in 1972 by Edith and Doug Hanson. Their female, Ch. Bonnie Doon, WDX, has taken 15 Bests of Breed and is the dam of several champions. A profes-sional handler, Edith Hanson is best known for the fine job she has done handling Susan Steuben's Ch. Teal's Tiger, who has many Bests of Breed and became the first Western dog of the breed to go Best in Show.

Fireweed Kennels belongs to Linda Harger and was started in 1977. It is now located at Junction City, Oregon. Her Ch. Wildwood's Fireweed, WDX, received 3 Bests of Breed and had also placed in a Qualifying Field Trial stake before her untimely death. The foundation male of this kennel is Fireweed's Aleutian Widgeon, OFA-CB-291, who has placed in Open and Amateur stakes and gives every promise of earn-ing his Field Championship.

Cascade Kennels, located in Elkgrove, California, and operated by Carolyn Sears, started in 1974. She considers Ch. Wildwood's Prince Baronof, CD & WD (OFA CB-299 and CERF CD-113), to be her most important dog. Prince has won Bests of Breed, has produced 3 bench champions—all with CDs, and is the family's duck dog, as well.

Berteleda Kennels was reactivated in 1969 by Nancy Lowenthal, the daughter of William Dougal, who had started breeding Chesapeakes in 1923. Nancy has made a champion of their Berteleda Maggie, UD & WDX, who is one of the finest duck hunting dogs I have ever seen in ac-tion. Nancy's husband, Les, is an inveterate hunter and he justly brags of Maggie's prowess. Nancy also trained their Ch. Cub's Marin Echo, UD & WD, who has 22 Bests of Breed and a Group placement. Echo's son by a Baron son, Hatchet Man, is FC & AFC Bay-City Jake. In addition, the Lowenthals are the breeders of numerous bench champions and Obe-dience title-holders.

Coleman's Kennels, located at Stanton in southern California, is operated by Charles and Maureen Coleman and their daughter, Charlene. The whole family participates in field trials, Obedience trials and bench shows, and they have won ribbons in all three.

At *Baronland Kennels,* we concentrated on Dual Ch. & AFC Tiger's Cub, CD in the early '70s. He was extensively used at stud and many of his get became bench champions as well as Obedience title-holders. His son, Cub's Kobi King, became a Field Champion in 1972 and a Dual Champion in 1978. This was a third generation Dual Championship won by dogs from my kennel. Our star these days is my fourth generation field trial dog, Cub's Terrific Thor, WDX, who was High Point Derby Chesapeake in 1978 and who shows great promise in his advanced work. He is only two and a half years old at this writing, but is a proven sire.

In all, over 450 bench championships were made in the years 1970 to 1979. We now have a uniformity of type that we did not have a few years ago. There also is a growing insistence that the bench champions should demonstrate their ability to work in the hunting field, so that the Working Dog and Working Dog Excellent tests are becoming more important each year. Also, the majority of owners are getting OFA and CERF numbers on their dogs. Thus the average owner of a shooting dog is assured of a better and sounder physical specimen and one whose parents have proven their willingness to work in the field.

Eastern Waters won 20 of these bench titles. Ch. Eastern Waters' Chargn Knight, owned and handled by Nathaniel Horn, won over 40 Bests of Breed in addition to his Best in Show triumph. Rupert Humer's Ch. Eastern Waters' Yankee, CD, was a very much admired contender of the period. Betsy and Rupert Humer now call their kennel Eastern Waters' II. Janet Horn writes that she, Dan, and their family have made a total of 60 bench champions!!

Millie Buchholz *(Chesachobee Kennels)* topped all individual records by bringing in 14 championships. Her current champion, Chesachobee's Gemson, CD & WD, has made the fine record of 24 Bests of Breed and 2 Group placements. Millie writes that he is now being trained for WDX as well as Tracking. Millie's total record, through 1978, is almost unbelievable. She has made a total of 48 Obedience titles—30 CDs, 8 CDXs, 2 UDs and 8 TDs titles. In addition, she has finished 5 WDs and 35 bench champions! Quite a record—quite a gal!

Chesarab Kennel's exceptional female, Ch. Chesarab's Little Acorn, took 9 Bests of Breed. Born in December of 1970, she was sired by Ch. Eastern Waters' Oak CD ex Chesarab's Turkish Taffy. Sedge in color, 24 inches in height and weighing 85 pounds, she impressed with her free flowing gait—strong and correct. "She has," writes Sheila DiVaccaro, "the shoulders to extend and the rear to propel. It is beautiful to watch." Quite a personality, too. "Corny is a grinner, a squeeker and a clown," Sheila writes. "In Obedience I have never had a more frustrating dog to show. When Corny grins in the Obedience ring, I know she is going to give it to me again. She knows the recall perfectly in practice; but in a show, halfway to me she looks directly at me, then at the gallery, then grins. She then proceeds to roll over on her back, wiggle and wag her tail. She never fails to get laughs—and she never does it without grinning first."

Terrific new interest was shown in Obedience as the breed registered the astonishing number of 336 CDs, 83 CDXs, and 13 UDs in the years 1970-79. Many new owners were taking their Chesapeakes to Obedience events.

Of the CD titles, 14 went to the Horn family, 10 to Millie Buchholz and her co-owners, 6 to Dianna Blakey, 3 to the Lowmans, 3 to the Lowenthals and 3 to the Charles Cranfords.

Dianna Blakey, a new, young and very competent Obedience enthusiast, led in procuring CDX titles with 6. The Horns made 5, the Lowenthals 3, and Millie Buchholz and the DiVacarros each had 2.

UD titles were scarce. In 1973 Nancy Lowenthal put a UD on her Ch. Berteleda Maggie and on Ch. Cub's Marin Echo. Dianna Blakey made Utility Dogs out of her Ch. Chesachobee's Cocoanut, Chesachobee's Ovedio Millie B, and Ch. Chesavieda's Ornamental Buoy, TD.

Twenty-nine Tracking titles were made by Chesapeakes in the years 1970-1979. Seven were accounted for by the Horn family. The Doctors Stewart finished 3, as did the Charles Cranfords, the Ronald Andersons and Dianna Blakey.

Just as I was closing out this accounting, I received word that Dianna's Ch. Chesavieda's Ornamental Buoy, WDX, is now a UDT—the first male Chesapeake to achieve this title.

He also won a title I had never before heard of—the A. D. title. The A. D. (not an official American Kennel Club appellation) signifies passing an endurance test given to dogs on an asphalt track. To earn it, dogs must trot for two hours, with only two 15-minute breaks to have their hearts checked and their pads inspected by two judges. Our congratulations to Dianna for Buoy's amazing feat in passing this grueling ordeal.

Seven Field Trial Championships and an equal number of Amateur Field trial Championships were gained in the decade.

Only Mike Paterno's Ch. Koolwater Colt of Tricrown did well in the East. In 1970 he won both his Field Trial Championship and his Amateur Field Trial Championship, and as he was already a bench champion, he thus became our fifth Dual Champion.

I was equally fortunate in that same year with my FC and AFC Tiger's Cub CD (OFA CB-6 and CERF 136/77-147). Cub was trained by Rex Carr and handled by me. When he won his Field Championship, he became the breed's sixth Dual Champion, as well as being a direct third generation Field Champion of my line. (His grandfather was Nelgard's Baron; his father was Tule Tiger.)

Cub's son, Cub's Kobi King (OFA CB-92 and CERF 157/78-123), became a Field Champion in 1972, making this a fourth generation affair. Kobi was owned by Helen Hartley of Anchorage, Alaska, and was trained and handled by Chuck Crook—who has always been excellent with Chesapeakes. Kobi's interesting story is told more fully in the chapter "The Character of the Chesapeake" by Nancy Lowenthal later on in this book. He added a bench championship in 1978 (at age of eleven) to become the breed's seventh Dual Champion.

Another Field Trial Championship of this period was made by Chuck Crook; he trained and handled Alamo's Lucias, belonging to Ben Robertson of Sacramento, California. Lucias was an excellent competitor and extremely consistent.

Greg McDaniel raised Copper Topper Der Wunderbar, trained him himself and made him a Field Champion.

Bay City Jake, co-owned by Dr. Miles Thomas and Pete Van der Meulen, and trained by Rex Carr, became a Field Champion in 1976.

In 1978, yet another Carr-trained dog came through: Aleutian Surf Breaker, co-owned by Dr. Miles Thomas and John McRoberts.

Chesdel Chippewa Chief, who already was a CFC as well as a CAFC, became our 33rd American Field Trial Champion. He has always been trained and exclusively handled by his owner, Alex Spear, whom everyone admires for his great devotion to the breed.

Seven of the dogs listed above also made Amateur Field Trial Championships. They were Kolt, Cub, Copper Topper, Jake, Surf Breaker and Chesdel Chief. In addition, in 1975 Hans Kuck's stylish little CFC and CAFC Nanuk of Cheslang made an American Amateur Field Trial Championship for his owner.

Descriptions of all of our Field Champions and Amateur Field Champions, as well as important pedigrees, the list of points earned and their National and Amateur National records are given in our later chapter, Field Trial History and Records.

Our breed has never stood on firmer foundation than it does today. This is due to the efforts of the many people who have worked hard to bring it before the public. We all know that Chesapeakes are natural retrievers and hunters. But due to the efforts of so many individual owners who enjoy organized competition, our dogs have now been given the chance—in many diverse fields—to prove their ability to stand up to, and often surpass, the dogs of many other breeds.

A flying leap—by Dr. John Lundy's Big Fellow.

The famous Martiniuk Kennels' sled team of seven dogs from Tok, Alaska, going for a run with Sue Martiniuk driving. They have won many races.

APPEARANCE: Well-proportioned, well-balanced, general outline impressive; body length medium; not cobby, not roached; coat texture and color an essential consideration.

SIZE: Weight—males 65-80 lbs. bitches 55-70 lbs. Height - males 23-26" bitches 21-24"

Oversized or undersized dogs to be severely penalized

TAIL should extend to hock; medium heavy at base; moderate feathering permissible, but over 1¾" long a disqualification; not to curl over back or side kink

HINDQUARTERS trifle higher than shoulders, especially powerful to supply swimming power

HOCK to HEEL not too long or too short

FEET harelike, well-webbed, good size; toes well-rounded and close

DISQUALIFICATIONS: Black colored. Dewclaws on hind legs; white on any part of body except breast, belly, or spots on feet; feathering on tail or legs over 1¾" long; undershot, overshot, or any deformity; coat curly or tendency to curl all over body; specimens unworthy or lacking in breed characteristics.

EARS small, set high, hanging loose, medium-thick leather

NECK medium-length, strong, muscular, tapering

SHOULDERS sloping: full liberty of action with plenty power, unrestricted movement

BACK short, well-coupled, powerful

FLANKS well tucked up

PASTERNS medium length, slightly bent

SKULL broad, round

EYES medium large, wide apart, yellowish or amber

STOP medium

LIPS thin, not pendulous

MUZZLE medium, short; pointed but not sharp; teeth not undershot or overshot

CHEST strong, deep, wide; barrel round

LEGS medium length, straight, good bone, muscular, very powerful; dewclaws may be removed on forelegs, must be removed on hindlegs

COAT thick, short, not over 1½" long; oily; undercoat dense, fine wooly; outercoat harsh, water-resistant (as a duck's feathers); hair on legs, face, should be short, straight

COLOR: Dark brown to faded tan or any shade of deadgrass; white spot (smaller the better) on breast, toes and belly permissible; solid and self-colored dogs preferred.

3

Official AKC Standard for the Chesapeake Bay Retriever

Head—Skull broad and round with medium stop, nose medium short muzzle, pointed but not sharp. Lips thin, not pendulous. Ears small, set well up on head, hanging loosely and of medium leather. Eyes medium large, very clear, of yellowish or amber color and wide apart.

Neck—Of medium length with a strong muscular appearance, tapering to shoulders.

Shoulder, Chest and Body—Shoulders, sloping and should have full liberty of action with plenty of power without any restrictions of movement. Chest strong, deep and wide. Barrel round and deep. Body of medium length, neither cobby nor roached, but rather approaching hollowness, flanks well tucked up.

Hindquarters and Stifles—Hindquarters should be as high or a trifle higher than the shoulders. They should show fully as much power as the forequarters. There should be no tendency to weakness in either fore or hindquarters. Hindquarters should be especially powerful to supply the driving power for swimming. Back should be short, well-coupled and powerful. Good hindquarters are essential. Stifles should be well-angulated.

Legs, Elbows, Hocks and Feet—Legs should be medium length and straight, showing good bone and muscle, with well-webbed hare feet of good size. The toes well rounded and close, pasterns slightly bent and both pasterns and hocks medium length—the straighter the legs the better, when viewed from front or rear. Dewclaws, if any, must be removed from the hind legs. Dewclaws on the forelegs may be removed. A dog with dewclaws on the hind legs must be disqualified.

Tail—Tail should extend to hock. It should be medium heavy at base. Moderate feathering on stern and tail is permissible. Tail should be straight or slightly curved. Tail should not curl over back or side kink.

Coat and Texture—Coat should be thick and short, nowhere over 1½ inches long, with a dense fine woolly undercoat. Hair on face and legs should be very short and straight with tendency to wave on the shoulders, neck, back and loins only. The curly coat or coat with a tendency to curl not permissible.

The texture of the dog's coat is very important, as the dog is used for hunting under all sorts of adverse weather conditions, often working in ice and snow. The oil in the harsh outer coat and woolly undercoat is of extreme value in preventing the cold water from reaching the dog's skin and aids in quick drying. A Chesapeake's coat should resist the water in the same way that a duck's feathers do. When he leaves the water and shakes himself, his coat should not hold the water at all, being merely moist. Color and coat are extremely important, as the dog is used for duck hunting. The color must be as nearly that of his surroundings as possible and with the fact that dogs are exposed to all kinds of adverse weather conditions, often working in ice and snow, the color of coat and its texture must be given every consideration when judging on the bench or in the ring.

Color—Any color varying from a dark brown to a faded tan or deadgrass. Deadgrass takes in any shade of deadgrass, varying from a tan to a dull straw color. White spot on breast, toes and belly permissible, but the smaller the spot the better. Solid and self-colored dogs are preferred.

Weight—Males, 65 to 80 pounds; females 55 to 70 pounds. **Height**—Males, 23 inches to 26 inches; females, 21 inches to 24 inches. Oversized or undersized dogs are to be severely penalized.

Symmetry and Quality—The Chesapeake dog should show a bright and happy disposition and an intelligent expression, with general outlines impressive and denoting a good worker. The dog should be well proportioned, a dog with a good coat and well balanced in other points being preferable to the dog excelling in some but weak in others.

Courage, willingness to work, alertness, nose, intelligence, love of water, general quality, and, most of all, disposition, should be given primary consideration in the selection and breeding of the Chesapeake Bay dog.

POSITIVE SCALE OF POINTS

Head, incl. lips, ears & eyes 16	Elbows, legs and feet 12	
Neck 4	Color 4	
Shoulders and body 12	Stern and tail 10	
Hindquarters and stifles . 12	Coat and Texture 18	
	General conformation . . 12	

TOTAL 100

Note: —The question of coat and general type of balance takes precedence over any scoring table which could be drawn up.

APPROXIMATE MEASUREMENTS

	Inches
Length head, nose to occiput	9½ to 10
Girth at ears	20 to 21
Muzzle below eyes	10 to 10½
Length of ears	4½ to 5
Width between eyes	2½ to 2¾
Girth neck close to shoulder	20 to 22
Girth at flank	24 to 25
Length from occiput to tail base	34 to 35
Girth forearms at shoulders	10 to 10½
Girth upper thigh	19 to 20
From root to root of ear, over skull	5 to 6
Occiput to top shoulder blades	9 to 9½
From elbow to elbow over the shoulders	25 to 26

DISQUALIFICATIONS

Black colored.
Dewclaws on hind legs.
White on any part of body, except breast, belly or spots on feet.
Feathering on tail or legs over 1¾ inches long.
Undershot, overshot or any deformity.
Coat curly or tendency to curl all over body.
Specimens unworthy or lacking in breed characteristics.

Approved November 9, 1976.

MRS. JAMES EDWARD (Anne Rogers) CLARK, pictured here in her assignment as judge of the 1976 American Chesapeake Club Specialty, is the very embodiment of what a judge should look like when judging. It is obvious that she enjoys the challenge. She is in full command of the ring, is very good with the dogs, and draws tremendous respect from handlers and gallery alike.

And this chapter gives evidence that her judging lives up to the appearance. Her comments are most interesting, indubitably valid and will be seriously studied by all dedicated Chesapeake breeders.

Anne is a very special person. In 1978, she received the Gaines award for "Woman of the Year" for her "lifelong devotion to dogs as a breeder, handler, judge and active supporter of the University of Pennsylvania School of Veterinary Medicine's educational activities; for her example as a woman who brings honor to our sport by her personal standards of grooming, conduct, manners, courtesy and graciousness." She had also been honored as "Woman of the Year" in 1972, and as "Judge of the Year" in 1959.

We greatly appreciate her contribution to this book.

4

Commentary upon the Chesapeake Standard

by Anne Rogers Clark

WHEN I WAS A CHILD, I had a friend for two whole summers at the seashore at Montauk Point, Long Island. This was a long time ago, and certainly long before I entertained any thoughts of being a dog show judge. The friend was a Chesapeake Bay Retriever bitch who belonged to the skipper of the Coast Guard station just across the wide lawn at our family place. Her name was Gyp and she was of moderate size, about the color of the clay cliffs at Montauk, and was all heart. As there were few kids around to play with, and as her main use to the skipper was during the hunting season, Gyp and I became fast friends. We were fond of long walks together along the dunes and cliffs, exploring clay caves, beachcombing for small treasures and swimming in the surf. The latter was second nature to Gyp as she was happiest in the water and really in her element if you would stand seaside and throw sticks for her to retrieve.

The surf at Montauk is always lusty and the undertow a little tricky, but never did I see Gyp falter, or refuse to get what she had been sent for. She would race headlong into the water, sometimes scrambling down a 50-foot cliff to make her retrieve. She would literally duck her head under oncoming waves, reach her retrieve and strike out for shore riding the waves when she could, or at least getting an assist from them. She was lithe, agile, hard as nails and never had a spare bit of flesh on her. She was my first acquaintanceship with this grand breed, and while I have never owned one myself, I have known many down through the years that I have admired tremendously.

In judging the breed I have relied on past experience with dogs that have been of the working type. These were dogs that I was privileged to watch work or to have work for me, in the job they do best, retrieving ducks and geese. I also have been lucky to have them perform in the land of their birth, the Eastern Shore of Maryland. The Eastern Shore offers water work in small fresh water ponds, wide brackish rivers and the Chesapeake Bay itself. As the weather is generally quite mild at the outset of the gunning season, the summer-lazy dogs gradually come into form in comfortable water temperatures. By mid-season, however, the winter starts to set in and by late December and January of a cold winter it is not unusual to see this hearty breed dodging ice chunks, breaking skim ice and working in a frozen Eastern Shore snowy marsh.

The Chesapeake is considered a dog for all reasons on the Shore. His love of family, work and water (not necessarily in that order) are legion. He is an extraordinary farm dog and by nature is a very good watchdog. There are few farms on the Shore guarded by a Bay dog that have ever had a robbery, and with good reason, as his size, piercing expression, agility and strength stand him in good stead. He has turned his hand to seeking out and helping eradicate the woodchuck, the bane of the farmer's existence. He is loyal to his family to the death, adores the youngsters and will work long hours in the duck blind for his master, combining the two main loves of his life, water and retrieving.

In exploring the standard of the breed, we find the word "medium" used repeatedly. I feel this was to point the way to a balanced symmetrical outline that would not be overdone in any way: the sum of all parts to equal a rugged sporting dog that could fulfill what was required of him in his daily work, without being unduly burdened with superfluous frills and for "show-purpose-only" extras.

Let's look at the standard together:

> **Head**—Skull broad and round with medium stop, nose medium short muzzle, pointed but not sharp. Lips thin, not pendulous, Ears small, set well up on head, hanging loosely and of medium leather. Eyes medium large, very clear, of yellowish or amber color and wide apart.

Comment: The head of the Bay dog resembles a blunt wedge or triangle. Though it is perhaps an "old wive's tale," it is averred by the old-timers that this shape of head gives a good-sized "brain box." If the ability to cope and learn, as evidenced by this breed, attests to the fact, it has good backing. The stop is not sharply cut. And this is true in all retrieving breeds. The length from stop to point of nose is not extreme, but is of sufficient length to allow for a mouth large enough to grasp his game, which can be as large as a 14 pound goose! Of course, the bite should be a normal scissors, the only mouth acceptable in a retriever. The lips are thin and fit very tightly with no hanging lip that would be a place for wet feathers to lodge. The ear is small and relatively water-tight being set high enough on the head to be clear of the water while the dog is swimming. The rather short to medium leather hangs loosely to allow air free access to the inner ear helping to guard against ear canker problems. The yellow or amber eye that appears to look at you fearlessly is to be a very important part of the Bay dog's type and character.

> **Neck**—Of medium length with a strong muscular appearance, tapering to shoulders.

Comment: The neck must be strong and muscular, once again to handle game as big as a Canada goose. While in the water the Bay dog pushes the bird, grasped firmly in his mouth, in front of himself, much as a tug pushes a barge. On reaching shore the bird must be raised to about the level of the shoulder and carried cleanly to his waiting master. These actions require a neck so described.

> **Shoulder, Chest and Body**—Shoulders, sloping and should have full liberty of action with plenty of power without any restrictions of movement. Chest strong, deep and wide. Barrel round and deep. Body of medium length, neither cobby nor roached, but rather approaching hollowness, flanks well tucked up.

Comment: This paragraph is rather self-explanatory, but if you have trouble with it, imagine that a Bay dog should be built like a rowboat with legs! The body "approaching hollowness" has some relation to the swimming dip that is found in some retrievers and also in the Poodle that started life as a retriever in Germany. This is a slight but perceptible hollow just behind the shoulders. This paragraph also says to me that the Bay dog is round and deep of chest, rib and body for stamina and breathing ability, but that his flanks are well tucked up denoting that he is hard and lean.

> **Hindquarters and Stifles**—Hindquarters should be as high or a trifle higher than the shoulders. They should show fully as much power as the forequarters. There should be no tendency to weakness in either fore or hindquarters. Hind quarters should be especially powerful to supply the driving power for swimming. Back should be short, well-coupled and powerful. Good hindquarters are essential. Stifles should be well-angulated.

Comment: Sometimes in evaluating a class of Chessies the above paragraph gives me pause, for invariably I feel that the hindquarters could show more bend of stifle, the hocks could be shorter, and that when asked to trot the whole animal could go away from me a little more soundly, and not incline to crab or move sideways which so many do. Then I stop and I remember many a frosty morning when striding ahead of me was a Chessie made just as these dogs are and I stop to reconsider what I am looking at. Here is a dog with over-long hind legs, as required by the Standard, for the purpose of swimming and not trotting. This dog can leap in tremendous forward bounds, pushing off with both hind legs and landing on both front ones. This is the only way to travel through a muddy marsh or water that is not deep enough to swim in. And this same Bay dog that I would like to see trot a little more soundly in the show ring can swim all today and tomorrow and for as long as you want him to. I am not saying that improvement cannot be made along the lines of "show dog soundness," just let's not do it to the detriment of proven working ability. Viewed in side movement, most Bay dogs constructed as above will be comfortable in their stride and will show good coordination between front and rear quarters providing that the shoulder and hind-quarter angulation are in close balance.

> **Legs, Elbows, Hocks and Feet**—Legs should be medium length and straight, showing good bone and muscle, with well-webbed hare feet of good size. The toe well rounded and close, pasterns slightly bent and both pasterns and hocks medium length—the straighter the legs the better, when viewed from front or rear. Dewclaws, if any, must be removed from the hind legs. Dewclaws on the forelegs may be removed. A dog with dewclaws on the hind legs must be disqualified.

Comment: A word of the Chessie's legs while we are in these two paragraphs. The legs all-round are of bladed bone. That is to say, not the fat round bone of the Foxhound but a flattish bone that allows for a long sinew and muscle attachment and that is of a hard, not soft or brittle texture. There is always prominent veining present, that can be clearly seen on the forelegs and while less prominent can be easily seen on the rear legs. The feet are of great importance. They are large without being spread or broken down in any way. Upon examination they fill the hand with very thick pads, very muscular toes, and when the toes are spread manually there is noticeable and very heavy webbing between each toe. The toenails are important also to this breed. They are very strong claws, of medium length—which length is naturally achieved in an active dog, and are of great assistance to the Chessie giving him extra traction and purchase behind and a hand over hand action in front when mounting a steep bank. They are also put to handy use when digging the woodchuck from his den!

The look of a bandy legged dog is aesthetically unpleasant and there is good reason to believe that a straight front leg will stand up better in the long run, stamina-wise, and that it will perform a swimming function more efficiently than a crooked one. Further a cowhocked dog does not walk, trot, gallop or swim efficiently. The need is to have a limb that while functioning will straighten almost completely and then return for its next stroke. A cowhocked or twisted leg cannot perform this function. I have found that rear dewclaws in many breeds that we breed, very often will occur on a dog that is not made correctly behind. I wonder if this was the reason that a dog with hind dewclaws is disqualified under the Standard? My feeling is contrary to the Standard, as I feel that a man-made fault, i.e., leaving dewclaws on the hindleg of a Chessie, should not be disqualification but rather a very serious fault. I believe the front dewclaws should come off as they can be torn and ripped in the normal course of activity of this very active breed.

> **Tail**—Tail should extend to hock. It should be medium heavy at base. Moderate feathering on stern and tail is permissible. Tail should be straight or slightly curved. Tail should not curl over back or side kink.

Comment: The tail is such an important part of any dog for it is the barometer of that dog's temper, fitness, alertness and sometimes his intelligence. I always pity the tailless breeds as they must do all of their signaling with their entire rear end. The functional use of the Bay dog's tail is to act as a rudder and balance in the water. It should not be heavily coated and its action when out of the water should be light rather than heavy non-expressive. A Bay dog trundling down the lane of his farm has his tail about the level of his back. There is nothing very important on his mind. He is just having a general check of his territory. A Bay dog guarding, barking an alarm or showing concern with a strange person or car on his property will raise his tail somewhat higher than we like to see in the show ring. In searching a marsh for downed birds the action of the tail can be a side to side lashing or wagging action particularly when the scent of the game reaches the dog. The length of the tail is natural and undocked and is the length required on most undocked sporting dogs.

> **Coat and Texture**—Coat should be thick and short, nowhere over 1½ inches long, with a dense fine woolly undercoat. Hair on face and legs should be very short and straight with tendency to wave on the shoulders, neck, back and loins only. The curly coat or coat with a tendency to curl not permissible.
>
> The texture of the dog's coat is very important, as the dog is used for hunting under all sorts of adverse weather conditions, often working in ice and snow. The oil in the harsh outer coat and woolly undercoat is of extreme value in preventing the cold water from reaching the dog's skin and aids in quick drying. A Chesapeake's coat should resist the water in the same way that a duck's feathers do. When he leaves the water and shakes himself, his coat should not hold the water at all, being merely moist. Color and coat are extremely important, as the dog is used for duck hunting. The color must be as nearly that of his surroundings as possible and with the fact that dogs are ex-

posed to all kinds of adverse weather conditions, often working in ice and snow, the color of coat and its texture must be given every consideration when judging on the bench or in the ring.

Comment: Of this breed's many unique attributes, his coat color, texture, and pattern of wave—not curled—hair is most unusual. The texture, of course, is most important, as he must have protection in bad weather. The correct coat will, with a quick shake, be left moist, and not dripping and freezing on him or the floor of the blind or boat. The double coat consisting of the thick woolly undercoat with the outer, crisp, waved coat is made waterproof by its oilness. When in proper coat the Chessie should not be bathed with soap or detergent, as this will remove the natural protective oil. Not only does this oil render the dog nearly waterproof, incidence of grass or flea allergies, hot spots or other skin problems occur very rarely in this breed. In the spring and early summer shedding may be quite prodigious with a Chessie that has spent the entire winter in unheated quarters. A warm bath or two with a mild soap and thorough rinsing will speed the unwanted old coat and provide a clean base for his new one.

The Chessie has a unique pattern of waved hair that starts just back of his skull, and proceeds rearwards, down the back of his neck and over the shoulders, and then on to the back, loins and tail. He has very slight breeches on the rear legs. On no account should the wave extend below a mid-point on the sides of the dog's body, and his face, legs and feet must be short and smooth. The balance of the body should have moderately short, straight hair. Once again this is related to work and function, there being no long hair on his sides, legs, face or chest to catch and hold water or to provide a place for icing in bitter weather. In summer the new coat may lie rather close and hard on the dog's body, but as fall comes on the typical waving, and very heavy undercoat will again be apparent. Trimming should not be condoned in this, one of the most natural of all sporting dogs.

Color—Any color varying from dark brown to a faded tan or deadgrass. Deadgrass takes in any shade of deadgrass, varying from a tan to a dull straw color. White spot on breast, toes and belly permissible, but the smaller the spot the better. Solid and self-colored dogs are preferred.

Comment: The color is to me very interesting, as it ranges from quite a dark brown through the reddish clay color and on to the dead-grass and sandy or sedge colors. I was glad when the disqualification of liver color was removed from the Standard as it was difficult to describe what the Chesapeake fanciers meant by the word liver, as opposed to the Springer fancier's idea of the color. Depending on the surrounding cover the Chessie can be of a color so like his background that he is undetectable, a great help in a fairly open blind.

Weight—Males, 65 to 80 pounds; females 55 to 70 pounds. **Height**—Males, 23 inches to 26 inches; females, 21 inches to 24 inches. Oversized or undersized dogs are to be severely penalized.

Comment: The thing to remember here is that the Chessie must be big enough to be a rugged, hardworking sporting dog, but must not be so large as to crowd you out of a blind, or swamp your boat on his retrieve.

Symmetry and Quality—The Chesapeake dog should show a bright and happy disposition and an intelligent expression, with general outlines impressive and denoting a good worker. The dog should be well-proportioned, a dog with a good coat and well balanced in other points being preferable to the dog excelling in some but weak in others.

Courage, willingness to work, alertness, nose, intelligence, love of water, general quality, and, most of all, disposition, should be given primary consideration in the selection and breeding of the Chesapeake Bay dog.

Comment: Unfortunately, in the two minutes or so that a judge is allotted per dog in the show ring, many of the Chessie's important points of symmetry and quality may go unrecognized. This is because many dogs are not mentally prepared by their owners to enter the show ring. The most magnificent working retriever may slink into the show ring looking for all the world as if he was waiting his turn at the vets. If this breed is to be a show dog as well as a worker, and I hope that the reverse proposition will not be implied, a little time must be taken to insure that the Chessie will greet a trip to the dog show with the same intense interest that he shows when on his way to the bird field. It must be fun for him, and he must be prepared mentally and physically for the demands of the show ring. Only then will the attributes of alertness, willingness to work and to comply with demands, intelligence and a bright and happy disposition be there for the judge and everyone else to see.

J. Tietelbaum's six-weeks-old "Matt" ponders a problem.

5

Choosing A Puppy

CHOOSING A PUPPY should be thoughtfully done, as this is no light matter. You are going to invest in a companion for many years to come, so, of course, you will want to get the best puppy you can to suit your needs.

First of all, do choose a reputable breeder, one recommended by the parent club, which is the American Chesapeake Club. Chesapeake owners find it well worthwhile to pay the moderate annual dues that the club charges its membership. The club publishes six bulletins each year. The bulletin discusses all breed problems, has articles on the latest health procedures, records the achievements of the dogs in bench, Obedience and field trial competition, and is a terrific source of general helpful information. To become a member of the American Chesapeake Club, write to the current club secretary. You can get the address by contacting or writing the American Kennel Club, 51 Madison Avenue, New York, N.Y. 10010.

If you are only looking for a dog for your family and/or for hunting, you will obviously have a wider choice of breeders than if you are looking for a dog to show on the bench, or in Obedience, or to compete in field trials.

Different breeders specialize in strains particularly suited to one or another of these categories. *But any Chesapeake, in my opinion, should come from working stock.* It is not enough to just be a fine specimen; he should also work.

The whole trend in retrievers today is to keep them doing the job for which they were intended—retrieving. A dog who demonstrates his willingness and ability to work is a much more intelligent and pleasant companion than one who does nothing.

I admire the Labrador Club, which has taken a stiff position on this for many years. They will not recognize the bench championship of any

Labrador who does not obtain a Working Dog Certificate. Although this stand is not condoned by the American Kennel Club, I personally wish that the American Chesapeake Club would take the same position. Perhaps they will in the future, for now more and more of our bench championships are earning their Working Dog Certificates. There no longer is the gap there once was between the bench champions and the Obedience and field trial dogs. For dogs with both Obedience titles and field trial dogs who have had any success, have both demonstrated their ability and willingness to work.

Any reputable breeder should not object to a prospective buyer asking him legitimate questions about the puppies he has for sale.

One of the things you should find out is if both parents have a certificate from the Orthopedic Foundation of America for sound hips. When this is issued the dog is also given an OFA number, and it should appear on the pedigree that the breeder has made out for the pups.

Chesapeakes are a hardy breed and, on the whole, eminently sound. But dogs of all large breeds—Great Danes, Saint Bernards, German Shepherds, Labradors, Goldens, Chesapeakes, etc.—could carry a recessive gene for hip dysplasia. The only way hip dysplasia will ever be completely eliminated is when conscientious breeders only mate dogs where both are completely sound.

In addition to this, ideally both parents should also have a CERF certificate and number. CERF stands for Canine Eye Registration Foundation, which was started about 1975. A CERF number means that the dog has been examined by a board certified veterinary ophthalmologist and found to be free of such hereditary eye diseases as cataracts and progressive retinal atrophy, both of which can be inherited and can cause blindness. Although Chesapeakes as a breed have a low incidence of these, the CERF number should be a requirement for each dog before breeding.

When you go to buy a puppy have the owner of the litter show you the dam of the pups. If the sire is on the premises, also take a look at him. In addition, try to see all the dogs the kennel has on hand. It has been said that the status of a kennel lies in the quality of its *average* dogs, not just in some individuals.

Breeders who are reputable, feed their dogs properly, give them any necessary veterinarian care, and do not aim for a large margin of profit. This is not true of the puppy mills, so be sure not to patronize such places. Taking proper care of a pregnant bitch involves special feeding, special vitamins, and careful supervision of whelping. It also means constant observation of the progress of the pups after they are born. The female should be wormed when she first comes in season, and the puppies should be wormed at four weeks and again at six weeks, to prevent any infestation.

An attractive and healthy Berteleda litter.

Only thing cuter than one pup is eight of them. These are from the Chesachobee Kennels.

A careful breeder gives the puppies supplemental feedings from the time they are about three weeks old and usually weans them by the time they are six weeks.

Are both parents of the puppies friendly and well adjusted? Ask to see them retrieve, as any Chesapeake should do a simple retrieve. Do they perform with zest and enthusiasm? For you must remember that the puppies will, without doubt, take on many of the characteristics of their parents. Ask if the dam, and/or the sire have been used as shooting dogs. Do either of them have a Working Dog Certificate?

If you are looking for a show dog, inquire if the parents have been shown successfully. There should be some bench champions in the pedigree.

If Obedience is your thing, ask if either the parents or the grandparents have earned any of the Obedience titles: CD, CDX, UD, TD, or TDX.

If you are looking for a field trial prospect be sure to buy your puppy from a breeder who has a record of success in the field trials. The pedigree of the puppy should contain the names of some of the current Field Trial Champions or Amateur Field Trial Champions. Remember that the dogs four or five generations back are not as significant an influence as the parents and grandparents.

In 1978, $200. was the going price for a good puppy, both of whose parents were OFA and CERF certified. If you expect the choice of the litter, the price could be more. Field trial prospect pups could well be $300. for a male, $250. for female, if sired by a Field Champion or a dog who has done well in the trials.

Most puppies are sold when they are seven or eight weeks old. I will not ship a puppy that is less than eight weeks old, and most airlines will not take them until they are that age. As we all know, Clarence Pfaffenberger's book *The New Knowledge of Dog Behavior,* a bible on the subject, advocates taking your puppy home when he is 42 days old.

When you are first shown the litter of puppies, carefully observe the attitude of the group as a whole. They should be happy to see visitors, and come charging up to the fence, wagging their tails, and competing for attention. If there is one that is timid and hangs back, do not for a moment consider getting him.

Do the pups, as a group, seem healthy and robust? What is the condition of their kennel run? Is Is clean and sanitary? There should not be any unfinished food pans sitting around to attract flies.

There should be no dewclaws on the pup's hind legs, and most good breeders also have the front dewclaws removed when the pups are only a few days old.

Look at the puppy's mouth. His teeth, at this early age, should be slightly overshot, as these teeth will straighten out later on. He should not be undershot, which means that the lower jaw protrudes further out than the upper jaw.

Hanging them out to dry? Skyline and her pups.

Golden Haze, playing tug-o-war with her four-months-old puppies. Owner, Shirli Hayes.

The bone on the puppies should be heavy and their chests should be wide—but they should not be clumsy.

After you have decided which two or three you like the best, ask if you may take them for a little walk so you can observe their reactions to new things and new places.

Where the pups have never been given any retrieves, if you will bring a golf or tennis ball with you and bounce it in front of them a few times, you will see which pups are the most alert. They also should show an interest in retrieving any ball that is rolled on the ground in front of them.

At Guide Dogs for the Blind, in San Rafael, California, many years ago Stanley Head, Clarence Pfaffenberger, and I, devised some puppy tests which helped us select the puppies that we thought were most trainable and bold enough to do the work of a guide dog. This program is still being continued at the institution. Retrieving was one of the things we carefully observed, for it denotes the trait of willingness on the part of the dog. We also observed the reaction of a small puppy to a loud noise. A pup should be startled by it. But he should adjust to it. You can clap your hands quite loudly and watch the reaction of the pup. In a few seconds he should be willing to come back to you to be petted.

If you are considering an older pup, remember that young dogs do not stop growing until they are a year old. They go through some awkward looking stages until that time. Most dogs are not really mature, nor do they have their full physical development, until they are at least a year and a half old.

Okay! You have picked out a puppy that you like and you are satisfied that the people who own the litter were happy to answer your questions. They also impressed you with their sincerity, as well as the good quality of their dogs.

Before you leave you should be given a pedigree of your pup, as well as the registration certificate that you must send in to The American Kennel Club in order to have the puppy registered in your name.

You also should find out the feeding schedule used for the puppy, so that you can continue it. Ask what kind of food has been used. Perhaps the owners of the litter will give you enough food for one day, so you will have time to buy the same kind. Changing foods can be upsetting to a puppy's stomach.

Small puppies should be fed three times a day until they are three months old, and they should have vitamins, bone meal, and cod liver oil added to their food. They should be fed twice a day until they are about six months old. After that, unless the dog is too thin, once a day should be enough.

I am assuming that you have anticipated your puppy's arrival at home by preparing a box, basket, or crate for him to use as his bed. Of

Proper introduction to the water, with Mama nearby to give them confidence.

Maggie Hoagland's puppies being properly introduced to the water, with Maggie wading in with them.

course this should be placed in a sheltered spot, out of any draft, and not in the full sun where it may get too hot in the middle of the day. You should provide access to a space outside of his box where he can relieve himself, and you will usually find he will not soil his sleeping quarters.

His first night away from all his littermates may be a lonely one for him. If you place a clock or softly playing radio nearby, he may feel that he has company.

If you plan on keeping him in the house, it will only take a short ime to housebreak him if you are careful about it. Every time after feeding him, put him outside in an enclosed yard *almost immediately* and leave him there until he has relieved himself. Then bring him in for a while. The last thing you do in the evening is let him out before you confine him to his bed. And the first thing you do in the morning is the same—rush him out to his yard. If this is done regularly your pup will very rapidly establish the habit of being clean.

When your pup is about three or four months old, if you are interested in training him yourself you should contact the American Chesapeake Club Regional Director in your state, and find out from him when the club will hold the next "Training Day". These Chesapeake Days are usually held almost every month, and their purpose is to help Chesapeake owners to train their own dogs. They have an instructor for all their classes. In the puppy classes you will be shown how your dog should work both on land and in water.

Properly introducing a young dog to water is very important. The novice should be started in wading water and after he is satisfactorily performing in that, the retrieves can be gradually lengthened so that he has to swim a little. As he becomes more confident you can give him retrieves that are *only* in swimming water. Never make the mistake of throwing your dog in the water—you can ruin him for life. If he is reluctant to go, hold him on leash and let him watch other dogs retrieving. Most dogs have a very competitive spirit, and they will want to do the same thing. You can even let two dogs go after a bumper at the same time.

The Practice Days of the Chesapeake Club usually involve retrieving birds as well as bumpers. But again, your dog's introduction to feathers should be carefully done, and be supervised by a knowledgeable person.

It is good for any young dog to go to such classes, for they become accustomed to seeing groups of people and other dogs. It definitely makes your dog a better adjusted pet as well as a better hunting dog.

If you are going to have your dog professionally trained, be sure to inquire about the "pro" you are considering. Some trainers dislike Chesapeakes, and if they do they will not give them a break. By judicious inquiring you should be able to locate a trainer who likes Chesapeakes as well as Labradors and Goldens.

Cub's Nessa, her ball, and her private swimming pool, provided by owner Ernest Pfaff of Deerfield, Illinois.

A lot has been written about individual outstanding Chesapeakes. Many have had phenomenal wins on the bench. Quite a few have gained outstanding records in Obedience competition. And the successful field trial Chesapeakes are well-known from one part of the country to another.

But we tend to overlook the hundreds of Chesapeakes who are, in their own way, the most important of all—the average hunting dogs who also serve as the family pet. Lorraine Wermecheichik writes that we must not forget the importance of "the dog who lives within the family, giving them the love only a Chesapeake can give. The dog who is, day after day, part of the family life. The dog who, on the days that you are feeling down and out, will do some silly thing to let you know that he is there and cares."

She continues: "If they sense danger, these dogs stand ready to defend those they love. In addition to being the children's playmate and pet, they are eager and ready when Father calls to go hunting—no matter how cold the weather, the water, or the snow."

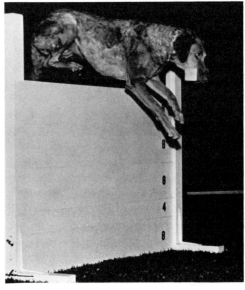

MISS EVE KEELER, author of the chapters on Early Puppy Training and Teaching Formal Obedience in this book, has been training dogs for Obedience for 25 years. She has judged at many matches and has served as Obedience Director for the Los Encinos Kennel Club.

As a member of several southern California Obedience clubs, she trained with such trainer-judges as Peggy Mellen, Howard and Sandy Cross, Joanne Weaver and Linda Penagaleck.

Her two present dogs are trained through Utility. Although her Chesapeake, Golden Boy's Titian Eve CDX (pictured here), is retired from competition, she remains active by attending advanced workshop training classes, seminars and AKC-supported shows, where she photographically records the entries.

Miss Keeler has spent several years in studying the methods for preliminary teaching of puppies presented in her chapter. She stresses procedures that will not in any way destroy the dog's confidence in himself or in his master, and that will at the same time tend to stimulate the dog's mental growth.

6

Early Puppy Training

by Eve Keeler

"The purpose of Obedience trials is to demonstrate the usefulness of the purebred dog as a companion of man, not merely the dog's ability to follow specified routines."—*From the preface of the official Regulations for licensed AKC Obedience Trials.*

As a COMPANION of man, a Chesapeake's usefulness depends on obedience, whether he is a family pet, gun dog, field trial dog, breed dog, or an Obedience trial dog.

Your Chesapeake can be a super dog, willingly obedient. All dog obedience is communication, implemented during kindergarten puppy training (at 7 weeks of age to 6 months) and refined for precision during formal training (starting at 6 to 8 months).

KINDERGARTEN PUPPY TRAINING

The Chesapeake personality is unusual. Most puppies appear very self-assured, often mistaken for aloofness. They do not *demand* your attention as other retrievers do. But do not be mistaken. They must receive intensive kindergarten puppy training (KPT) and socialization to fulfill their maximum potential.

Your Chesapeake puppy will grow, mentally as well as physically. Just as physical growth requires nourishment, maximum mental growth and psychological adaptability result from exposing your puppy to words, sounds, objects and sensations during the first six months of his life.

KPT is pre-Obedience training, programmed with the dog's point of view in mind. The full KPT procedures (along with training for formal

Obedience) are contained in *The Pearsall Guide to Successful Dog Training* by Margaret E. Pearsall (Howell Book House Inc.). Basically, communication is formulated in the mind of your puppy by your praise and encouragement, accompanied by *gentle*, manual corrections, never shouting or harshness. The key to successful training is consistency in your requests and in the words you use for a specific action.

However, be aware of a puppy's limitations during his early developmental stages. Training must be in the form of *guided* play. It must fit your puppy's attention span—very short. Never repeat an exercise more than three to five times, and include directed play periods. Always break the lesson before you both become bored. Remember that training sessions are *short*; it is daily repetition, not length of time, that instills any lesson. Your puppy is going to learn, but it's up to you to properly expand his learning capacity so that he develops into a happy, secure, out-going adult.

Preparing for Your Chesapeake Puppy

Prepare to receive your puppy by setting aside a draft-free, confined, area just for him. The area should include his bed, a water dish, and his toys. A good early bed is a crate, the size for a full-grown dog, or a cardboard box which is easily replaced if chewed on. The area should *not* be the run of the house. Restriction provides security, especially when it prevents him from learning bad habits, and you from having a reason to shout at him, which you never should do anyway. Most bad habits are born out of boredom. Therefore, your attentiveness through regular exercise and guided play is necessary.

All puppies use scent as their primary means of identifying people and objects. Your keen-scenting Chesapeake will associate the scent on his toys as being OK to play with—*anything* with that scent. Playing is chewing. Puppy toys must not be family discards. Training and grooming items must not be left for your puppy to play with.

Your memory-keen Chesapeake puppy will be eager to explore. Anything he is allowed to do now, he will try to do throughout life. The basic rules of what's acceptable must start from day one   It is much easier to prevent bad habits than to break them. Bend down to the puppy's level to pet him so he doesn't try to jump up. Make him wait until his food dish is on the floor and you say OK before he dashes in. Imprint on his mind all the rules that will make living pleasant and comfortable with a large, strong and quick minded Chesapeake.

Verbal Communication

Your voice can turn your puppy on or off. Verbal enthusiasm is infective. Praise is not an occasional pat; it must be verbally expressed. To

"Let's be friends."

Chow time, and everyone is ready.

"It's your move now." Two of George Balthazar's pups.

accomplish a specific action from your puppy, consistently use the same word every time, e.g., "Good boy!" "No!" Always praise correct action and always praise after a *manual* correction. Use a coaxing tone of voice to excite him into action. Use a happy tone for praise. Never use a harsh tone when training, even if your puppy is slow to learn—you might be to blame! Use a demanding tone only when you are positive that your puppy knows what's wanted, but refuses; however, don't be too quick to demand.

Physical Communication

As the trainer, you will be your puppy's new pack leader. Dogs interact through physical communication. Challenging signs are staring, erect ears, tail up, hackles, the head laid over another's withers, corners of the mouth pushed forward, and the lips retracted vertically. Signs of submission are ears flattened against the head, tail down or tucked be-tween the legs, deliberate exposing of the underside, head lowered, and lips pulled back horizontally to form the submissive grin. Understanding dog language, you should not stare (threatening gesture) at your puppy when he is coming back to you.

Touching, stroking, and handling your puppy all over is physical communication, vital for instilling confidence in your handling during formal training, and during home treatment of wounds or grooming. Early is the time to introduce nail cutting, teeth cleaning, whisker scissoring for show, combing and other forms of grooming.

Fetch Games

Pre-Obedience learning of fetch games is critical, especially for Chesapeakes. The breeder should start your puppy at 5-½ weeks (in the second critical period of socialization) on retrieving socks in a narrow hall or passageway so that the puppy has to come back. Fetch games expand the puppy's mind for learning growth; they teach the puppy *how* to learn. When the puppy goes to his new home at 7 weeks (the beginning of the third critical period), the continuation of fetch games is vitally important. Reinforce the previous training with a sock. Gradually advance to a small ball, a tennis ball, or a puppy bumper. Exercise care that any ball is not too large for your puppy's throat.

Remember the puppy's short attention span. Stop your fetch games before he tires. One or two retrieves are fine. If two are too much, keep it at one until he shows the desire to advance. Never exceed five retrieves in one session.

At this stage, you are teaching your Chesapeake how to learn, not perfection in retrieving. If he drops the article while coming back, do not

The first lesson from Mama.—*D. Carter*

Eastern Waters' puppies, belonging to Nathaniel Horn.

make him pick it up again (which teaches your retriever to play with the article). When he comes back (with or without the article), he *has* come back to you, usually eagerly—this is important. Don't grab for the article; let him enjoy it a little (grabbing teaches freezing). Hold your puppy and pet and praise him. Usually, he will drop the article; if not, open his mouth so it drops into your hand. Teach him the thrill of going out and the joy of hurrying back to you.

An economical, super puppy bumper is the fuzzy cover for a paint roller (about 7 inches long), fitted inside with styrofoam. Cover this with canvas-like material, nonpenetrable by puppy teeth—no rings or strings (prevents learning to pick up by the end or string). This bumper is lightweight, floats, and is soft for the mouth.

Housebreaking

Usually, your first obedience communication, for teaching your Chesapeake how to learn, is housebreaking. Your puppy can learn not only to not relieve himself in the house, but (1) to use a specific area, (2) to relieve himself on command, and (3) that verbal praise is a desirable reward.

To avoid accidents, you must watch for your puppy's needs—which usually are: after waking up; after a short period of play; and after eating—when you should take him to a specific area of the yard. The area may be simply a designated corner or a specially built area that is out of the way and easy to clean up and disinfect. Give him a word (command) in a normal tone of voice, "Hie on", "Get busy", or "Duty". Do not use words such as "Go", "Out", or "Hurry up" as these are words that will be used in formal commands or are commonly used in conversation. When he starts to use the area, praise him. Communication begins and housebreaking time is cut in half. He has learned that your command requires his action, and that his correct action brings him the reward of praise.

Pre-Obedience Commands

Caution about teaching pre-Obedience commands: Chesapeakes are smart and have keen memories. They can frequently outwit you. They are innovative in achieving their goals. They must see the usability of any command as a direct application to their needs. If you let your Chesapeake get away with not minding a command in these early stages, he will never forget.

Socialization

Socialization must occur prior to your Chesapeake's sixth month. Up to this time, he will readily accept new situations, environments, and objects. After six months, anything new to him will be suspect. You are going to have to go out of your way to find some of the forms of exposure for your puppy. KPT philosophy applies to socialization: your assured introduction, praise for curiosity, and short exposure times. What you react to, he will react to. The following paragraphs discuss suggested socialization:

Crating and Kenneling: Show and field dogs are almost always crated. Bitches in season are shipped in crates. Even a family pet may need to be crated as the result of an injury. A puppy that has been introduced to a crate is pre-conditioned to have no fear of it; therefore, when the necessity arises, the crating is security in the familiar. If your puppy has been pre-conditioned to a kennel run, he will feel right at home, knowing that you will come back to get him. If he hasn't been pre-conditioned, he will feel that he is being abandoned when kenneled after 6 months of age.

People and Objects (Sights): Your puppy will visualize all people according to those he is exposed to prior to 6 months. Things about people that affect him can be beards, hats, helmets, age (children and the elderly), clothes, and objects people use and carry. After 6 months, the *different appearing*—dog show judges and stewards; gunners, marshalls, and field personnel; the veterinary; people in homes he may visit, etc.—are to be suspect.

Sounds and Sensations: Pray for thunder, rain, sleet, and hail while your puppy is in this formative stage. If not, you might have to stimulate these sounds. Most gun dog owners know that you bang doors, pans, and the like while the puppy is eating—a pre-conditioning to the gun noises. Besides sights and sounds, introduce scents (birds and fields), motions (car, boats, etc.), and textures and environments (carpets, wood floors, stairs, tiled surfaces, ashphalt, concrete, water, hills, reeds and weeds, etc.).

You have been developing your Chesapeake to his fullest potential. At 6 months he will be so receptive and eager to learn more, that you will look forward to teaching formal Obedience training, which is discussed in Chapter 15.

End of a hard day's training session.

NANCY LOWENTHAL, author of this chapter, has had Chesapeakes all her life.

Nancy served on the Board of Directors of the American Chesapeake Club for four years and was in charge of the Regional Directors Program during that time. She still managed to show dogs, breed several excellent litters, and go hunting with her husband, Les.

Nancy and Les have helped countless other Chesapeake owners solve whatever training problems they might have. She is pictured here with her Ch. Berteleda Maggie, UD, CDX, and Maggie's daughter, Ch. Berteleda's Purdy Game Girl, whom Les runs in field trials.

7

Chesapeake Character

by Nancy Lowenthal

EVERYONE who has ever owned a Chesapeake seems to have a tale illustrating the nature of this individualistic breed. The Chesapeake's personality is as American as apple pie, and as difficult to generalize about as is the character of the American people.

The Chesapeake's beginnings were similar to those of the early settlers. The dog survived because of his ability to cope with life as he found it, do a more-that-honest share of work, and fulfill the needs of those upon whom he was dependent. He learned, and earned, the rewards of perseverance and loyalty, developing great self respect. He learned the advantages of accepting discipline, but he developed a pride that would not tolerate abuse or abasement. These traits are apparent today.

The Chesapeake is at his best when he can be part of a human family. When he enjoys this privilege he will work long and hard. Although he accepts confinement reasonably well, he cannot accept a solitary state devoid of people; he needs, and must have, love from humans.

This dog is serious about his work and responsibilities. An understanding, fair, loving (though demanding) taskmaster will receive unsurpassed loyalty and devotion. The Chesapeake is inclined to ignore strange people and animals as long as they do not interfere with what he considers the proper performance of his duties, one of which is to protect his family's property, real and otherwise, including house, lot, acreage, cars, trucks, children, dogs, cats, and birds—indeed anything that he considers worth protecting. A Chesapeake does not need to be taught to protect property; it is instinctive. A wise owner will not encourage this propensity, but will control and channel it. A Chessie is a calm, gentle, patient friend and guardian of children and will gladly endure and enjoy roughhouse and hard play.

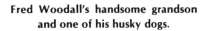

Fred Woodall's handsome grandson and one of his husky dogs.

Lonn Peige Wood, darling daughter of John and Karen Wood, with their great brood bitch, Chapel Jene, CD.

Douglas Smith, son of the Gary Smiths of Salina, Kansas, and his best pal. Ch. High Plains Ruff 'n Ready, CD.

Foxridge's Duffy, age ten, giving a ski tow to owner Shirli J. Hayes.

Two dominant traits found in almost every Chesapeake are the intense desire to retrieve and the love of water. A Chesapeake's idea of heaven is to retrieve waterfowl from rough, cold water every day, all day, year in and year out. This king of retrievers will retrieve almost anything that he can find. My Chesapeakes become very restive, particularly after duck season's close, about retrieving things about the house. They bring me shoes, boots, toothpicks, bobby pins, and once three goldfish from our outside pond, carefully delivered to the front doormat.

To say that Chespeakes love water is an understatement: they have a *passion* for water. Tom Williams, a well-known trainer, once told me that he would pray to have a Chesapeake with him if he were ever lost in the desert because, if there were one pothole of water within 500 square miles, that dog would find it.

Friends of mine were given a Chesapeake named Portola Pete by a field trialer, who rejected the dog from trials because he had a "water problem." My friends, who just wanted a pet, assumed that the dog didn't like water. One sunny weekend they drove to the Fort Cronkite beach on the Pacific Ocean for a picnic and took the dog along. Pete, escaping his leash in the parking lot, dashed for the ocean, with his owners running hard behind, shouting, ordering, whistling, and pleading for Pete to stop. Rushing through the pounding surf, Pete swam on and on in the general direction of Japan. Finally he paused to splash, bark, and play at an outcropping reef. Observers on the beach alerted the nearby Coast Guard rescue team, who launched a boat to rescue Pete. Despite the crashing surf and powerful riptide, they managed to reach the big wet dog, drag him into the boat, and return him to his grateful owners. Pete gobbled up a proffered ham sandwich to renew his strength, had a good roll in the sand, and again escaped to make his determined, powerful swim. . . .straight back to the same reef. This time the Coast Guard crew ignored him. When the sun began to sink, Pete swam back to the beach, shook himself, rushed back to the car, and crawled underneath to await condemnation. When told about the incident, the former owners explained that Pete's water problem was getting him out of the water, not getting him in it.

Another Chesapeake with a passion for swimming was Koko. Koko's owner was traveling across a bridge high over the Snake River in Idaho with the Chesapeake in the back of his truck. He slowed the truck and looked to see if there were any ducks in the water. There were, and Koko saw them too. The dog jumped from the pickup, over the bridge's rail, and 168 feet down into the water. After a long, fruitless swim, Koko responded to his owner's anxious call, calmly proceeded to shore, climbed the steep bank, and jumped back into the truck. Koko's jump was reported in headlines in the *Idaho Statesman,* January 9, 1975.

I remember another dog who liked to jump into water. Ch. Puff O'Smoke, the eleventh AKC bench champion Chesapeake, was purchased by my father in the East and brought to California in 1920. To acquaint Californians with the breed, he regularly entered "Bud," as Puff O' Smoke was nicknamed, in the annual Santa Cruz Kennel Club's high diving contest for dogs. My most prized silver trophy is inscribed: "Best 35-foot High Diver in the High Diving Contest at Santa Cruz, California. July 21-22, 1923."

My friend, Charlie Sambrailo, told me this unusual story about Bayberry Pete. One cold, drizzling, ordinary-duck-hunting-weather morning, Ed Fleischmann and Snuffy Belliveau took big, old, friendly Bayberry Pete out to the duck club for a day's shooting. It was necessary to travel in a small motorboat from the clubhouse to the blind, as it was quite some distance. Pete had a dim view of motor boats and repeatedly tried to jump out. He soon was thoroughly convinced by Snuffy and Ed that "STAY" meant stay in the boat as well as stay on the line, and he sat disconsolately, but obediently, in the boat's bow. Motoring smoothly through the channels, the boat suddenly hit an underwater berm and threw both men into the water. Not Pete, who remained in the boat where he had been told to stay. Lightened, the boat bounced off the berm, turned about, and with motor still on, made its way back eventually to a place near the clubhouse dock with Pete still firmly ensconced in the bow. When the keeper discovered the boat, Pete decided to be "on guard," as Chesapeakes usually do with their owner's possessions. Surmising that the hunters had met with mishap, but unable to get into the guarded motorboat, the keeper took the remaining boat, which had no motor, and rowed slowly out to rescue the stranded, cold, wet, disgusted hunters. (Chesapeakes take orders seriously and well when they have been impressed to do so. Sometimes too well.)

Another story which illustrates Chesapeake nature came from Monroe Coleman, the original owner of FC—AFC Nelgard's Baron, the sire found most often in the pedigrees of today's best Chesapeakes. Mr. Coleman related this incident to Eloise Heller Cherry when she purchased Baron from Cliff Brignall.

Monroe took the very young Baron hunting to grounds about five miles from his home, on a poor day for duck shooting. It was late morning before the hunter finally shot down a very high flyer. Unknown to both Monroe and Baron, the bird landed in a channel and drifted some distance from where they had seen it go down. Baron hunted in vain and finally was called back to the blind. Monroe lined him again to the original mark. Again Baron returned with nothing. Monroe, enraged about the loss of his only duck, recast the dog for the third time and got into his truck and drove home, leaving Baron to his own devices.

That evening, after dinner, Monroe relented and started out the door to look for Baron. On the doorstep sat Baron with the duck on the doormat. It had been nearly seven hours. The development of this natural perseverance and intelligence led to Baron's becoming one of the truly great retrievers of his day.

Many tales have been told about tough old Dual and Amateur Field Champion Baron's Tule Tiger. CD. Practically all the negative terms that have been applied to Chesapeakes were applied to him: stubborn, hard-headed, difficult to train, impossibly tough and irascible. His famous trainer often carried a garbage-can lid for armour, as well as a dog whip, whenever he expected to apply high-pressure training methods to this dog. If all this is true, one wonders how Tiger became the High-Point Field Trial Chesapeake of all time.

Here are some other facts about Tiger: he had an overwhelming desire to retrieve birds, particularly under difficult circumstances. He enjoyed hard work and approached his arduous training sessions eagerly. Tough and enduring, Tiger was never known to quit. He ran hundreds of trials and traveled thousands of miles by air and car. He advanced to the line in each test in every trial with deadly serious concentration, oblivious of adverse weather or water conditions. The dog ran his last trials with only one eye, but with the same honest, gallant drive that was so much a part of his nature.

According to his lifetime owner and handler, Eloise Heller Cherry, Tiger was a superb housedog. He welcomed all of her many guests and particularly enjoyed cadging snacks at cocktail parties. Eloise loved him better than all her other great dogs and he adored her; they understood one another.

His Chesapeake pride and self respect were evident. Tiger took his just punishment, as most Chesapeakes do, when he understood that he performed or behaved badly. But he would not tolerate punishment he considered unjust. (He and his trainer often disagreed on this point.) Tiger also determined exactly how much punishment was fair and, if it was carried beyond that point, he would look up and plainly indicate that he would not tolerate one more "lick." It was then that he became stubborn, hard-headed, tough and irascible.

When Tiger's trainer was developing the use of the shock collar for training trial dogs, he invited a young woman trainer to watch a demonstration. He considered Tiger tough enough to withstand possible mechanical problems due to the collar's imperfections at the time. (Airplanes flying closely overhead, for example, sometimes caused the collar to shock the dog.) So Tiger's trainer, the young woman, and Tiger traveled in the training truck far out into the fields for the demonstration. Something definitely went wrong. Although the trainer was armed with the garbage-can lid, the shock collar and the whip, Tiger decided that he had been treated unfairly and that his pride was at stake. He came through lid, whip, and collar and chased both trainers up onto the top of the truck's cab. And there they stayed until the kennel man, completing his evening chores back at the kennels, noticed that they had been gone an inordinately long time and came out to find two humans perched precariously on the truck's cab and Tiger on guard below.

"It's all right, Tiger. Time to go home for dinner," the kennel man said. Tiger agreed; so did the trainers, and that's what they did.

Dual Champion Cub's Kobi King is an intelligent and perceptive dog with a very intense personality. He has learned to communicate his desires to humans in numerous interesting ways.

Raised in Alaska by owner Helen Hartley, he showed enormous field potential at a very young age. He was sent to be trained for trial competition to Wayne Crook, who loves and appreciates the breed's individuality and prideful nature. Crooks' Kennels are on the Pacific Ocean's shores in California and Kobi lived there for eight years.

Confined to a kennel (of which he never became protective), Kobi ignored most of the kennel boys and male visitors. But as he was brought up by a woman, he acknowledged female visitors with a sniff or two and a tiny wag with the tip of his tail. When his owner came to visit, which she could only rarely do because she lived so far away, Kobi greeted her happily but not effusively. Although he respected both Wayne, and his son Chuck, co-trainer, enough to work for them, Kobi never really liked to be petted after a good day's work. He would dodge his head away from that kind of advance. But he did enjoy voluble praise and would respond with a few wags of his tail.

Kobi's protective instinct guarded what he considered his right to privacy while breeding bitches. Three times Kobi knocked Wayne to the ground for attempting to assist the dog with a difficult bitch. He never bit Wayne, but would stand over him, sometimes lightly but firmly holding Wayne's arm or leg, and growled formidably. Wayne had to try to relax and enjoy his position until someone came along to convince the dog that he could attend his bitch with no interference.

The Chesapeake learned, too, how to demand his freedom from confinement. Kobi began to work sporadically, became deaf to whistles, refused to get in or out of the truck kennel, and exhibited other annoying habits. However, Chuck discovered that if Kobi were let out of the truck at the training area adjacent to the ocean to take a long swim in the surf, followed by a few minutes play with rocks on shore, the dog would trot back to the truck, jump in his kennel, and be ready to go to work. These trips were taken entirely at the dog's volition. Only after this daily performance would Kobi turn his considerable talents with enthusiasm and

Life is a serious matter for Jerry Stotts, age three, son of the Richard Stotts of Baldwinsville, New York. Their pup, Noble Rex—You're My Delight, at eight weeks seems equally serious.

Two old-timers.

concentration toward training. Kobi's field trial performance improved to such an extent that he earned his coveted Field Championship.

Kobi was sold to Charlie Sambrailo, who treated him kindly, but Kobi never related to his new owner enough to work well for him. However, he continued to run well for Wayne and Chuck Crook and he earned an enviable record of points in field competition. Perhaps Kobi's poor response to Charlie was caused by Charlie's affection for his Labrador, Drummer. Probably Kobi sensed that he could only hold second place in his owner's affection, Kobi never earned his Amateur Championship title. Charlie nicknamed Kobi "Grumps," which aptly described the dog's attitude towards his world and the people in it.

Charlie took "Grumps" hunting when the dog was about nine. They had a wonderful time. But Kobi soon forgot his steady ways and began to jump in front of the shotgun every time it was raised and aimed. To break this dangerous habit, Charlie applied the electric shock collar. It worked so well that Charlie tried it in field trial work to make Kobi respond better. Only after Kobi had ignored numerous whistles and shouts was the shock applied. Immediately Kobi went down on the ground and refused to move or make a sound, an unusual performance for a dog that has had shock applied. Kobi glared up at Charlie as if to say: "If you are going to kill me, do it now. I would rather be dead than accept or respond to this kind of humiliation." So the collar was discontinued, except for duck hunting.

Charlie and Kobi continued to enjoy hunting together at Charlie's duck club. Kobi's lines out to shot birds were straight and true but, after a time, his delivery lines back to his owner became circuitous. Kobi stayed in the water and did not try to run on dry banks as dogs often do. He would turn this way and that, run straight for a while and then turn sometimes away and sometimes toward his owner — but eventually he always retrieved the bird to Charlie's hand.

Many gravel paths traversed Charlie's duck club, but during duck season when water is let in to fill the ponds, the paths are almost all submerged. Kobi had discovered how much easier it is to run on the underwater paths than on the sticky, mucky, mudflat bottoms. It took the human much longer to discern what the dog had discovered in a short time.

Retired from trial competition at eleven years old, Kobi was entered to try for his breed championship; his bone structure and conformation were excellent. Charlie took him to a show kennel to be conditioned and prepped for the show ring performance. Kobi began to show affection for Ellen Loftsgaard, the kennel girl. She adored the old campaigner,

Helen Fleischmann, walking her puppies.

Taking the babies for a swim—the author and her daughter, Jill, in Sonoma, California.

bathed and groomed him, threw balls for him in the neighboring park, and rewarded his every sign of affection with liver treats, cadged from the kennel's unending supply. The show handler began to teach him show ring gaiting and stacking techniques, always rewarding him with snacks and kind words, and never punishing him. Kobi thrived. Bare spots on his legs, feet, and body, worn by years of lying in a concrete kennel, became less conspicuous as his sparse coat improved with daily grooming and special show diet.

Old "Grumps" began to show the animation and spirit necessary for successful ring performance. His body's strong muscling from years of field endeavors far outbalanced his worn teeth (diminished by playing with those rocks on the ocean shore). He was defeated only twice in his short show career before winning his AKC breed championship at age eleven. Bede Maxwell, one of the most celebrated and respected judges in the show world, who had put him up for championship points, heard about him completing his championship and sent him a special letter congratulating him on his feat. It was even addressed to Dual Champion Cub's Kobi King.

Kobi no longer lives in a kennel. Now he is back in Alaska with Helen Hartley, his first owner, whom he adores.

Cappy is a large, powerful, and exceedingly gentle Chesapeake. A nephew of Kobi, he exhibited the same tenacity towards his objectives, but employed an entirely different technique in obtaining them.

His first loyalty was to his young owners, who had raised him from puppyhood. They trained him in the basics of field work, took him hunting, brought him in the house every evening, and loved him dearly. His immense talent in field work was soon apparent to everyone who saw him and his owners were encouraged to trial him. A professional trainer was employed to perfect his training and Cappy began to win. He was sold for a prodigious price to one of the breed's most successful and prominent field trialers and he became the California All-Breed Derby Champion.

At the end of his Derby career, Cappy was sent to one of the nation's top training kennels for advanced training. This kennel uses the electric shock collar methods in training retrievers for competition. Confined in unfamiliar quarters, under absolute control of a strange trainer, who showed him little affection, Cappy became unhappy. He was trained there for two years and he endured. But he became aloof from both trainer and owner and would not truly relate to humans in that situation. He learned his lessons well, but he would not work hard enough, nor exhibit the style and speed needed to realize his potential in trial competition.

His owner took him home at times to brighten him up but his attitude did not improve. Praise or correction was met with passive resistance. His trial performance was lackluster. His natural tendencies to guard were never exhibited, as he greeted strangers in a most obsequious manner. Everyone who knew the dog at this time remarked about his friendliness to strangers and how atypical of the breed he was.

So Cappy was sold to an amateur owner in the East. His new owner fell in love with him on sight. Although Cappy had been a "kennel dog," she brought him into the house with her other dogs and he soon became part of the family. His response was a happy and devoted attitude. She began showing Cappy, a magnificent specimen of the breed, in the breed ring and he is well on way toward his bench championship.

Cappy was sent to an excellent Eastern field trainer, who had a real understanding of Chespeakes and who does his share of winning in field trial competition. This trainer understands the breed very well indeed; he decided that Cappy should sleep in his house by his bed every night. He explained that a California raised dog could not possibly sleep outside until he was acclimated to the cold Eastern winter.

An observer who knew both trainers pointed out that going from the first trainer to the second was like going from the depths of hell to the heights of heaven. Could a Chesapeake stand such prosperity? (Chesapeakes are believed by some to need sustained and pronounced authority to perform well.)

After a winter of renewing his spirit, personality, and field expertise, Cappy won the Qualifying stake in the first spring trial in which he was entered.

His new owner purchased a new Airstream Trailer so that she and Cappy can be together and enjoy air-conditioning while traveling on the field trial circuit. Cappy can sleep near his beloved owner, on his own mat, on his own bed, in his own trailer, all of which he defends in the typical Chesapeake manner.

These few stories are told to illustrate the character and some of the facets of the temperament of our Chesapeakes. They are loyal and devoted to their masters and they will give their all for them. But, in turn, you must establish a good relationship with them, showing them respect and real affection.

Mike McLemore, who has won many of the National Duck Calling contests, calls them closer while his Chesapeake, Duke, watches the sky. — *Jerry Hard.*

8

The Chesapeake—
Hunter and Companion

THE OLD TIME MARKET HUNTERS and their big guns has always been a fascinating subject, for duck hunters of every era. The best description I have ever read of this appears in James A. Michener's exciting· book, *Chesapeake,* published by Random House in 1978. It relates how these guns were used on the Chesapeake Bay.

Michener says, "Duck hunting with a big gun was an exacting science best performed in the coldest part of winter with no moon, for then the watermen enjoyed various advantages: they could cover the major part of their journey by sliding their skiffs across the ice; when they reached areas of open water they would find the ducks clustered in great rafts; and the lack of moonlight enabled them to move close without being seen. The tactic required utmost silence; even the crunch of a shoe on frost would spook the ducks. Sometimes it took an hour to cover a quarter of a mile; the barrel of the gun was smeared with lamp black to prevent its reflecting such light as there might be.

"With one explosion of a big gun like this, the watermen sometimes got themselves as many as 80 or 90 ducks. On rare occasions they would be able to fire twice in one night."

Speaking of Twombley's gun, Michener tells us, "It was one of the proudest guns ever to sweep the ice at midnight. It was a monstrous affair, eleven feet six inches long, about a hundred and ten pounds in weight, with a massive stock that could not possibly fit into a man's shoulder, which was good, because if anyone tried to hold this cannon when it fired, the recoil would tear his arm away. The gun was charged with three quarters of a pound of black powder, over a pound and a half of Number Six shot, plus one fistful.

"This gun was mounted in a fourteen foot skiff with an extremely pointed bow and almost no deadrise, chocks occupying what normally would have been the main seat, and a curious burlap contraption built into the stern area. The gun barrel was dropped between two chocks, a wooden lock was secured over it, and then the heavy butt was fitted into a socket made of burlap bagging filled with pine needles in the stern area. You don't point the gun; you point the skiff. And when you get seventy, eighty ducks in range, you put a lot of pressure on the trigger. The gun explodes with a power that seems to tear a hole in the sky. The kickback is absorbed by the pine needles in the stern." Twombley's Chesapeake was then expected to retrieve all these birds.

Michener describes another waterman who "mounted seven guns in his boat, each with a barrel two inches in diameter. They fanned out like the tail of a turkey gobbler. There was a trough just below the powder entrances to the seven guns. It was filled with powder all the way across the trough, and it was lit at one end. It then fired each of the seven guns in order."

Let's turn back the clock about 80 years, to read a story written by C. L. Hancock of Cody, Nebraska who wrote:

We were going hunting at the Ankeny Clubhouse, 22 miles south of Lakeside, Nebraska. I was a 14 year old kid driving teams for the Lundsford livery barn. There were no automobiles at that time, and no roads, only cow trails through the sandhills. Twenty-two miles was a long hard day for a good team hitched to a spring wagon, loaded with hunters and their dunnage. It was a tough trip, jolting along in the old wagon.

Sandy Griswold, sporting editor of the *Omaha World,* had come to shoot ducks, as this was a very famous place. Although we did not arrive until shortly before sundown, Sandy still thought he had to shoot a duck before he called it a day. As soon as we arrived he hopped out, put on his shell vest, grabbed his old gun, and took off for a lake over the hill about three quarters of a mile away.

Came dark and dinner time, but Griswold did not come in. His pals decides they were going to go out to hunt for him. Just then Griswold came dragging in, completely exhausted.

Sandy reached for a hankerchief in his hip pocket and discovered he had lost his billfold. He then went wild, and the boys couldn't quiet him down because besides the $200 in his billfold, it contained papers that he felt that he just couldn't lose.

Mr. Ankeny told Griswold to come outside with him and show him the path he had used coming back. It was dark as ink outside, raining some, and getting cold. Ankeny said to Griswold, 'Give me your hankerchief.' He then called Mike, a big, beautiful Chesapeake dog, and had Mike smell the hankerchief. Then Ankeny talked to Mike as one would to a person. He said, "Mike, this man has lost his billfold and you must go find it. Go find." The dog whined a little but then disappeared into the dark.

Griswold said to Ankeny, "That was a foolish thing to do because I was in the water, out of the water, and all around the lake. There is no possible chance for a dog to find that billfold."

Mike did not return that night but next morning at daylight I saw Mike laying on the top step of the bunkhouse with a billfold between his paws.

Typical hunting scene—bringing back a big one.

Day's work done. Ed Apple's Chesapeake now guards the birds.

John E. Hurst and William B. Hurst, Jr., who in the old days owned the famous Chesacroft Kennels in Lutherville, Maryland, wrote in their circular, which was put out in 1925:

How many times, brother sportsman, have you wished for some method to get that crippled mallard who, falling too far from the blind for you to reach, was making his way to the reeds. You knew if you went to get the boat, the duck would beat you to the marsh and become the victim of some preying raccoon or mink in the coming night. How many times have you spoken about the rotten pattern of your gun as you watched the spray of shot about the head, which was the only visible part, of that wing-struck redhead who was making away from your decoys, and laughing at your ineffectual attempts? Or the time when your patience was exhausted and you jumped into your rowboat to get that redhead or die in the attempt? And, of course, that would be the very moment when a bunch of bluebills would pass by, just aching to decoy!

All these, and countless other trials and tribulations, are not the fault of anyone but yourself. The properly trained Chesapeake is the cure-all of the wild-fowl hunter. True, he can't make the birds fly, nor set out your decoys, nor build your blind, nor kill your ducks, but he can and will do about everything else. The cripple moving rapidly away will be in your bag if he has to follow it for a mile. He is as able a trailer of the crippled bird in the marsh as any Bloodhound, and when he comes back with his quarry in his mouth, and his tail wagging with the knowledge of a deed well done, you will then know the acme of sport; humane elimination of wastefulness by the co-operation of your best pal. And you'll find he is more than a dog—he is a most intelligent pal.

As a further instance of the Chesapeake's almost human intelligence, I will relate an incident which occurred about ten years ago at Lego's Point, a promontory which marks the dividing line between Bush River and the Chesapeake Bay, and where we built a large, permanent, concrete blind. We had then in our possession a dog named Prince of Lego's (whose name appears in nearly all our pedigrees). This old chap, as fine a type as I have ever seen, was accustomed to lay along the side of the blind toward the river and about on a level with our heads. Little attention was paid to him as he lay as still as a log. The tremors which from time to time we noticed, were attributed to the cold. These were soon forgotten in a spasm of shooting. It was not long, however, before we began to notice the coincidence between these tremblings and the shooting which generally followed, and we commenced to watch the old fellow. He would sight a duck coming from the river at a much further distance than our eyesight permitted, and his eyes would never leave it. From that time on we left the watching on the river side to Prince, and contented ourselves with watching him, knowing that his incredible eyesight would not fail us.

At another time, my father left the point blind to take refuge from a sudden storm in a little cabin which was situated a short distance away. He intended to return after the storm and so left the rubber cushions which he used for a seat covering in the blind. Finding that the storm was not going

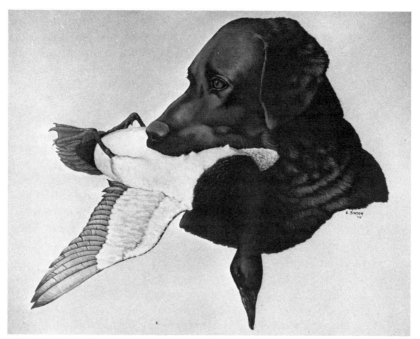

Ch. Crosswinds Flying Gee Bee, WD, with canvasback, a painting by Arthur Sinden, which the three Lowman children had done as a gift for their parents, Kent and Fran Lowman of Illinois.

Winston Moore and friend in their duck blind on the Snake River of Idaho, with AFC Chesnoma's Louis, who expertly retrieved their limits.

to let up he continued back to the house. That afternoon at feeding time one of the young puppies which were being trained that day was missing, and no trace could be found of him. Early the next morning when my father returned to the point he was first greeted by a fierce puppy growl from the depths of the concrete box, followed by hilarious and happy barks of welcome. That seven-month-old puppy, who incidentally became Champion Chesacroft Tobe, had stayed, without a word of command, without food, and by his own will, faithfully guarding his master's property.

The well-known writer, Ray P. Holland, is a real Chesapeake enthusiast. In his book *Bird Dogs,* published by A. S. Barnes and Company in 1948, he makes some interesting comments on our breed:

"There are a number of reasons why I like the Chesapeake better than any other retriever. He has a better coat for the work than any other dog. This explains why he can take rough weather that will freeze out other breeds. I have seen Chesapeakes with ice frozen to their coats lie on a wet sand bar and not shiver unless it was from the excitement of an approaching flock of ducks. The reason they can do this is because of their under-coat which does not get wet.

"I like Chesapeakes because they get along well with other dogs that may be along on a hunting trip. I can't say they are friendly with other dogs. Rather they are tolerant. The Chesapeake is not a fighter—unless the other dog starts it. Then he can more than take care of himself. Yet I have never known one that would follow up an advantage with intent to kill, as will so many dogs.

"Instead, most Chesapeakes will run into another dog that wants to start something, and when that heavy shoulder hits the quarrelsome one it sends him rolling. Then the Chesapeake will stand over such a dog and give him a good growling. After that is over he will walk off and never look back. Usually that is all it takes. The other dog doesn't want any more of the same kind. Apparently he realizes just what the big retriever could have done to him."

Mr. Holland identifies qualities he especially admires in a Chesapeake:

". . . courage and stick-to-itiveness, plus the ability and nose to get what he goes after, and all the time enjoying his work. I have seen these dogs lie on a cake of ice and pant with excitement as ducks flew over. Often I have hunted when the weather was so cold that the drops of water on the outer coat of the dog would freeze almost immediately when they climbed out. Yet when the duck was dropped they would plunge in to retrieve and come out with the ice all washed off, only to have it form again until they would rattle when they walked.

"I have seen Chesapeakes swim out into a lake after a diving duck until you had to strain your eyes to see the little brown spot that was the head of your dog—and come back with the duck. When the old Missouri

Brandon West, son of Findley West of Texas, and his Canadian honker.

Learning to call them. Mike Ray, son of Robert Ray, Jr., starts in early. Here shown with his father's field trial dog, Blue Valley Jimbo.

River was filled with large cakes of floating ice after the spring break-up, it took a he-dog to go out and bring back a duck. I've seen a Chesapeake climb up on an ice cake, cross it and plunge in on the far side time and again to reach his duck, and then have to do the same thing to get back to shore. That takes courage, super-dog strength and a love of the game.''

Fred Woodall, a famous Illinois hunter, was asked for a tale about 'the good old hunting days' and wrote us:

"As near as I can recall the year was 1920 when the shooting season ran from September 16th to January 5th and the limit was 15 ducks a day or 60 in possession. I was running a Duck Club when the 'feed-pens' were in their hey-day. I had 17 of these 'feed-pens' or 'feed-holes,' in the river bottom land and one 'feed-pen' in the corn fields of the prairie. All 18 of these pens had 50 to 100 live ducks in them. The ducks were fed daily with these mallards cleaning up 20 to 50 bushels of corn each day.

As everything except the Sangamon River, itself, had been frozen solid for days, I had decided to break camp January 7th. This meant gathering up one thousand to twelve hundred live ducks and getting them and all my other paraphernalia back home.

To accomplish this, I had hired a local trucker and three helpers to assist in this back-breaking job.

Quite unexpectedly, two Chicago hunters who felt they had not had their money's worth, showed up despite the freezing weather.

The gang went down to the far timber-hole near the river to bring in the first 90 ducks and also in the hopes of getting a few shots.

The trucker, gun in hand, was the first to walk to the river and Bang! Bang! Bang! He yelled, "Send Butch over!" This command was needless as Butch was practically there before the last shot rang out! By the time I got around to reaching the scene, Butch had three of the fat mallards already, and was going for the fourth one a couple hundred yards downstream. Butch brought in the fourth duck, but the fifth one was centered on a six-foot cake of ice, which was rapidly gaining distance downstream.

Butch tried and tried, but it was impossible for him to get that duck off the cake of ice. It was the only one, in a lifetime of spectacular retrieving, that he ever failed to get.

The Sangamon River on this day was alive with ducks, for as everything had been frozen solid for days they were probably coming to this open water to get their feet warm. Crane Lake, a great concentration place, about two miles away, had an estimated one million ducks sitting on the ice at this time.

Seeing the thousands of ducks milling up and down the river, was more than we could stand regardless of the job we had come to do.

I always had a few ducks at each stand with rings on their legs for 'tieouts' or 'decoys' and I carried lines with snaps on them in my hunting coat. It took us but a few minutes to put a few of these ducks on the line and stretch the line across a narrow opening along the back of the river.

This, along with our calling, was quite sufficient to bring those fast-flying mallards within gun range.

In this crude manner, with the gang lined up alongside trees on the river bank, and with no boat within miles of us and fifteen feet of water in front of us, we were shooting ducks just about as lively as possible with every duck falling out into the flowing current. Old Butch did not miss another duck! Each time he came out of the water, pebbles of ice froze to the hair on his back so that he actually rattled as he ran.

When we had a count of 105 dead mallards for the seven of us to carry, we called it a day.

In the cabin that evening, one of the boys felt sorry for Old Butch lying out on the back porch—'with all that ice on his back.' He coaxed him into the cabin. In a few moments we noticed that Butch's tongue was out and he was panting as though it was the month of August. The minute someone opened the cabin door, he promptly ran out again to his gunny sack bed on the porch. The next morning he greeted me with gusto and rattled around with some of those ice balls still on his back! Gay as a robin in May!

Today, I have about the 'teenth' Retriever by the name of Butch. Although I never expect to again see a day when a dog will retrieve 105 ducks in zero weather, from a fast-flowing river, I am quite sure that my present day Butch is a "chip off the old block."

Several years ago, we asked Winston Moore, of Boise, Idaho, who is an avid hunter, to write us about some of his experiences. We think that you will enjoy his Salton Sea Story. He tells us:

"One of the first and finest I've owned was my Stormy. He was not big as Chessys go, weighing about 65 pounds, but he was extremely fast and eager. We used to hunt the Salton Sea in Imperial Valley, California. This body of water is perhaps 40 miles long and several miles wide and with a little wind certainly resembles the ocean. We used to put out over one hundred wooden decoys and shoot redheads and canvasbacks from a boat. As any duck hunter knows a crippled redhead or 'can' is a real challenge for motor boat or dog. Many is the time that Stormy, swimming through three or four foot swells, was completely out of sight for a matter of ten to fifteen minutes, only to always return with the bird. These were, of course, extremely tiring retrieves, but he was always just as eager to get the last bird as he was the first.

The fact that the Chesapeake is without question the supreme duck dog is backed up by professional guides all over the United States. A friend of mine at Tulelake, California, guides for a living during the duck season, and will tell you story after story of the other breeds quitting when the weather and going gets tough, while his Chesapeakes keep right on bringing in the birds.

My Chesnoma's Louis demonstrated to me, time after time, not only what tremendous courage and heart these dogs have, but also that they have the fantastic ability to think things out, and cope with a new situation. Last season a doctor friend of mine invited me to shoot with him on an island in a very treacherous river in Idaho. Neither Louis or I had ever hunted this particular island before so it was all new to us. The island was perhaps a half mile long, but only two hundred yards wide, with slack water on only one side. Shooting from this spot we had to be careful and pick our shots so that the birds would fall in the slack water. If they fell in the current, and it was a swift and rough one, they would be carried far away.

The shooting was fantastic and within a short time we were limited out on mallards but kept calling in bunches of ducks, trying to spot a pintail or a widgeon—as they were bonus birds. Finally in one nice bunch of mallards there was a drake pintail. The pressure was on as we didn't care to shoot another mallard—yet we wanted this prime pintail. We both fired and unfortunately, merely wing-tipped the bird, who sailed two hundred and fifty to three hundred yards away, landing in the the swift water. Louis saw the fall and was on his way. After about five minutes I decided to have a look, so stood up. I saw a dot that might be Louis. The binoculars proved it was—Louis, still swimming after our crippled pintail! Finally he captured the duck, and for a moment tried to head up-river, all the time being carried further down-stream. He was easily one-half mile away and was now barely visible in eight-power binoculars. He finally came into sight directly opposite our island. He stopped, looked at me, then ran further up-river till he was opposite the up-river end of the island, and plunged back into the river. The current here is known to be 12 miles per hour. Even though Louis entered the river above our island, and is a very powerful swimmer, he just barely caught the down-river end of this island. Finally he came trotting through the brush and presented me with a beautiful drake pintail, who was very much alive.

After seeing a performance like this I wonder how people can think that dogs have no reasoning power. This retrieve involved swimming almost a thousand yards in zero weather. Louis had already brought in two limits of mallards but he merely shook himself and was ready to go again.

In 1957, by actual diary count, he retrieved 588 ducks and 4 honkers. Last year I estimate his work at nearly 700 ducks. Often he was the only dog working for several hunters and he never, ever, let us down.

In our time not very much has been heard about tolling ducks and geese although many of the old hunting stories tell how retrievers were trained for this. However, Ernest Pfaff, an American Chesapeake club member from Deerfield, Michigan recently told us that his six months old female, Thor's Nessie, was doing it naturally.

He wrote, "My hunting partner and I were goose hunting on the shores of Lake Michigan and the breakers were running about three and a half feet high. The waves would knock Nessie down and wash her up on the beach. She would then chase them as they ran out. She really loves the water as most of our Chessies do.

"Nessie devised her own system of tolling the geese until they were within about fifteen feet of the shore—and in front of our blind. She ran,

Jonathan Kronsberg of Charleston Heights, South Carolina, calls them in closer so that he can get a shot. Mullet is known as a fine retriever.

Texas David Sheaff got a white one, which was handily retrieved by his Independence Sweetback Bay.

George Balthazar's Baltz Whitefoot Bay and Findley West's dog, Fin's Bay Boy Buckshot, bring back a couple of fat mallards.

Jim Batte and his friend Bob Schlemmer took his Missy on an Alabama duck and goose hunt, getting the limit.

In the days of larger limits — the Dan Bilboa family had a day of wonderful shooting.

barked, splashed, swam out into the water, and back again, until the curious geese had traveled about a hundred yards, over to our side of the lake. Then when the geese came quite close, Nessie sat quietly, until we shot at the ones we could reach. I had never seen this done before. Nessie is a really smart puppy.''

Chesapeakes also are excellent performers in the field on upland game. They can easily be taught not to range out too far, so that when they flush birds they are usually in range. You can readily tell when your dog has scented a pheasant, or quail, because of his increased tail activity, and his excited and alert attitude.

Chesapeakes are often used on doves, most of whom are shot in the hot weather of the early fall. You will invariably see Pointers, setters, and other hunting breeds, overcome by the intense heat, but Chesapeakes seem almost impervious to it.

In chukkar hunting, in the West, the birds are hunted on high mountain sides. When shot, they often fall across a steep canyon, and must be retrieved from a considerable distance. It takes a rugged dog to stand up to these lengthy retrieves, which necessitate his climbing up and down these precipitous canyons.

Winston Moore writes, "Generally in pheasant hunting my Chesapeakes take me hunting, I don't take them. I will stop the car near some likely looking cover, but from then on I follow the dog. And more often than not we come in with the birds while the dogless boys come in birdless and with complaints about 'no birds' and 'all hens,' etc. I will never be a bit interested in hunting pheasants without a good Chesapeake.

"Several years ago my wife and I, hunting pheasants, were working a long draw, always good for a rooster or two. My dog was down in the bottom charging through brambles and thickets, putting up numerous hens but no roosters. I noticed his tail suddenly go into action, indicating at last he was on a rooster, which promptly erupted from under Stormy's nose. I got off two shots and while the bird did not collapse, as a dead one will, I knew he was hard hit. He sailed about a hundred yards before disappearing into the thickest cover in the draw. Away Stormy went. before he reached the area where the bird went down, he stopped, checking a rabbit hole. He insisted on staying there and smelling the hole. I insisted he leave it and come with me to find the bird. As he paid no attention to my commands, I put a collar and leash on him, swore a little, and literally dragged him away from this hole. About 30 yards up the draw I released him telling him to 'hunt' em up.' He immediately turned around making a mad dash back to the hole and beginning to dig very vigorously. He dug and dug, snorted and snorted. Finally he made one furious siege, backed out of the hole, presenting us with a big rooster pheasant who was very much alive. Apparently when this bird hit the ground he ran toward us instead of away from us, and took shelter in this hole, and the dog winded him there as we approached the spot where the rooster went down.

"Last year I had one dog that on two different occasions froze over a bunch of cover. As I moved in, getting ready for the shot, he charged the brush, flushed the bird and actually caught a live rooster in each case."

Dan Russ, Federal Game Warden, has a Chesapeake he loves. He proudly writes, "Last summer Miss Mockery and I were assigned to Alberta, Canada, to band waterfowl for the period July 1 to August 5. This assignment was in accordance with studies conducted on the Canadian breeding grounds by the Fish and Wildlife Service and cooperating agencies. My assignment was to band 'local' mallards on a permanent check area between Bassana and Drumheller, Alberta. The term 'local' is applied to a young duck that has not yet attained flight, and can be considered as having hatched in, or near, a pot-hole or slough where banded. From records maintained, Miss Mockery retrieved 776 locals during twenty-five days worked. Of the total number of locals retrieved, twelve died of injury and 764 were banded. Miss Mockery had her best day on August 2nd when she retrieved 73 ducks.

"Because of weather conditions on the prairies, it was necessary to begin banding at 4:00 A.M. and conclude activities at about 9:00 A.M. The maximum temperature recorded was 108 degrees during the week of July 11-16. Following a thunderstorm or a hailstorm, the temperature would fall to 56 degrees. I witnessed a severe hailstorm during which the hailstones measured two inches in diameter. In spite of the abnormal weather, Miss Mockery showed excellent stamina and adaptability. She required no veterinary care; however, I supplemented her diet with vitamins.

"A few weeks ago I received instructions that tentative plans were being formulated for this summer's Canadian banding assignments. Miss Mockery and I look forward to bettering our past record. We would not consider splitting up the team."

From another source we have heard that Warden Russ was far too modest in his story of Miss Mockery. Although the banding is not a retrieving contest, we understand that Miss Mockery caught and retrieved three hundred more ducks than the next highest scoring team. All this in her first season of experience. Her small record of injury to the ducks is almost incredible, when you consider that these young ducks are far more active than most cripples, flapping at high speed across open water, and skulking or running in heavy marsh grass.

Older club members will remember Miss Mockery as a young trial dog, having placed in the Derby at the 1959 Specialty in Kansas City. She was sired by Ralph Mock's AFC Chuck's Rip Joy and was out of Charleton Lady.

Aside from their hunting prowess, there are many other fine attributes inherent in our breed, illustrated by the following stories, which show the courage, intelligence, and the adaptability of the Chesapeake.

Many years ago I was approached by a game warden I knew asking me if I could find him a good Chesapeake he could use in his work. He was stationed on one of the state hunting preserves in Northern California, where I often shot. He claimed that quite a few of the hunters who came from the city were shooting over their legal limits. Then, as they came through the checkout stations, they would hide these illegal birds in the hub caps of their cars. He intended to train a dog to sniff at the hub caps of each car, as the hunters drove their cars up to check out. He wanted, and I sold him, my year old Pruneface.

The following year several hunters I knew were among those discovered storing their extra birds this way, as Pruneface had become very proficient in sniffing out the hub caps. They knew Pruneface, they knew me—and it did not add to Pruneface's popularity, or mine, or that of the Chesapeake breed.

Many people who do not know Chesapeakes have heard, and believe, that they are extremely aggressive dogs, always looking for a fight. I can attest to the fact this this is not so!! Many of them are perfect gentlemen, and William Hoard's Deerwood Trigger and my Storm Cloud II were fine examples.

In 1953 at the Chesapeake Field Trial Specialty, both "Bill" Hoard and I had flown in, and both of us had rented cars. By chance, they gave us identical blue Ford sedans. Trigger was the only dog in Bill's car. But as I was competing with Sasnakra Sassy, a female, as well as with my big, strong male Storm Cloud II, these two were in my car. When I went to the line with "Stormy," I left Sassy sitting in the back seat of my car. Stormy performed quite well, and I was extremely excited. Evidently, I was so overcome with success, that when I returned to where the two blue Fords were parked, I opened the back door and told Stormy to get into the wrong car. Then I got into the front seat—where I looked for my purse and cigarettes. Instead, I saw a man's hat and pipe!

I quickly turned around and there on the back seat sat Trigger in the left corner, looking out the left window. Stormy had gotten in, and was sitting in the right corner, looking the other way, out of his right window.

I was petrified! No one ever got herself out of a car faster than I did, calling Stormy to come with me.

Both Trigger and Stormy were fully grown males, both had been used at stud. Yet they got along even though they had never been properly introduced, or even seen each other before. Who says Chesapeakes don't have good temperaments?

Brown Dog was the name given to the Chesapeake Bay Retriever, owned by Mr. and Mrs. W. A. McKay of Campbell River, British Columbia.

Mr. McKay was working at his logging camp near Campbell River, when he was attacked by a cougar. The cougar cornered McKay, knocked him down, and broke his leg. Brown Dog charged for the cougar's head, barking all the way. The big cat turned and ran with Brown Dog pursuing until the cougar was treed. According to Mr. McKay he would have sustained far more serious injuries had it not been for the timely intervention and pursuit of his dog.

On September 12, 1974, at the Maple Leaf Gardens in Toronto, Ralston Purina of Canada Ltd. presented Brown Dog with an award in recognition of his heroism and intelligence.

Another interesting tale concerns Duchess, who was obtained by her owners under unusual circumstances. She was donated to the Immaculate Conception Church in Baltimore, Maryland, to be raffled off at a church fair, at ten cents a chance. The wife of Baltimore's Assistant Chief Fire Investigator, John H. Farrell, won the dog.

He really intended to find her another home. But since she showed unusual ability to learn, and was very easily trained, he decided to keep her and attempt to train her for bomb searching work, as the city of Baltimore uses dogs for this purpose.

Farrell took Duchess to the Canine Center at Edgewood Arsenal, where the army trains their sentry, narcotic sniffers, and bomb dogs. Duchess learned rapidly and since then has often been used for explosive incidents and bomb threat calls at the Baltimore Airport.

Dr. Brenda Stewart, a vice president of the American Chesapeake Club, tells of having trained one of her Chesapeakes to help her take care of 32 Holsteins. The dog learned to help turn them out to pasture in the morning, and to go gather them up at night. Her friends were amazed at how gently this was always done.

Each year a dog is saluted as the Ken-L-Ration Dog Hero, and given national attention and acclaim. The 1978 hero brought particular pride to Chesapeake owners. He was Chester, a Chesapeake, owned by Mr. and Mrs. Gary Homme of Livingston, Montana.

Chester won this honor as the result of saving the Hommes' son, five year old Kenny, from drowning. One day in the spring of the year, Mrs. Homme says, she was washing dishes, periodically looking out of the kitchen window to check on the boy, who was watering the flowers outside. Suddenly, Mrs. Homme noticed that Kenny was gone. She ran outside and heard him shouting, "Help me! Help me!"

The boy had fallen and could not help himself from sliding down a steep hill nearby, and into a creek that was swollen, and surging with a powerful current. Chester was in the water trying to save the child. As the dog swam towards Kenny, the water pulled the boy into a culvert. Chester battled the raging stream for ten minutes. Kenny grabbed Chester's hair twice, but lost his grip both times. Kenny then climbed on-to the dog's back and rode him out of the tunnel to safety.

"If we didn't have Chester, we wouldn't have a son right now," Mrs. Homme said.

Five-year-old Kenny Homme of Livingston, Montana, with Chester, the courageous dog who saved him from drowning in a raging creek. For his brave deed, Chester was honored as Ken-L Ration Dog Hero of 1978. — *Courtesy, Ken-L Ration Awards.*

Ʌ Hunting Dog's Prayer

I thank Thee, Oh Lord, for the rivers, woods, and fields wherein lie the game birds I love to hunt. I thank Thee also for the men who protect and preserve wild life in all its forms so that future generations will have the healthful pleasures of hunting and fishing. My master means more than life or death to me and I pray for intelligence, ability and strength to understand and execute his commands and desires. May our companionship lead to complete understanding so that our moments together will be the happiest of all. Help my master to comprehend that I will gladly give my life for him, be he millionaire or pauper. His love and confidence are all I ask. I beseech You to guide him and protect him from thoughts, deeds, or actions which will disturb the faith of others in him. I want my master to be respected by his friends as I look up to him. The wag of my tail indicates the feelings of my heart and no blows, privation, or hunger will ever keep me from being happy when I hear my master's voice or footsteps. When the curtains of death are about to close my active life, I pray Thee, Oh, God, that my master be near, his hand caressing my head as my eyelids close.

9

Training Your Hunting Dog

HUNTING WITHOUT A DOG just isn't any fun for those of us who have been lucky enough to shoot over a well-trained Chesapeake. It really isn't very difficult to educate your dog—and it can be great fun. There also is satisfaction in knowing you will conserve game when your dog can be counted upon to bring in all the birds you shoot. Chesapeakes are determined dogs and they persevere in their search for cripples.

Several thousand Chesapeakes are kept as a combination hunting dog and family pet. Actually it is an ideal arrangement. There is no reason why your dog can't be the children's playmate, a household guardian, and an excellent performer in the field. It is really up to you. If you go about it properly, it is easy to have an eager and obedient hunting companion who happily retrieves all the birds you shoot.

Chesapeakes are natural retrievers, and you will see this trait clearly exhibited, even in puppies who may only be six weeks old. Throw a ball in the pen with some very young puppies, and in no time at all you will see them competing for it, and one of them carrying it around in his mouth. You often will see a puppy chase a leaf that the wind has blown by, pick it up, and carry it around—just for fun.

You certainly want to encourage this instinct, for after all, that is what your dog is meant for, to find and carry to you the birds you shoot.

Of course, the best hunting dogs are those that have been properly trained. But there is no reason why the average hunter can't train his own dog, if he is willing to expend a little time and energy.

As Eve Keeler points out in her chapters in this book, we do not *train* a young dog as much as we *teach* him.

A definite time should be set aside each day for you to be with your puppy, even if it is only for fifteen or twenty minutes. You should work with your dog in a place where there are no distractions, such as loud noises, other dogs, or people passing by.

You start by putting a choke collar on your puppy; attach a leash to that and put him on your left side. Give him the command "HEEL," pat your left side and encourage him to come along with you. After he is moving with you in a satisfactory manner, and you have praised him for his cooperation, put him away until the next day. You may have to do this several days before you can move on to the next command, "SIT."

To teach him to "SIT," on leash of course, you gently force his rump down with your left hand, meanwhile pulling up a little with your right hand which is holding the leash. Praise him extravagantly when he does it well. Then combine the two commands "HEEL" and "SIT" until he performs properly. Again be sure to praise him enthusiastically — "Good boy! Good boy!" Do not make your training sessions too long, and play with him when he is through working.

The next command he must learn is "STAY." This is an enormously valuable word, with all kinds of practical uses. After you have heeled him, and have told him to "SIT," then introduce him to the word "STAY," while he is still on leash, of course. Move away from him and make him "STAY." Then return to him and make him "STAY." You should be able, in a few days, to walk all around him while he remains motionless. When he is doing this very well, discontinue the lesson and end up by playing with him.

The distinction between work and play is basic. You are *insisting* on his working, and when he does it properly he receives a lot of praise. You should be loving but firm. Following his work time, a puppy must also have a separate play time that is fun.

The next command your dog must learn is "COME." I prefer that word to "Here," because "Here" and Heel" sound so very much alike. Have the dog "HEEL," "SIT" and "STAY," and while he is still on leash, give him the new command "COME." When you do this you gently pull him towards you and back up a little bit. When he comes to you, he should receive a world of praise. He must like to come to you for it should mean that he will be made over and petted.

Now, in an enclosed spot, do all of this off leash. If he starts to disobey any of these commands put the leash back on again, and make him do it properly.

Not every amateur is successful in forcing his dog to retrieve. I personally think that if you have a willing retriever, you can teach him to "HOLD" the boat bumper or dumbbell, and this should be sufficient for the average hunting dog. If your dog drops the bumper, put it back in his

Training retrieving could start with a ball which all dogs seem to love. Douglas Smith, son of the Gary Smiths, with Ch. High Plains Ruff & Ready, CD.

John Urben and daughter, Terrie, training their Ch. Cherokee Tanya's Carbon Copy, CD.

Starting early! Kobi retrieves Mike Scattini's first duck which he shot at Charles Sambrailo's duck club.

Working on a diving duck—it takes patience, practice and know-how, which only comes with age.

Setting out the "dekes" is always fun. Tim Covey and his Duke.—*C. Connor*

mouth, force his lips to close over it, and make him hold it while you heel him on leash. He should soon get the idea that he is not to drop it. When you take your dog hunting, if he drops a crippled bird, and the bird starts to get away, that alone should teach him that he must "HOLD." Be sure that you are teaching your dog with bumpers, *not* with birds.

I must repeat that you should be generous with your praise and keep your training periods short so that you do not lose your dog's attention. "STAY" is the command you will later use when you start to teach your dog double retrieves. It is also the command you will use when you steady him to shot.

"NO" is an extremely important command—with innumerable handy uses. It should be said in a harsh and unpleasant manner. It really means "Stop immediately what you are doing." Sometimes it even means "Don't dare do what you were thinking of doing." Like wetting in the house, or chewing up a shoe, or thinking of fighting. The command "NO" could, and often should, be accompanied by a swat on the dog's rump, just for emphasis.

I would not permit the children to work a young, green dog on retrieving. Ask them please not to do so, until he is older and really knows his work. Just in case they might be tempted to do it when you are not around, hide the bumpers so they can't. You should also explain that they should not throw sticks or stones for the puppy, as this will tend to develop a hard mouth. Ask them to please not throw anything for him and tell your wife, so she can see that they don't. After a season of hunting it will not make any difference, but it surely will complicate the early training of a puppy.

When your pup or dog is retrieving properly on a single, bringing it back to you, sitting at your side, and releasing the dummy on the command "OUT," you can then, but not before, start to teach him double retrieves. But do not overlook the importance of cooperation on the command "OUT," or "GIVE." No tug-of-war here, please. You don't want to do anything to make your dog "freeze" on the bird, which is the expression used when a dog will not give his handler the bird. The new plastic small boat bumpers are the best to use. The old-fashioned canvas bumpers, filled with feathers, have the drawback that most dogs like to "pop" them. This may cause the habit of biting into the bumper and subsequently biting into the bird, which will surely make them unfit to eat.

After single retrieves are being smoothly performed in the yard you should get someone to go into a field with you and throw the bumpers for you, so that you can increase the distance of the falls.

But when you start to teach double retrieves initially do them on the lawn or in the open, so the dog can see both falls. Throw the first one, and say "STAY," then throw a second bumper. Naturally you send the dog for the last bumper thrown. When he picks it up you say "COME," and when he comes to you you should say "HEEL," and make him come to your left side. Then you say "SIT," and "OUT," and after he has given you the first dummy, you then send him for the other one. It sounds complicated, but it really is easy. If you can train with some field trial people, they can demonstrate it for you, for all field trial dogs, even those in the Derby, have to do double retrieves.

In field trials the dogs are sent to retrieve by calling their names. Many hunters just use the command "FETCH," which is okay as long as you and your hunting buddy don't both say "FETCH" and send both your dogs at the same time. In that case, the result could be a glorious dog fight.

When you commence doing double retrieves have the bumpers fall about 180 degrees apart. Then the dog will have to come by you with the first bumper, before he can go for the other. This gives you the chance to call him to you and make him deliver, before you send him for the second fall. Some upland game hunters don't bother to train their dogs on doubles, as they feel they will probably only get one shot. But duck hunters often get a chance to shoot two, or even three times, if a flock comes in to the decoys. So a duck dog would benefit by learning to do double retrieves.

When you start working on water, pick a warm day. It is ideal to take your pup to a pond with an older experienced dog. At first it should be wading water, and the puppy should be allowed to just play in it. After a short time he probably will start following the other dog into the deeper swimming water. Let him set his own pace here, so that he develops confidence. Then give the older dog a retrieve in deep water, and you usually find that the pup will follow him, and start to swim himself. His first retrieves should be short ones, where he can run in for them. The distance should be gradually lengthened, so that he is swimming a little farther each time. Although Chesapeakes are wonderful water dogs, never throw a puppy or dog into water until he has been properly introduced to it. He could easily become water shy, and be afraid of water for a long time.

Introduction to feathers is very important. Pheasant or duck wings should be used at first. Then progress to dead birds. Then, live birds which are shot for your dog. Last would come shackled ducks. Avoid discipline on birds; do not give your dog any birds to retrieve until you are completely satisfied with his performance on bumpers.

Securing birds with which to train is not easy, if you don't know where to go. If they are having a Chesapeake Day in your area, by all means attend it, for they will shoot pigeons and also have live shackled ducks for the water marks. They also will have some experienced people there to coach beginners. You will meet other Chesapeake owners, and as your dog improves, be able to compete in the Hunter's Stake. Bring your family and a picnic lunch and make a day of it. Your dog will become accustomed to a crowd, and also, to working when there are other dogs around.

If your dog growls at the others, or shows any tendency to fight, stop it right now. Give him an unpleasant jerk with your leash and collar, and a stern command "NO." If that does not work do not hesitate to use a willow branch or whip, and give him several hard cracks on his rear end, accompanied by several more hard "NO's." Make him stop it right now. A fighting dog is not only a nuisance, but is also dangerous to have around. Even your wife and children can get hurt if your dog is allowed to fight. Don't stand for it for one moment—stop it immediately!

Of course, if you want a perfect dog, you may wish to send your puppy, when he is about six months old, to a professional trainer to be force-broken. This process usually takes a couple of months. Be sure to send your dog to a trainer who likes Chesapeakes, for, unfortunately, not all trainers do. Your local American Chesapeake Club Regional Director should be able to help you select a man with a good reputation and one who is not too hard on the dogs. People think of Chesapeakes as tough dogs, but most of them respond much better to an affectionate trainer than to a handler who is tough with them.

If you are a duck hunter you usually can arrange to place a tie-down in your duck blind. Then, if your dog is not steady to shot, you can release him when you want him to retrieve. However, this can get to be a nuisance for you, and you may decide that you will, after all, *make* him steady to shot. Anyone can miss, and you certainly don't want your dog charging out into the pond while the ducks are still working. He can spoil any subsequent shots for you, as well as the hunters in the next blind. This is no way to win friends and influence people.

Teaching your dog to quarter and hunt for upland game is not difficult, if you a have a field in which to work. Leave your dog in the car or put him in a place where he is not able to watch you. Walk out and drop three or four bumpers in the field, in spots that you can remember. Dead birds are better, of course.

Then walk diagonally across the field with him, and when he finds the bumper or the dead bird, and brings it to you, make a big fuss over him. This is a fun game, and should result in his hunting very eagerly.

Ideally, you would want to dizzy and plant some pigeons, and shoot them for him when he flushes them. But sometimes local ordinances do not permit this. Besides, birds, even pigeons, are hard to procure.

In addition, you could have trouble with the members of the Society for Prevention of Cruelty to Animals, who seem to be completely unable to understand the concept of conservation. You are, of course, training your dog so you will not lose any wild game that you have shot. As both wild ducks and pheasants are scarce, if a hunter's dog retrieves every bird that has been shot, and none are lost, he is conserving game. Also, if your dog will bring in every crippled bird he comes across, you leave more live birds for other hunters, and you may save wounded birds from a prolonged death.

If you, as a hunter, want a fancy dog who will handle, and go out on a blind retrieve of about 150 yards, you will probably decide that professional training for your dog is necessary. Many hours of work go into teaching a dog to "take a line," to stop when the whistle is blown, and to take arm signals directing him to the blind. If you have the opportunity to watch the major stakes at a field trial you will see the advanced dogs doing this. But a lot of training has gone into this process, probably more than you would think of spending on your shooting dog. It is also necessary to have the "know how." Most Chesapeakes are both intelligent and willing—so teaching them to handle is no great chore—if you know what you are doing.

Chesapeakes are used on every type of upland game: pheasants, quail, partridge, sagehens, grouse, chukkars and dove.

There is something about the taste of doves that almost all dogs dislike. The first time they pick one up they usually spit it out, with a definite expression of distaste on their faces. However, insist your dog "HOLD" and after two or three retrieves, he will become accustomed to fetching them.

On land, an experienced dog should hunt in close. You should insist on this—for if your dog ranges out too far he will flush a bird that will be out of range. I have seen only a few Chesapeakes who would point—but it is not required of them. Most handlers can tell when their dog is on the trail of a bird, as the dog will become visibly excited. His tail will wag and he will be concentrating, and will pick up speed. You may want to teach him the command "EASY," which means slow down. At first you might have to put a check cord on him, and when he starts to go out too far in front of you, pull him back and say "EASY, EASY." If he flushes a covey of quail, and is not too far away from you, you may get two shots instead of just one.

Most Chesapeakes are sturdy dogs and can hunt all day long—if you will only keep them in condition throughout the year. It would be eminently unfair of you to expect him to immediately hunt hard, if he had just been sitting around all year in your back yard.

Goose hunting in Texas, with excellent shot George Balthazar and Baltz getting their share.

Sneaking up on them—George Balthazar and Whitefoot in the Blessing, Texas reservoir.

"Snuffy" Beliveau, a famous Western retriever trainer, is very emphatic on a refresher course before the hunting season starts. He feel you should:

1. Harden up your dog if he has not been regularly exercised.
2. Check on his obedience—"SIT," "STAY," and "COME." "EASY" if he knows that command as well.
3. Work on live game, even if you can't shoot it until the season opens. Go to fields where there are pheasants or quail. When your dog flushes them, shoot a blank pistol, or just shoot in the air, and check the fact that he is steady to shot. If there are no fields near you where game can be found, buy some pigeons and take them to a field where you can work your dog on them.
4. If you have had trouble with your dog chasing rabbits, try to take him into an area where rabbits are plentiful. Then if he chases them, you must severely discipline him. It is wise to do this before the hunting season starts.
5. Put a leather collar with identification on your dog's neck so that if he should be lost, he could be returned to you.

Tattooing a dog's ear or flank with a number or name, if properly done, is a positive means of identification. But the fellows who steal, and sometimes sell hunting dogs, take the dog first and inspect him later. If they discover him to be tattooed they will want to get rid of him quickly, so the dog will be either killed or abandoned.

When you are downtown, or even shopping in the neighborhood, if your dog is a friendly type, be sure to lock the car doors. Also be doubly sure to leave enough of the windows down for proper ventilation.

At the end of a day's hunting, Beliveau also advocates checking out your dog to see if he has picked up any foxtails or burrs. Look over his feet carefully, to be sure there are no thorns of foxtails between his toes. If so, they should be promptly removed.

Also look in his ears. Avoid a lot of discomfort for the dog and a veterinarian bill for yourself.

If his eyes are red, or look irritated, use a little two percent yellow oxide of mercury, easily obtainable from a drug store without a prescription, as it is often used in babies' eyes.

Weekly brushing is advised, and an ordinary scrub brush can be used to remove the dead hairs in your dog's coat. He will smell a lot better if you will do this.

You should have a properly enclosed place in which to keep your dog at home. He should have a dry, draft free doghouse on a platform raised from the ground. His run should contain some sun and some shade.

The proper place for your Chesapeake is on your premises, guarding your house and family. You certainly don't want him roaming around the countryside. Besides he could easily get run over or poisoned.

Do not encourage your dog to become mean, and certainly, do not allow him to attack people. Your wife will feel more secure when your dog is home, so that he can protect her, or the children, if need be. The fact that a large, impressive looking dog is on the premises is a great deterrent to trespassers or possible thieves. Dogs have an uncanny instinct about people's motives, and even the friendliest of dogs seem to sense when an intruder does not mean well. A low growl from a big, tough looking dog is usually sufficient to discourage any intruder.

Do everything you can to keep your dog safely at home when you are not there, for you surely don't want to lose him. After all your hours of working together your dog is undoubtedly devoted to you, and would be miserable without you. You have, ahead of you, many fine years of companionship as well as fun in the duck blind or in the hunting field.

"I'm really awful tired." — D. Carter

A typical scene at a National Field Trial, with one contestant sending his dog for the bird, while the next two must stay in holding blinds until it is their turn to run. — *Retriever Field Trial News*

10

A Short Explanation of Field Trials

ENGLAND, in 1900, was the scene of the first Retriever Field Trial ever held. Each subsequent year these events became more popular. Many Americans visiting abroad attended them and were intrigued. However, it was 1932 before the first American trial was put on by the Labrador Club—for Labradors only. In 1933 the American Chesapeake Club followed suit and held one for Chesapeakes only. It was 1934 before an All-Breed Retriever Trail was held in this country.

Every year since then the number of trials held in the United States, and the number of competing dogs, has steadily increased. In 1978, according to statistics given in *Retriever Field Trial News,* 169 licensed field trials were held with a total of 29,014 dogs competing in the four stakes: Open, Amateur, Qualifying and Derby. This tremendous increase of interest and participation has changed the whole character of American field trials—today they are somewhat of a rat race. Judges are not given enough time to adequately evaluate their fields. Unfortunately, many of today's tests are tricky ones which do not concern themselves with the dogs' innate abilities.

Today in England, Open entries are limited to 24 dogs, with two alternates, and this is done by a draw system. Also, their Field Trials are only permitted to be held in the fall, during the regular hunting season. Game is shot as it is flushed in the field, and they shoot whatever is encountered. The bag may be pheasant, grouse, partridge, snipe, and an occasional duck. Often a hare. For the English people would think it highly unsportsmanlike to throw and shoot birds. They would feel that the bird did not have a fair chance.

In 1975 I had the privilege of observing one Irish and two English trials. No professional handler was permitted to compete with more than one dog. Throughout each event the atmosphere among the contestants was friendly and relaxed.

All old-timers! Guy Burnett with Nelgard's Baron; author Eloise Heller (Cherry) and her Sasnakra Sassy; Snuffy Beliveau, who handled Bayberry Pete for Ed Fleischmann (with tray) and "Pat" Montgomery with his Montgomery Sal.

A royal family. From left to right: FC Mount Joy's Mallard, Ch. Sasnakra Sassy, FC & AFC Nelgard's King Tut and AFC Chuck's Rip Joy. Sassy bred to Tut produced 3 Field Trial Champions.

American field trials of the same year, and even more so in the subsequent three years, often saw an entry of sixty, seventy, or eighty dogs — sometimes even a hundred, entered in the Open All-Age Stake. Often a professional would run four, five or (on the East Coast) even eight or nine dogs. For judges to put on tests, in a three day period, that adequately separates such a field is almost impossible. Dogs are often dropped from the first tests for any small error they might make, while in the later tests, the same fault may be overlooked in the winner or placing dog performance. Definitely, something must be done to cut our enormous and unwieldy entries.

But, returning to a discussion of the early field trials in the United States, we find that our practices were copied from the English. Several dogs were held on the line at the same time. This is still done in England. After a gunner shot a bird, one of the two judges would call a dog's number (number in the draw) and the owner of that dog would send him to retrieve. Meanwhile, the other dogs are expected to sit quietly at their handlers' sides. If the first dog failed to find the bird, that dog was recalled and a second dog was sent. If he, also, failed, they sent a third dog, and if he was successful it was said that he "wiped the eye" of the other two. There was no equality in this test, as one dog might get a fall in the open, and the next dog be sent for one that fell in heavy cover. There were no "bad falls" as we know them today. The dogs were supposed to hunt until they found the game, and to work out their own problems. Since there were so few dogs competing, time was unimportant as the judges had all day.

If a dog "broke" (or "ran in" as they say in England) he was eliminated, as he was supposed to wait until the judge called his number and his handler sent him for the bird. This is also true today, as is elimination for "hard mouth."

In our early trials, when ducks were plentiful, they were shot from a boat, falling into tules or weeds. Live decoys, attached to weights, were used. But if a dog brought back one of these decoys, he was through for the day. The early handlers prayed that the guns would make a clean kill, for a live decoy, and a crippled duck that was swimming in the decoys, could easily be mistaken for each other.

Often an American handler had two dogs with him, one on each side. The judge would call the number of the dog he wanted worked. Meanwhile, the handler's second dog was expected to sit still, be quiet, and just watch. It took a lot of training to obtain such control and discipline.

American trials are very different today—more complicated, and the dogs are supposed to do a tremendous number of different kinds of tests and combinations of tests.

They say you have to be a little crazy to constantly run in field trials, so maybe I am. For I still find them completely fascinating, even after attending them for some 35 years. In that time I probably have participated in over 300 trials and judged several dozen, including one National Amateur Championship Stake.

Field trials no longer are composed of hunting tests, as so naively described in The American Kennel Club's gray booklet. Today the tests are SUPER hunting tests; they demand much more from a dog than any sane hunter would think of doing.

How often, when out shooting, will a hunter and his pal have three pheasants down at the same time? If they should be lucky enough to do so, would they expect their dog to remember where all three fell? The average hunter certainly would *not* expect his dog to immediately bring in all three of these birds. But when a "triple" (the field trial term for three shot birds) is given, the field trial handler *demands* that his dog find all three, and with speed and style. He is trained to do so.

Again, certainly, the average hunter would not expect his dog to retrieve a bird that has been hit, and sailed out some 200 yards before it landed, without the dog even seeing the fall. But in field trials the dogs must be trained to do this. This type of test is known as a "Blind Retrieve." The dog must take a line towards the bird for a considerable distance, stop if his handler whistles to him, and take arm signals to the fall. This test is often set up so that the dog has to cross a number of obstacles on the way (such as a deep ditch, swim through a pond, and run through a heavily scented field) before he reaches the place where the bird has been hidden.

All of these things, and more, are required of the field trial dogs of the late 1970s. These dogs have more than a college education. They are Ph.Ds!

Naturally, if you are interested in participating in field trials you would be foolish to buy anything except a dog that comes from good field trial lines, which have proven their trainability. The pedigree should contain the names of some of the recent field trial champions and other dogs who have proven their worth, by winning places in the various stakes.

Anyone interested in field trials can write The American Kennel Club, 51 Madison Avenue, New York, NY 10010 and ask for, and receive, a copy of the two booklets that they have on this subject: *Field Trial Rules and Standard Procedures* and *Standing Recommendations of the Retriever Advisory Committee*. These publications discuss in detail all field trial matters, and a beginner should familiarize himself with them before he starts to run a dog.

Today the regular stakes at a Retriever Trial are the Derby, Qualifying, Open All-Age and Amateur All-Age. We will discuss each in detail.

Dr. Marston Jones and his attractive little female, Chemin De Fer, who is trained by John Dahl and run by him in Open Stakes, while Jones runs her himself in the Amateur All-Age.

Charlene Coleman, a terrific young handler, with four of her family's field trial dogs. L. to r.: Dale's Cinnamon Chip, Cub's Dale Mullica, Snap's Crackle and Chip's Pestering Pacer.

DERBY STAKE

The little gray book (commonly referred to as the "Bible") says in Section 10, page 57, "A Derby Stake at a Retriever Trial shall be for dogs which have not reached their second birthday on the first day of the trial at which they are being run."

For the benefit of beginners I will describe the test normally held in this stake. For many years the usual sequence was to start with a land single, followed by a water single, then have a land double, and usually end with a water double. Pigeons were normally used in the land tests, but because they became quite scarce and because their uneven flight pattern makes them difficult to shoot, many clubs now use shot pheasants instead. In the water tests most clubs use shackled ducks, which means that the wings and feet of the duck are tied, and they are thrown into the water, which does not hurt them. Ducks also are scarce today, so shot ducks are a rarity.

Due to the greatly increased number of field trials held in the 1970s, with their attendant large entries, many judges felt that they did not have time to put on single marks, and often started out with doubles. Also, where marks used to fall a reasonable distance of sixty or seventy yards, now the dogs must be trained to make much longer retrieves, and 100 yards is not uncommon in the later tests. It is becoming ridiculous, as often the guns are so far away that the handlers have to point them out to their dogs.

In addition to this, the Derby dogs are now being given "right-angle" falls. The well trained Derby dog of today has to learn a sophisticated bag of tricks to win or place. It is no longer the natural ability and marking of the dogs that is being tested.

David Elliott, a famous old Scottish trainer and one of the first to succeed in the early Eastern field trials, commented that we have become "idiotically obsessed" with the idea of cramming a year's training into a few months. He feels we consequently ruin, and have to discard, many good dogs that, if given a longer time to learn, would do very well.

My personal feeling is that most Chesapeakes mature much later than Labradors, and they should be taken along slowly while they are young.

The little gray book says, about Derby dogs, that speed, style and class, as well as outstanding marking ability, are what the judges are supposed to look for and appreciate. It also says that Derby dogs should ideally have a fast departure, on land or into the water. They should make an aggressive search for the fall, have a prompt pick up, and have a reasonably fast return. They are supposed to eagerly come to the line, with an obedient attitude. They must have a "good nose," and they are supposed to persevere in their hunt for the bird.

If you win, you sometimes have to swim! This is what happened to Les Lowenthal at the
Chesapeake Specialty Field Trial, after he won a Derby.

It is not hard to train a Derby dog, and any work that you do give him will certainly improve his ability as a shooting dog. Start with a simple single retrieve and do not start double retrieves until you have taught your dog to hold the bird, return to your side, and give it to you on the command of "GIVE" or "OUT." If you have not yet steadied your dog, you should work him on a long cord and forcibly restrain him, until you call his name. After you have thrown the dummy, hold him for a silent count of five, before you let him go for it. This wait will become a habit with him—and will make him a lot steadier than he would be otherwise. It also will make teaching doubles much simpler.

When you start to train on birds, ducks or pigeons, commence with a cold dead bird first. Then proceed to a freshly killed bird, and finally shot birds. Never forcebreak on birds—always on dummies.

Not everyone has experienced people with whom to train. Your best bet is to attend a picnic trial, or practice session held by the Retriever Club in your area. It is essential that you have someone else throw for you, because otherwise your dog will only go out the distance you can throw. At these training sessions you will meet other people who are interested in training their dogs, so you can work together.

If you will contact the American Chesapeake Club Regional Director in your area, you will find him very helpful and informative. Try to attend any local Chesapeake Days that are held, and try to get to know other Chesapeake owners who are also interested in Field Trials.

QUALIFYING STAKE

The next stake for you, after your dog has become two years old and is no longer permitted to run in the Derby, is the Qualifying. The little book says "A Qualifying Stake at a Retriever Trial shall be for dogs which have never won first, second, third or fourth place or a Judges' Award of Merit in an Open All-Age, or won first, second, third or fourth place in an Amateur All-Age Stake, or won two first places in Qualifying Stakes." In other words, this is an intermediate stake, where the dogs who are just starting their advanced work can compete with each other.

Many field trial judges feel that the Qualifying Stake is the hardest to judge. Until the judges run a couple of tests, they cannot tell whether this group of dogs is just out of the Derby or if they are pretty experienced. You, as a handler, will have no way of knowing until the Stake starts how hard the tests will be. But you will know, that, in addition to being steady to shot, your dog will have to "Honor." This means that after the dog has had his turn retrieving a bird, he will be expected to sit quietly next to you and watch the other dog on line with you be sent for *his* bird.

Qualifying dogs are supposed to be able to mark triple falls. They also are supposed to be able to do simple "Blind Retrieves," often a hundred yards long.

In a "Blind Retrieve", the dog handlers are called up to stand next to the judges, which is the starting point. From there you are allowed to watch where the bird is placed. The dog has *not* seen this plant. When you run, you are supposed to tell your dog to "GET BACK," and he is supposed to run into the field on the line you gave him and look for the bird. If his direction deviates from the original one you gave him, you are allowed to blow your whistle. When you do this your dog is supposed to stop, sit, look at you, and then take the direction you give to him with a hand signal. It really is simpler than it sounds, but you certainly will either have to have a trainer start your dog on this, or train with some knowledgeable people to understand how to do it.

Your dog must be trained to do "Triples" on both land and in water. In other words, he must remember each of three fallen birds which have been shot and thrown by three separate gunners.

Until recently, the Qualifying Stake's first test was always a "Double" land mark. Then you would be expected to do a "Land Blind." Normally the field would then move to water and you would have a "Water Triple." Most Qualifying Stakes used to end with a "Water Blind."

Like all the other stakes held today there are really too many dogs entered to have enough time to adequately test the ability of the participating dogs. So the tests have become more complicated, which in my opinion is a shame. Few judges of today will start with a mere "Double" on land. What is more usual now is to commence with a "Single," combined with a "Blind." Obviously, unless your dog has been taught not to return to his former mark, you are in trouble. It takes a long time to teach a young dog all these new things. It is usually a year or more after they are out of the Derby before they can successfully place in a Qualifying.

It is absolutely essential that the dogs be trained with other people and other dogs. Practically no one has successfully trained a Qualifying winner if he works alone.

Another important factor is having several different kinds of places to train. On land, you need some green fields, some rice checks, some hilly country, as well as some land that is bisected by creeks. Do not think you can always work on the same pond, or the same kind of pond. You will find, as you attend various trials in different areas, that some lakes are fringed with heavy tules. Other water tests are held through a series of ponds. Some ponds have islands and peninsulas. If your dog has not been shown these different types of water, he may well become confused.

Dual Ch., AFC/CFC Baron's Tule Tiger, CD, in the seventh test of the Open National Stake in 1965.

AMATEUR ALL-AGE and OPEN ALL-AGE

The American Kennel Club booklet states that "An Open Age Stake at a Retriever Trial shall be for all dogs." It also says that "An Amateur All-Age Stake at a Retriever Trial shall be for any dogs, if handled in that stake, by persons who are Amateurs."

Both the Open and the Amateur Stakes carry points towards a dog's attaining his Field Championship or Amateur Field Championship.

Usually the tests are the same for both of these events. The Open is considered harder to win because you are competing with professional handlers, and their expertise. Also, many of the top "pro" handlers will enter five or six dogs, so that gives them a numerical edge over the average amateur with only one dog to run.

However, an astute and dedicated amateur handler, with one well trained dog, often can and does win the Open All-Age Stake. For the one dog owner is particularly successful in establishing complete rapport with this dog. He can give him two or three times the amount of work that the professional can give each of his dogs. Since the "pro" has a group of dogs to train he can only allot so much time to each dog.

Because the dogs are so versatile today, and so well trained on a variety of marking and handling tests, it is necessary to have extremely demanding series to separate the field.

A dog who is fast, stylish, a good marker, and in addition wants to please, is always a threat in any company. There are some special amateurs—hardworking, competent, and with a lot of time in which to train—who can hold their own against any professional. Some of these amateurs even win Open Nationals. During the years 1970 to 1978, six amateurs have won the National Open Championship Stake.

There is no pattern or ruling as to what the tests will be. Normally, the judges start on land, because when they have a large number of dogs to run, land tests go faster than water tests. But All-Age dogs are expected to do triples on land and on water. Sometimes they are even given quadruples on water. They are expected to do not only single blind retrieves, but also double blinds. And a combination of these tests can be given them in any order that the officiating judges wish.

If the stake starts early in the morning, the first test could be a triple mark on land, combined with a double blind retrieve. This would count as two series, after which the dogs that had performed properly would be "Called Back," or invited, to do the next test. The dogs who had poor work would be eliminated from further competition.

You can teach your dog to do "Blind Retrieves" when you and the dog are alone. But you will also have to school him in doing blinds with a combination of marks, so you will need to have gunners that will shoot birds, and then stand still in the field. Your dog may be asked to do blinds that are planted past the gunners, to one side of them, or even through two sets of them, to a spot that is further out.

The titles of Field Champion and Amateur Field Champion, are not lightly won. They are attained by a point system, and no points are earned unless there are twelve qualified "Point" dogs in the stake.

I have a great admiration for the Obedience dogs who have won their Utility Title. But training for that is simple compared to training for field trials. True, the Utility dog works on hand signals. But these are

Icy weather often prevails at Eastern field trials. Note snow on coat of Tule Tiger. — *Shafer*

given him in an enclosed ring, at a fairly short distance from the handler. In trials, the dogs are often two hundred yards out. When the handler blows his whistle, the dog must stop, and then respond to an arm signal given to him and be completely under control. It really is quite exciting to watch.

Some of the tests are called "Courage" tests, where the dogs have to go through very tough cover, like nettles or heavy tules. Some dogs will hesitate before entering these obstacles, and will receive a lower score than those who courageously plunge in and through.

In the spring of 1978, I ran in a field trial in Southern California, where they even had a courage test for the handlers. The announcement came over the loud speaker, "Will the handlers of all the dogs in this stake please bring your dogs down the road to the judges, as there are snakes in the grass." They were not joking either! As my dog completed the test and was delivering the duck to me, there were two shots behind me as the gunners ended the life of a large and long rattlesnake. I don't think I care to run there again!

Besides the trials held by the various field trial clubs in all parts of the country, once a year there are two national events.

The National Retriever Club, usually in November, holds its National Championship Stakes of that year. You have to win an Open Stake, plus two additional Open points to qualify to run. Here professional and amateurs both compete, and the finest dogs of the country run against each other. It is well worth your time to watch this event if it is held in your area.

The National Amateur Retriever Club also holds a National Amateur Championship Stake each year, usually in June. Here, only amateur handlers may compete. To participate you must qualify by winning an Open or an Amateur first place, as well as two additional points. The winner of this event is known as the National Amateur Champion of that year, which, of course, is a big honor.

The entries in both of these National Stakes are now uncomfortably large, and the judges are hard pressed to properly test such enormous fields in the four days allotted to the events. Every year some of our Chesapeakes qualify for both of these Nationals.

In the year 1978 there were 43,500 Labradors, 34,249 Golden Retrievers, and 3,059 Chesapeakes registered with The American Kennel Club. Obviously, our breed is greatly outnumbered. But, percentage wise, Chesapeakes are winning more than their share of field trial awards.

If you have a good dog, lots of time to train and travel, you will enjoy running in field trials. I can't think of a hobby that is more fun. But then, I am an avowed field trial nut!

Linda Harger and her Fireweed's Aleutian Widgeon, who is a real threat in the All-Age stakes. He will undoubtedly win his Field Championships.

CFC, CAFC & AFC Nanuk of Cheslang, pictured with his owner-trainer-handler, Hans Kuch of Canada. Nanuk was a favorite with the crowd.

FC Shagwong Gypsy, lovely and able female of the early field trials, owned, trained and handled by E. Monroe Osborne of Long Island, N.Y. Portrait is by the famous artist, Edwin Megargee.

FC Guess of Shagwong, as depicted by Mr. Megargee. Guess was also owned and capably trained and handled by Mr. Osborne.

11

Chesapeake Field Trial History and Records

$\mathbf{T}$HE COVETED TITLE of Field Champion or Amateur Field Champion is not easily won. Probably, in all breeds, approximately one out of every fifty good Derby dogs are promising enough to go on and be trained for Open and Amateur stakes. Then, alas, many of them prove to be only mediocre in their advanced work.

Behind each dog who wins a Field Trial Championship, or Amateur Field Trial Championship, are many arduous hours of training. To please the judges a dog must be eager, stylish and fast. He must also be intelligent and a willing worker. Outstanding marking ability is required to remember the fall of three, and sometimes, four, birds that are shot in the big stakes. Trainability is a definite requisite in learning to do land or water "blinds" (where birds are hidden, and where the dog is directed to the location of it by his handler). These birds may be planted 200 yards away from the handler and starting point, and all the handler is permitted to do is to blow his whistle, and give his dog arm signals. Absolute control is needed for a good performance, which when it occurs, is thrilling to watch.

In each stake only four places carrying championship points are awarded. The best Labradors and Goldens in the country run in field trials, so the Chesapeake is not just competing against his own breed. He is required to defeat other breeds, as well. In addition, today's entries are larger than they have ever been.

Relatively few Chesapeakes are run in field trials, and we constitute a very small percentage of the All-Breed entry. But, fortunately, we have a high percentage of success. It is with pride and pleasure that I give a description of the Chesapeakes who have made our Field Trial History.

CHESAPEAKE DUAL CHAMPIONS

	Breeder:	Owner:
1936 SODAK'S GYPSY PRINCE (Makota's Gypsy Prince ex Bandy Lindy)	Chesacroft Kennels	Chesacroft Kennels
1959 MOUNT JOY'S MALLARD (Nelgard's King Tut ex Sasnakra Sassy)	Mount Joy's Kennels	E. C. Fleischmann
1965 BARON'S TULE TIGER (Nelgard's Baron ex Joanie Teal)	Eloise Heller	Eloise Heller
1965 MEG'S O'TIMOTHY (Beewacker's Chester ex Meg O' My Heart)	Quincy Hunt	Dr. F. A. Dashaw
1970 KOOLWATER COLT OF TRICROWN (Bomarc of Southbay ex Welcome of the Willows)	Margaret Long	Michael Paterno
1970 TIGER'S CUB Tule Tiger ex Napolitano's Ladybug)	Eloise Heller	Eloise Heller
1978 CUB'S KOBI KING (Tiger's Cub ex Chesareid April Echo)	Eloise Heller	Charles Sambrailo

CHESAPEAKE FIELD TRIAL CHAMPIONS (1932 through 1979)

		Owner:
1935	SKIPPER BOB (Prince of Montauk ex Sou West Sal)	Harry Conklin
1936	Dual Ch. SODAK'S GYPSY PRINCE (Makota's Gypsy Queen ex Bandy Lindy)	Chesacroft Kennels
1937	DILWYNE MONTAUK PILOT (Prince of Montauk ex Sou West Sal)	Dilwyne Kennels
1939	SHAGWONG GYPSY (FC Skipper Bob ex Princess Anne)	E. Monroe Osborne
1941	SODAK'S RIP (Dual Ch. Sodak's Gypsy Prince ex Chesacroft Darky)	E. K. Ward
1942	GUESS OF SHAGWONG (FC Chesacroft Baron ex Shagwong Swamp Fire)	E. Monroe Osborne
1945	CHESACROFT BARON (Dual Ch. Sodak's Gypsy Prince ex Chesacroft Teal)	R. N. Crawford

1946	BAYLE	Vance Morris
	(Big Chief ex Delshore Wilde)	
	TIGER OF CLIPPER CITY	Dr. George Gardner
	(FC Chesacroft Baron ex Belle of the Wolf River)	
1952	DEERWOOD TRIGGER	William Hoard, Jr.
	(Water King Cliff ex Del Monte Ginger)	
	MONTGOMERY'S SAL	L. P. Montgomery
	(Corporal Jan ex Klamath Gypsy Nell)	
1953	NELGARD'S KING TUT	Mount Joy Kennels
	(FC Chesacroft Baron ex Sunbeam of Cocoa King)	
1954	RAINDROP OF DEERWOOD	P. J. Gagnon
	(Johansen's Major ex Del Monte Ginger of Deerwood)	
1959	CFC NELGARD'S BARON	Eloise Heller
	(Rex of Rapids ex FC Tiger of Clipper City)	
	AFC ATOM BOB	Dr. John Lundy
	(Ch Nelgard's Riptide ex Aleutian Keeko)	
	CH & AFC MOUNT JOY'S MALLARD	E. C. Fleischmann
	(FC & AFC Nelgard's King Tut ex Ch Sasnakra Sassy, CD)	
1960	AFC MEG'S PATTIE O'ROURKE	Dr. F. A. Dashnaw
	(Beewaker's Chester ex Meg O' My Heart)	
	AFC STAR KING OF MOUNT JOY	
	(FC & AFC Nelgard's King Tut ex Ch Sasnakra Sassy, CD)	
1962	MT. JOY'S LOUISTOO	E. C. Fleischmann
	(Dual Ch. AFC Mount Joy's Mallard ex Frosty Milady)	
1963	AFC MEG'S O'TIMOTHY	Dr. F. A. Dashnaw
	(Beewacker's Chester ex Meg O' My Heart)	
1964	SLOW GIN	Dr. L.B. Reppert
	(Tealwood's O'Lord Farouk ex Lake Lady)	
1965	AFC BARON'S TULE TIGER, CD	Eloise Heller
	(FC & AFC & CFC Nelgard's Baron, CD ex Joanie Teal)	
1966	CHESONOMA'S KODIAK	Dr. W.E. Pelzer
	(AFC Chesnoma's Louis ex Dinie's Miss Priss)	
1968	AFC MOUNT JOY'S BIT O'GINGER	Mrs. E.C. Fleischmann
	(Dual & AFC Meg's O'Timothy, CDX ex Mount Joy's Jug Ears)	
1970	AFC KOOLWATER COLT OF TRICROWN	Michael Paterno
	(AFC Bomarc of Southbay ex Welcome of the Willows)	
	AFC TIGER'S CUB, CD	Eloise Heller
	(Dual Ch, AFC & CFC Baron's Tule Tiger, CD ex Napolitano's Ladybug)	

1972	CUB'S KOBI KING (Dual & AFC Tiger's Cub, CD ex Chesareid April Echo)	Daniel Hartley
1974	AFC COPPER TOPPER DER WUNDERBAR (Hector ex Bonnie La Bonita)	Greg McDaniel
1976	ALAMO'S LUCIAS (FC & AFC Chesnoma's Kodiak ex Dobe's Atom Agnes)	Ben Robertson
	BAY CITY JAKE (Hatchet Man ex Ch Cub's Marin Echo, UD)	Dr. Miles Thomas and Pete Van Der Meulen
1978	ALEUTIAN SURF BREAKER (Big Fellow ex Chopper's Bobbie)	Dr. Miles Thomas and John McRoberts
	AFC CHESDEL CHIPPEWA CHIEF (Dual & AFC Koolwater's Colt of Tricrown ex Chesdel Longwood Lassie)	Alex Spear

DESCRIPTIONS OF THE FIELD TRIAL CHAMPIONS

FC Skipper Bob, owned and trained by Harry Conklin, was our first Field Trial Champion. Anthony Bliss tells us that "Bob was fast, steady and keen. He followed his handler's directions perfectly on land and water. He made quick finds and he had a perfect delivery. But his most important characteristic was his uncanny ability to mark the fall of a bird and remember it, sometimes for as long as an hour and a half. He could do this when one, and sometimes two, dogs had already failed to find the bird."

Dual Ch. Sodak's Gypsy Prince was owned and trained by Anthony Bliss who says of him, "Prince was fast and stylish with a natural ability to take direction. He was one of the greatest sires in the history of the Chesapeake. Not only did he sire field trial champions but his descendants dominated the Chesapeake field trial dogs for many years. Almost every Chesapeake field trial winner in the past twenty years can be traced back to Prince. Due to faulty early training, Prince was occasionally hard-mouthed. Had it not been for this fault, I believe that he would have been the outstanding field trial contestant of all breeds."

FC Dilwyne Montauk Pilot was owned by the Dilwyne Kennels of the Carpenters. Pilot was a full brother to Skipper Bob. Bliss gives us the information that "Pilot was a bigger, stronger dog and at times was Skipper's equal in the field. However, he was not as easily controlled and, although a good marker, he lacked the exceptional marking ability that carried Skipper Bob to first place in so many trials." In 1936 Pilot won the Field and Stream Trophy for the best field trial dog in the country.

FC Shagwong Gypsy, owned by E. Monroe Osborne, was the first Chesapeake female to succeed in trials. She was spectacular and handsome although Osborne writes, "She was the runt of the litter at four months. She completed her first trial at 11 months, and was always an excellent marker and a great dog in a duck blind or a field trial. She was a pleasure to handle although I never used a mechanical whistle but blew through my teeth. This was difficult to do in cold weather or when my mouth became dry in the heat of competition." Gypsy ran in and completed the 1941 Open National.

FC Sodak's Rip, owned by E. K. Ward of the Middle West, was a rather tall, light-boned dog and dark dead-grass in color. He was an excellent marker and a good handling dog. Handled by Charles Morgan, in the 1941 Open National Rip completed all ten tests. In the '44 event he broke in the sixth series.

FC Guess of Shagwong, also was owned by E. Monroe Osborne, who says of him, "He was a big dog but very agile, an excellent gun dog, and quiet in the blind. He was exceedingly easy to handle. I called him 'Guess' because of his odd color. No one believed he was a Chesapeake and when people asked me what kind of a dog he was, I said 'Guess!' He ran in the '41 Open National and completed all tests with E. Morford handling. Guess also qualified for the '42 event, but was unable to run, since Osborne had gone overseas to serve in World War II.

FC Chesacroft Baron, owned by R. N. Crawford, was trained and often handled by Charles Morgan, and made his Field Trial Championship in 1945. Unfortunately, I have not been able to procure a picture of him, nor an adequate description of his abilities, except that we have been told that he was an excellent marker and a hard running dog who liked his handling work. He was the only Chesapeake to run in the 1945 Open National and handled by Morgan, he completed three series.

FC Bayle was owned by Vance Morris, an amateur at the time, but who subsequently became one of the best known professional trainers on the East Coast. It has been said that Bayle was an exceptionally fine marker. He was an unusually long-coated dog who did not pass this characteristic on to his pups, but did endow them with his fine marking prowess. Morris ran him in the 1946 Open National, but he broke in the second test.

FC Tiger of Clipper City, a female belonging to Dr. and Mrs. George Gardner. He tells us that "Tiger was dead-grass in color and not a large dog in either height or weight—at best never weighing more than 65 pounds. Her outstanding quality, and the place where she was superb, was her ability on handling tests in water. She amassed a total of 32 Open

Dual Ch. & AFC Mount Joy's Mallard, who was Ed and Helen Fleischmann's favorite dog. Mallard was trained by Rex Carr, and besides being a good marker, ran a fine diagonal "Carr" line.

                              Dual Ch. Sodak's Gypsy Prince
                    FC Chesacroft Baron
                              Chesacroft Teal
          FC/AFC Nelgard's King Tut
                              FC Sodak's Rip
                    Sunbeam of Cocoa King
                              Lake Delavan Dolly
DUAL CH/AFC Mt. JOY'S MALLARD
                              FC Sodak's Rip
                    Ginger Buck
                              Laddie's Ginger
          Ch. Sasnakra Sassy CD
                              Dilwyne Con-Kell
                    Lake Andes Lassie
                              Miss Flight of Sun-Tu

All-Age points, a record that stood until her son, Baron, broke it in 1959. In the 1946 Open National Tiger finished the sixth test, handled by Charles Morgan. In '47, Dr. Gardner ran her himself and she finished the seventh test.

(In 1951 the American Kennel Club established a point system under which dogs could earn the title of Amateur Field Trial Champion. Some of the following dogs are both Field Champions and Amateur Field Champions.)

FC & AFC Deerwood Trigger was trained and owned by William Hoard. Trigger was an attractive, bright, personable male who was dead-grass color and had a wonderful temperament. He was one of the most consistent dogs ever to participate in field trials. He was an excellent marker, a willing handling dog, and had the honor of being awarded for two consecutive years the title of "Outstanding Retriever," by the Wisconsin Amateur Field Trial Club. Trigger went two series in the '51 Open National, and in the '52 National he completed the sixth test.

FC Montgomery Sal was owned by a hunting dog guide, Pat Montgomery of Klamath Falls, Oregon. During the hunting season she retrieved hundreds of ducks, as ducks were plentiful in those days in the Klamath Falls basin. Sal was a rugged bitch although she was small. Light brown in color, she was not a pretty dog but had an attractive personality. Her water work was exceptional and her marking ability on triples was renowned. Sal ran in the Open National of 1951, completing her third test.

FC & AFC Nelgard's King Tut, owned by Robert Brown, was trained and often handled by Charles Morgan. Tut was a tall, dark dead-grass dog, a little rangy in appearance. He was a good marker and a good handling dog, but in my mind, he lacked self-confidence and style. Bred to Champion Sasnakra Sassy, CD, he produced well—two Field Champions, Mallard and Star King, and one Amateur Field Champion, Chuck's Rip Joy. Tut ran in the Open National of 1951, finishing two series, while in the 1952 event he finished six tests.

FC & AFC Raindrop of Deerwood was a fast and stylish bitch, dead-grass in color. She was an extremely tractable and both an excellent marking and handling dog. Her owner, Phil Gagnon, trained her himself and only he ran her in trials. She made the fine record of 20½ Open and 33½ Amateur, a total of 54 points. Raindrop represented our breed in the '54 Open National and finished seven series.

FC, AFC & CFC Nelgard's Baron, CD., was bred by Munro Coleman of Canada, where he had been the National Derby Champion. Cliff

Dr. John Lundy with his FC & AFC Atom Bob, who was a stellar field trial performer. Bob was bred, owned and trained by Dr. Lundy.

<pre>
                                    Ginger Buck
                        Rex of Rapids
                                    Elder Cove Boots
            Ch. Nelgard's Riptide
                                    FC Chesacroft Baron
                        FC Tiger of Clipper City
                                    Belle of the Wolf River
FC/AFC ATOM BOB
                                    FC Bayle
                        Ch. Bayberry Pete
                                    Sheeza Natural
            Aleutian Keeko
                                    Aleutian Water Chief
                        Aleutian Fantasy
                                    Hi Test Pride of Marcroft
</pre>

Brignall bought him from Coleman when he was running in their National Championship Stake. Brignall irritated Coleman by criticizing his handling ability. They had an altercation that day. The next day when this event was over, Brignall asked Coleman to give him the dog. Coleman's gruff reply was, "He's tied to that tree over there, go get him yourself." From the first moment Baron saw Brignall he apparently seemed to dislike him. He growled and would not allow Brignall to come near him. It was not until he was bribed with food that he could be untied from the tree.

When Baron was seven years old, I was able to buy him from Brignall. He was definitely hard-mouthed, and undoubtedly this was caused by pressure, for in a short time he stopped crushing ducks and carried them properly. This took some work on my part, and I blew a special encouraging whistle for him that the fellows called the "lovey-dovey" whistle.

Baron had a tremendous amount of energy and drive, marked well, and had a fine water entry. But like his mother, Tiger of Clipper City, water handling was his forte, and he was hard to beat on water blinds. He was a classy dog and a real crowd pleaser. Baron established an excellent record of 48 Open and 27½ Amateur points, a total of 75½, and he stands sixth on our list of High Point Chesapeakes.

Baron had a fine record in Nationals. He completed seven tests in the Open National of '59 and was a finalist in the Open National of 1960.

FC & AFC Atom Bob was bred by Dr. Lundy, and was out of his good Field Trial bitch Aleutian Keeko. Dr. Lundy had owned Chesapeakes for many years and hunted them on the swift and treacherous Snake River, where a dog of courage was required to handle the tough current. Bob was a snappy and fast field trial performer, best known for his retrieving ability on difficult triples, on land or water. He was a husky, stocky, medium-sized dog, with no resemblance to his sire, Champion Nelgard's Riptide. He was medium brown in color and had a nice temperament. Bob was used a lot at stud. He won 8 Derby Points, 47 Amateur, and 47½ Open, a total of 94½. He stands fifth on our High Point list.

Bob ran in the 1958 Amateur National, completing four tests. In the Open Nationals, in '59 he completed four series; in '61 he completed the second, and in '63 he went three series.

Dual Ch. & AFC Mount Joy's Mallard belonged to Ed and Helen Fleischmann, and was a gift from Robert Brown. Mallard was trained by Rex Carr who taught him the famous fine diagonal line, for which Carr was noted. Known for his outstanding triple marking, Mallard made a fine record. Mallard was a large, dark dead-grass dog who became the second Dual Champion in our breed. He was extensively bred and produced one Open Field Champion, Louistoo, and an Amateur Field

Champion Chesnoma's Louis. Mallard did very well in the Derby, garnering 18 points. He also won 36½ Amateur points and 20½ Open, a total of 57.

Mallard never ran in an Open National. But he was a participant in the first National Amateur ever held, in Park Rapids in 1957. In the sixth series Mallard broke when Helen discharged the shotgun, as the handlers were required to shoot a blank cartridge. Helen was not a hunter and never before had shot over him. He ran in the '59 Amateur National completing the fourth test.

FC & AFC Meg's Pattie O'Rourke, affectionately known as "Missy," had a fabulous Derby record of 90 points in two years and was the National Derby Champion of 1958. She started in 27 Derby stakes; miraculously she placed 26 times. In 1960 she easily won both her Field Trial and Amateur Field Trial Championships. She was one of the outstanding markers in our breed, and practically never missed a bird. She was Dr. F. A. Dashnaw's first dog, so he had Rex Carr train her for him. She ran long lines on her blinds and was spectacular on her marks. "Bud" Dashnaw became a fine handler and it was unfortunate that his health forced him to quit trials when "Missy" was at her peak. Sad to relate, she was only bred once—to her full brother Meg's O'Timothy! In 1961 "Missy" was the first Chesapeake to win an All-Breed Double Header. In '62 she also won both the Amateur and Open Stakes at the Chesapeake Specialty.

Her National record is excellent. She ran in the Amateur National Stakes of '60, '61 and '62, and was a finalist in all three of these. She also ran the 1963 Amateur National and she finished three tests. In the 1960 Open National she completed six tests, and in the 1962 event she, again, was a finalist. Altogether she finished four of the six National events in which she was entered, a wonderful record.

FC & AFC Star King of Mount Joy belonged to Harold Johnson of the Midwest. King was a full brother to Mallard and to Chuck's Rip Joy. King was a large dog, dark dead-grass in color, with a friendly temperament. Johnson taught him to mark and handle well. King was never bred, to my knowledge. He was only run in one Derby where he placed second. Harold Johnson did not have the time to run in very many trials, but percentage-wise, King's record was very good as he gathered 28 Amateur and 10 Open points, a total of 38. He never competed in either an Open or Amateur National Championship Stake.

FC & AFC Mount Joy's Louistoo, a Mallard son, was bred by the Fleischmanns. He, also, was trained by Rex Carr, but exclusively handled by Helen Fleischmann. Louistoo was a large, rather thin, light brown dog who was a fine triple marker. He was an extremely consistent

FC Tiger of Clipper City, who was owned by Dr. George Gardner of Chicago. Tiger was a good marker and a fabulous handling dog.

FC Alamo's Lucias, who belonged to Ben Robertson of Woodland, California, and was trained and always run by professional "Chuck" Crook. Lucias' record in field trials was excellent.

Dual Ch. Cub's Kobi King, with Charles Sambrailo, who purchased him from his original owner, Helen Hartley of Alaska. Sambrailo ran him in quite a few trials and also took him duck hunting. — Carter

performer who won two All-Breed Double Headers. As he proved to be sterile, the Fleischmanns could not go on with their male line. Louistoo is third on the Chesapeake All-Time High Point list with a total of 111 licensed points of which 51 are Open and 60 are Amateur.

He ran in the 1962 Open National and failed in the fifth. He also participated in the '63 Amateur National completing three series, in the '65 again finishing three, and in the '67 event he completed the second test. He qualified for the '68 Amateur National but did not run.

Dual Ch & AFC Meg's O'Timothy, CDX., a full brother to Meg's Pattie O'Rourke, was a good looking brown dog who was extremely tractable. Also trained by Rex Carr, Tim performed well in trials for his owner, "Bud" Dashnaw. But Obedience was where he really shone, and he rolled up impressive scores for his trainer and handler Douglas Bundock. Tim is still the only Field Trial Champion Chesapeake to attain the CDX title. In '65 he became the fourth Dual Champion in our breed. He won 2 Derby points. His All-Age point record was 20½ Amateur plus 12½ Open, a total of 33.

FC Slow Gin, owned by Dr. L. B. Reppert of Texas, was a large, well-built, brown dog who was very affectionate and had a great personality. He was professionally trained but ran extremely well for his owner. Unfortunately, Dr. Reppert was a very busy physician and could not spare the time for many trials. Slow Gin was only bred once or twice, although none of his get subsequently ran in trials. Slow Gin won 18 Derby points. In addition to this, he had 3 Amateur and 11½ Open points—a total of 14½. He ran in the 1963 Open National, going three series.

Dual Ch. CFC & AFC Baron's Tule Tiger, CD, was a handful, as he was determined and willful. Rex Carr trained him and they had their battles, which Rex always eventually won. Tiger was extremely capable, a fine marker, and ran a good line on land. But his water blinds were where he really excelled. Tiger loved me—but was most indifferent to other people and all dogs except his son, Cub, whom he liked. Tiger's right eye was punctured by a rice straw, resulting in blindness. But with vision in only his left eye, he still continued to place and win. He was good looking and won his bench championship in three straight shows, as he did his Obedience title. Tiger won 55 Derby points against some really hot Labrador contenders of his day. He won an All-Breed Double Header and 3 Chesapeake Specialty Double Headers. Tiger's record of 112 Amateur and 96 Open points, a total of 208, has stood for the past 11 years, and may never be equalled.

His performance in National competition was excellent, probably because he was such a consistent worker. In the Amateur National Stake

Dual & AFC, Can FC Baron's Tule Tiger CD, bred, owned and always handled by author Eloise Heller. Tiger owns the top record of 208 All-Age points.

```
                              Ginger Buck
                    Rex of Rapids
                              Elder Cove Boots
          FC/AFC/CFC Nelgard's Baron CD
                              FC Chesacroft Baron
                    FC Tiger of Clipper City
                              Belle of the Wolf River
DUAL CH./AFC/CFC BARON'S TULE TIGER CD
                              FC/AFC Nelgard's King Tut
                    Dual Ch./AFC Mt. Joy's Mallard
                              Ch. Sasnakra Sassy CD
          Joanie Teal
                              Wisconong Joe
                    Wisconong Joe's Sandy
                              Aleutian Wisconong Trace
```

FC & AFC Chesnoma's Kodiak with owner, Dr. "Wes" Peltzer of Salt Lake City. "Kody" was a fun dog, and well trained by Rex Carr.

FC/AFC Nelgard's King Tut
Dual Ch/AFC Mt. Joy's Mallard
Ch. Sasnakra Sassy CD
AFC Chesonoma's Louis
Willows Dime
Frosty Milady
Jacqueline
FC/AFC CHESONOMA'S KODIAK
Rex of Rapids
FC/AFC/CFC Nelgard's Baron, CD
FC Tiger of Clipper City
Dinie's Miss Priss
Ch. Captain Culpepper II
Sam's Low Country Lady
Ch. Duxbury Blondie

of '64, he failed on a bad bird in the first test. But he was a finalist in the '66 and '67 events. He qualified for 5 Open Nationals. In '64, he went 5 tests, but in '65 he was a finalist. He completed 4 tests in both the '66 and '67 trials, and was qualified for the '68 trial, but had died by that time. He was my once-in-a-lifetime dog.

FC & AFC Chesnoma's Kodiak was a zippy little brown male, owned and always handled by Dr. "Wes" Peltzer of Utah. "Kody" was another Rex Carr product, which meant that he, too, learned to run long, long lines on blinds. In addition, "Kody" was a good marker. He was merry and gay and loved all people, but sometimes took a dim view of other males. He was seldom used at stud. It was a traumatic experience for his owner when "Kody" died of heat prostration. "Kody" won 6 Derby points. In All-Age Stakes he took 33 Amateur and 30 Open points, a total of 63. He ran in the 1966 Amateur National Championship Stake, where he completed 5 series.

FC & AFC Mount Joy's Bit O'Ginger was bred by the Fleischmanns, the sire being Meg's O'Timothy. Ginger was sold to Barbara Ornbaun, who did well with her in the Derby, winning 21 points. When Ginger was two, Helen Fleischmann bought her back and gave her to Wayne Crook to train. Ginger was a bright sedge, medium-sized female, who was an excellent marker and ran a good line. It was sad when Ginger died of cancer at an early age. Despite this, she is one of our High Point dogs with a record of 70½ total points, 44 Amateur and 26½ Open.

Ginger qualified for the Amateur Nationals of '68 and '69, but ran neither. However, in '68 she ran in the Open National, finishing one series. In the '69 Open National she did her very best work, completing 7 excellent tests for her trainer, Wayne Crook.

Ch. & AFC Koolwater's Colt of Tricrown, a son of AFC Bomarc of South Bay, was the first Eastern Chesapeake to make a field trial title for the long, dry spell of 13 years. Mike Paterno of New York owned Colt and sent him to John Honore to train. Colt was a large, dark brown dog with a fine temperament and a good personality. He marked very well. To my knowledge, Colt never stood at stud. He died when he was about six years old, at the height of his career. Mike was crushed and never wanted, or had, another Chesapeake after that. Colt won 15 Amateur and 12 Open points, a total of 27.

In the 1969 Amateur National Stake, Colt completed the second test. In 1970 Open National, he finished the sixth series.

Dual Ch. & AFC Tiger's Cub, CD was a typey, handsome specimen with a broad chest and heavy bone. He was bred a lot, and almost all of his get resembled him, which is the sign of a prepotent sire. He was a gay, happy Obedience dog, as he seemed to love the close contact with his owner.

Unlike his sire, Tule Tiger, who was always deadly serious in the field, Cub had a sense of humor. To my great annoyance, this always got us into trouble in the field trials. Rex Carr trained Cub and he often tried Rex's patience because he would not work to his full capacity. Cub easily made his bench championship, and he won his first Open Stake when he was only 3½, but he would not settle down to business. His record is 37 Derby points. His All-Age record of 85½ Amateur and 29 Open, a total of 114½ points, is second only to that of his sire, Tiger.

He ran in the Amateur National of '69, completing the third test. In the '70 event he went four series; in the '71 trial he completed two, as he did in the trial of '72. He qualified in the '73, but had just lost a toe, and had to be scratched. I judged the Amateur of '74, which put him out. We ran in one Canadian National, where in the third test he broke on three dead birds!

To a deadly serious competitor, as I was in those days, Cub was most exasperating. However, he was a very ingratiating chap, who loved all dogs and people.

Dual Ch. Cub's Kobi King belonged to the Dan Hartleys of Anchorage, Alaska. Dan Hartley unsuccessfully tried to train him, so Kobi was sent to the Crook's Kennels to be educated. Wayne and Chuck Crook did a fine job with him, for he was both tough and determined. Kobi (CERF-157/78-123) was a dog of medium size, bright sedge in color, and quite handsome. He looked, and acted, more like his grandsire, Tule Tiger, than his own father, Tiger's Cub. When the Hartleys were divorced, Dan put Kobi up for sale and Charles Sambrailo bought him and ran him in Amateur stakes. But, as he got older, Kobi's vision and hearing started to fail. At the age of 11, Kobi was shown on the bench by Ellen Loftsgaard, whose expertise resulted in his winning his bench championship. He thus became the seventh Dual Champion in our breed. Helen Hartley, a charming little Eskimo lady, had been crushed when Kobi was sold. She continually corresponded with Sambrailo, wanting to know how Kobi was getting along. Sambrailo decided to give Kobi back to Helen and, happily, that is where he is now.

Kobi never ran in Derbies, and in very few Amateur stakes, although once Helen Hartley came down from Alaska to attend the Specialty, and took an Amateur third place with him. He won 30½ Open points, but never was a contestant in a National Championship Stake.

FC & AFC Cooper Topper Der Wunderbar well-built and a good worker, was medium brown in color. His owner, Greg McDaniel, of Southern California, did all of Copper's training himself. Copper was a fine marker and a good handling dog. As McDaniel was a school teacher, with little time to spare for field trials, Copper only competed in a few trials each year. He was only occasionally used at stud. He made 5 Derby points. His All-Age points totaled 30½, of which 18 were Amateurs and

FC, AFC & Can FC Nelgard's Baron always was an exciting dog to watch. Owned first by Munro Coleman of Canada, then by the author, Baron's achievements in the Nationals are so far unequalled.

FC & AFC Tiger's Cub, CD, painted by Thomas Quinn. Cub won 29 Open and 85½ Amateur licensed Field Trial points — a total of 114½, a record second only to that of his sire, Tiger.

12 were Open. In the 1973 Amateur National he did some splendid work in finishing six tests.

FC Alamo's Lucias was brown, tall and somewhat thin. His owner, Ben Robertson of Northern California, had Chuck Crook train and run Lucias for him. Lucias was an excellent marking dog and his blinds were more than adequate. He was only infrequently bred. He never competed in any Amateur stakes. He won 10 Derby points and 19½ Open points. His National record was three series in the '75 Open Championship stake, and he finished the sixth test in the '76 Open National.

FC & AFC Bay City Jake, a very large, and substantial dead-grass colored dog of about 90 pounds, is co-owned by Dr. Miles Thomas and Peter Van Der Meulen, both of Idaho. Jake was sired by a Baron son and his dam is a Cub bitch. Jake has an agreeable, attractive personality and is a willing worker. He was trained by Rex Carr, and alternately run by his co-owners. Jake sired one litter, and then, to everyone's dismay, was pronounced sterile. He won a Double Header in 1977. I don't believe he was ever run in the Derby. At the end of 1978 he had a total of 50 points, 34½ Amateur, and 25½ Open. He ran in the Amateur National Championship stakes of 1976, going five series, and in the '77 stake he completed six. He is qualified for the 1979 Amateur National. At the Open National of '76, Jake finished three tests.

FC & AFC Aleutian Surf Breaker comes from Dr. Lundy's line. Surf is co-owned by Dr. Miles Thomas and John McRoberts, both of whom handle him. A medium-sized dog and a husky specimen, Surf is very birdy. He marks well and is a capable handling dog, but a bit temperamental. He has been used at stud quite a bit recently. Through 1978 he had 5 Amateur and 7 Open points, but he has won quite a few more in 1979.

He competed in the 1977 Amateur National, finishing four tests. In the Open National of '78, he finished three series. He is qualified for the 1979 Amateur National.

FC, AFC, CFC & CAFC Chesdel Chippewa Chief, a large dog, is light brown in color. Alex Spear bred his Chesdel Longwood Lassie to Koolwater Colt, and Chief came from this litter. Chief is a pleasant, dependable, and willing worker, and a real credit to our breed. He has been entirely trained by his owner and always run by him. Despite the fact that Spear has not had the time to extensively campaign him, Chief's point record is excellent. He won 31 Derby points and was eighth in the National Derby listing of 1973. At the end of 1978, he had a total of 40 All-Age points, 28 Amateur and 12 Open. He has won and placed in '79, so his record will go up. He has been used as a stud for several years now.

He ran in the '77 Amateur National, finishing five tests. In the 1978 Open National he completed two. Chief is qualified for the 1979 Amateur National.

Dual Ch. & AFC Koolwater's Colt of Tricrown, who was owned by Michael Paterno of New York.

                        Ch. Nelgard's Riptide
                FC/AFC Atom Bob
                        Aleutian Keeko
        Ch./AFC Bomarc of South Bay (OFA 2)
                        Mount Joy's Tiger
                Aleutian Duchess
                        Aleutian Water Spray
DUAL & AFC KOOLWATER'S COLT OF TRICROWN
                        Cocoa King Tugboat
                Am/Can Ch. Native Shore Dan
                        Jill of Greenwood
        Ch. Welcome of the Willows
                        Ashby's Dynamite of the Willows
                Am/Can Ch. Dyna of the Willows CD
                        Sheerie of Greenwood

CHESAPEAKE AMATEUR FIELD TRIAL CHAMPIONS

(Note: It was not until 1951 that the American Kennel Club established a point system under which dogs could earn the title of Amateur Field Trial Champion.)

		Owner:
1952	NELGARD'S KING TUT (FC Chesacroft Baron ex Sunbeam of Cocoa King)	Mount Joy Kennels
	RAINDROP OF DEERWOOD (Johansen's Major ex Del Monte of Deer- wood)	P. J. Gagnon
1953	GYPSY (Buddy Brown ex Gypsy of Suffolk)	J. V. O'Shea
	DEERWOOD TRIGGER (Watercliff King ex Del Monte Ginger)	William Hoard, Jr.
1954	ODESSA CREEK SPUNKY (King LeRoy Jan ex Montgomery's Sal)	Triever Point Kennels
1955	CHUCK'S RIP JOY (FC & AFC Nelgard's King Tut ex Ch Sasnakra Sassy, CD)	Ralph Mock
1956	MOUNT JOY'S MALLARD (FC & AFC Nelgard's King Tut ex Ch Sasnakra Sassy, CD)	E. C. Fleischmann
1957	ATOM BOB (Ch Nelgard's Rip Tide ex Aleutian Keeko)	Dr. John Lundy
1957	RIP (Rip Van Winkle ex Raymond's Queenie)	Frank Holliday
1958	NELGARD'S BARON (Rex of Rapids ex FC Tiger of Clipper City)	Eloise Heller
	STAR KING OF MOUNT JOY (FC & AFC Nelgard's King Tut ex Ch Sasnakra Sassy, CD)	Harold Johnson
1959	CHESNOMA'S LOUIS (Ch Mount Joy's Mallard ex Ch Frosty Milady)	Winston Moore
1960	MEG'S PATTIE O'ROURKE (Beewacker's Chester ex Meg O' My Heart)	Dr. F. A. Dashnaw
1962	CH MEG'S O'TIMOTHY (Beewacker's Chester ex Meg O' My Heart)	Dr. F. A. Dashnaw
1962	MOUNT JOY'S LOUISTOO (Dual Ch & AFC Mount Joy's Mallard ex Frosty Milady)	E. C. Fleischmann
1963	CH BOMARC OF SOUTH BAY, CD (FC & AFC Atom Bob ex Aleutian Duchess)	August Belmont
1965	AFC BARON'S TULE TIGER, CD (FC & AFC & CFC Nelgard's Baron, CD ex Joanie Teal)	Eloise Heller

FC & AFC Raindrop of Deerwood, with just a few of her trophies. She was extremely consistent, and her record is quite amazing in the light of the few trials in which she competed for her owner, Phil Gagnon.

Dual Ch. & AFC Meg's O'Timothy, CDX, owned by Joyce and "Bud" Dashnaw, was an exceptional dog who excelled in field trials, on the bench, and in Obedience.

1965 AFC BARON'S TULE TIGER, CD   Eloise Heller
      (FC & AFC & CFC Nelgard's Baron, CD
      ex Joanie Teal)
1966 CHESNOMA'S KODIAK   Dr. W. E. Pelzer
      (AFC Chesnoma's Louis ex Dinie's Miss
      Priss)
1968 MOUNT JOY'S BIT O'GINGER   Mrs. E. C.
      (Dual & AFC Meg's O' Timothy, CDX ex   Fleischmann
      Mount Joy's Jug Ears)
1970 KOOLWATER COLT OF TRICROWN   Michael Paterno
      (AFC Bomarc of Southbay ex Welcome of
      the Willows)
      TIGER'S CUB, CD   Eloise Heller
      (Dual Ch & AFC & CFC Baron's Tule Tiger,
      CD ex Napolitano's Ladybug)
1972 COPPER TOPPER DER WUNDERBAR   Greg McDaniel
      (Hector ex Bonnie La Bonita)
1975 BAY CITY JAKE   Dr. Miles Thomas and
      (Hatchet Man ex Ch Cub's   Pete Van Der Meulen
      Marin Echo, UD)
      CFC & CAFC NANUK OF CHESLANG   Hans Kuck
      (The Big Fellow ex Atomalina Myrtle)
1978 ALEUTIAN SURF BREAKER   Dr. Miles Thomas and
      (Big Fellow ex Chopper's Bobbie)   John McRoberts
      CHESDEL CHIPPEWA CHIEF   Alex Spear
      (Dual & AFC Koolwater's Colt of Tricrown,
      CD ex Chesdel Longwood Lassie)

DESCRIPTIONS OF THE AMATEUR FIELD CHAMPIONS

*(Dogs who have won both Field Trial and Amateur Field
championships have been described in the previous section.
The following made Amateur Field Championship only.)*

AFC Champion Gypsy, owned by Vincent O'Shea of Long Island, was
sired by the great Buddy Brown. Gypsy was a small brown female with
great desire and ability. She only competed in a few trials, but made her
American Field Championship in 1953. I find no report on her Derby
career. However, she made 21 Amateur points and 10½ Open, a total of
31½. Gypsy ran in the Open National of '51, and gave a good account of
herself, completing six tests.

AFC Odessa Creek Radar, a son of Montgomery Sal, sired by King
LeRoy Jan, was bred by Pat Montgomery. "Spunky" was a dead-grass
male, rather slightly built, a pleasant dog of sound temperament, but
not particularly impressive in his work. Owned by Sandy MacKay of

FC Slow Gin, who belonged to Dr. L. B. Reppert of Texas. A handsome brown dog, Gin had an exceptional temperament, friendly and sweet to all.

FC Montgomery's Sal leaping a fence to bring a pheasant in to her owner, "Pat" Montgomery. Pat was a professional hunting guide in Klamath Falls, Oregon, and trained Sal himself.

AFC Gypsy, bringing in a pheasant for her owner, Vincent O'Shea of New York. Gypsy was fun to watch as she was always so enthusiastic and gay.

Southern California, who became ill, "Spunky" was not campaigned and just became Sandy's gun dog. "Spunky" won the necessary 15 points for his Amateur Field Championship, but did not qualify for either National.

AFC Chuck's Rip Joy was a product of the famous King Tut and Sasnakra Sassy breeding. Hence, he was a full brother to Mallard and Star King. Medium brown in color, a handsome, personable individual, Rip was an excellent marker and a good handling dog. He also was undeniably the most important thing in the life of his owner, Ralph Mock of Dayton, Ohio. Rip was bred often, but his progeny was all sold to hunters. His record is 17½ Amateur points, handled by Mock, and 9½ Open Points, handled by Charles Morgan, who trained him. He was never a National contender.

AFC Rip, owned by Frank Holiday of Omaha, Nebraska. Rip was of medium size, a bright dead-grass male who won his Amateur Field Championship in '57. He was known for his excellent marking, his consistency, and fine temperament. He was entirely amateur-trained. Rip was seldom bred, and we know nothing about his get. He was only run in a few Derbies — also, very few trials. His record is 21½ Amateur points and 3½ Open. In the first Amateur National of 1957, Rip completed seven tests.

AFC Chesnoma's Louis, a son of Mallard ex their female, Frosty Milady, was bred by the Fleischmanns. Louis was a powerful, heavy set dog, who was fast and stylish. He was medium brown in color. One of Louis's sons, Chesnoma's Kodiak, became a Field and Amateur Field Champion. All of Louis's training was done by Helen Fleischmann, who got 5 Derby points with him and made his Amateur Field Championship in '59. Shortly after this he was sold to Winston Moore of Boise, Idaho. Moore ran him in a few Field Trials but mostly used him as a shooting dog. Louis made 28 Amateur and 7½ Open points. He never qualified for either of the National Stakes, Open or Amateur.

AFC Bomarc of South Bay, CD, was bred by John Lundy, and was a son of Atom Bob ex Aleutian Duchess. A rich brown color, good looking, but a strong, and strong-willed dog, he was sold to August Belmont of Long Island. Belmont trained Bomarc, who would only do his best for his owner. His Derby record was excellent as he won 28 points. When older, Bomarc was sent to Rex Carr — an experience neither particularly enjoyed. After Bomarc made his Amateur Field Championship in '63, Belmont gave him to a top Eastern trainer, Jay Sweezey, to keep for a year in an attempt to win his Field Championship. It didn't work. Bomarc was definitely a one man dog! His record is 2½ Open and 24 Amateur points, all with Belmont at the helm.

FC & AFC Mount Joy's Louistoo, winner of two Double-Headers for her owner-handler, Helen Fleischmann. Louis was known as a super marker on water triples, and ran a good line on blinds.

Ch. Bayberry Pete, a fine field trial dog and Ed Fleischmann's personal hunting dog for many years.

Mount Joy's Bit O'Ginger, excellent field contender, was owned by Helen Fleischmann. Ginger was a great marker and a good handling dog.

AFC, CFC & CAFC Nanuk of Cheslang was bred by Paul Kimball of Boise, Idaho. He was purchased as a puppy by Hans Kuch of Langley, B.C., Canada, and was trained and always handled by his owner. His style, excellent marking ability, and spectacular water entry made him a favorite among judges and spectators. Small in stature and light brown in color, Nanuk was fun to watch. He made his Canadian Field Championship and Canadian Amateur Field Championship before he was three years old. He finished his American Amateur Field Championship in 1975. Nanuk was one of a handful of Canadian retrievers that earned both American and Canadian Field titles. He was retired with a record of 73 Canadian and 34 American licensed points — a total of 107.

He qualified for the '73, '74, '75, '76, '77 and '78 Canadian National Championship stakes. In addition, he ran in the '74 and '76 American Amateur Nationals, completing three tests in both events.

Other Notable Field Trial Dogs

Chesabob, belonging to R. R. M. Carpenter, was declared the 1937 Derby Champion of that year.

Native Shore Pink Lady, owned and trained by George Carmony of New York, exclusively represented our breed in the 1950 Open National. I saw her, in sleet, snow and icy water, complete three tests.

Ch. Bayberry Pete had a fine Eastern Derby career for his owner, Dr. W. L. Parrott. Ed Fleischmann saw Pete and bought him, and he did quite well in Open stakes. In 1952, handled by "Snuffy" Beliveau, Pete won 17½ Open points, making him third place dog in the country. But, unfortunately, Pete never could win a first in an Open All-Breed trial, which is required to win a Field Trial Championship. In the 1952 Open National, handled by Bud Hedges, he completed six series.

Beewacker's Chester, owned by E. J. Rowe of San Francisco, won 15 Derby points in 1953 and was fifth on the National Derby list. Chester was one of the finest marking dogs I have ever seen. He passed on this great ability to his daughter, Meg's Pattie O'Rourke. However, Chester did not like to handle.

Chessy Cocoanut won the 1977 Chesapeake Specialty Amateur stake and qualified for the '78 Amateur National. But his owner, Jesse Mitchell, was unable to attend. Mitchell has been a staunch supporter of our breed for a long period of years. He was often the only Chesapeake owner in many of the Eastern trials. He has had several really good dogs which he co-owned with R. R. M. Carpenter, Jr. — such as J. J. Hy Wyne Willows and Mount Joy's Jez O'Meg.

FC & AFC Bay City Jake, pictured with Pete Van Der Muelen, who co-owns him with Dr. Miles Thomas. Trained by Rex Carr, Jake thoroughly knows his work and is a splendid performer.

```
                              Rex of Rapids
                      FC/AFC/CFC Nelgard's Baron CD
                          FC Tiger of Clipper City
            Hatchet Man
                          Dual Ch/AFC Mt. Joy's Mallard
                      Ch. Trofast of Green Valley
                          Wisconong Joe's Sandy
FC/AFC BAY CITY JAKE
                          Dual AFC/CFC Baron's Tule Tiger CD
                      Dual CH/AFC Tiger's Cub CD (OFA 6)
                          Napolitano's Ladybug
            Ch. Cub's Marin Echo, UD/WD (OFA 42)
                          Ch. Chief Kamiakin
                      Ch. Chesareid April Echo
                          Can Ch. Heather of Carnmoney
```

FC, AFC, CFC & CAFC Chesdel Chippewa Chief, with veteran owner-handler, Alex Spear. Chief has been a standout example of the Chesapeake breed.

FC/AFC Atom Bob
Ch/AFC Bomarc of South Bay CD
Aleutian Duchess
Dual Ch/AFC Koolwater's Colt of Tricrown (OFA CB-19)
Can/Am Ch. Native Shore Dan
Ch. Welcome of the Willows
Can/Am Ch. Dyna of the Willows CD
FC/AFC/CFC/CAFC CHESDEL CHIPPEWA CHIEF (OFA-CB 175)
Dual Ch/AFC/CFC Baron's Tule Tiger CD
Baronland's Chesbay Beaver
Ch. Chesareid April Echo
Chesdel Longwood Lassie (OFA CB-96; CERF 142)
Chesdel Brandy of Kennett
J. J.'s Sassapeake
Rip Tide Lee

ALL-TIME HIGH POINT CHESAPEAKES
Combined Open and Amateur Points—1932 through 1978

	Open Points	Amateur Points	TOTAL POINTS
Dual Ch., AFC & CFC Baron's Tule Tiger, CD	96	112	208
Dual Ch. & AFC Tiger's Cub, CD	29	85½	114½
FC & AFC Mount Joy's Louistoo	51	60	111
FC & AFC Meg's Pattie O'Rourke	55½	52	107½
FC & AFC Atom Bob	47½	47	94½
FC, AFC & CFC Nelgard's Baron, CD	48	27½	75½
FC & AFC Mount Joy's Bit O'Ginger	26½	44	70½
FC & AFC Chesnoma's Kodiak	30	33	63
FC & AFC Bay City Jake	24½	34½	59
FC & AFC Mount Joy's Mallard	20½	36½	57
FC & AFC Raindrop of Deerwood	20½	33½	54

Winners of 25 or more Open Points

	Open Points
FC, AFC & CFC Baron's Tule Tiger, CD	96
FC & AFC Meg's Pattie O'Rourke	55½
FC & AFC Mount Joy's Louistoo	51
FC, AFC & CFC Nelgard's Baron, CD	48
FC & AFC Atom Bob	47½
FC Tiger of Clipper City	32
FC Shagwong Gypsy	31
Dual Ch. Cub's Kobi King	30½
FC & AFC Chesnoma's Kodiak	30
Dual & AFC Tiger's Cub, CD	29
FC & AFC Mount Joy's Bit O'Ginger	26½
FC Dilwyne Montauk Pilot	26
FC Skipper Bob	26
FC Montgomery's Sal	25½
FC & AFC Bay City Jake	25½

Winners of 25 or more Amateur Points

	Amateur Points:
Dual & AFC & CFC Baron's Tule Tiger, CD	112
Dual & AFC Tiger's Cub, CD	85½
FC & AFC Mount Joy's Louistoo	60
FC & AFC Meg's Pattie O'Rourke	52
FC & AFC Atom Bob	47
FC & AFC Mount Joy's Bit O'Ginger	44
Dual & AFC Mount Joy's Mallard	36½
FC & AFC Bay City Jake	34½
FC & AFC Raindrop of Deerwood	33½
FC & AFC Chesnoma's Kodiak	33
AFC Chesnoma's Louis	28
FC & AFC Star King of Mount Joy	28
FC, AFC & CFC Chesdel Chippewa Chief	28
FC, AFC & CFC Nelgard's Baron, CD	27½

Dorothy Traung, famous California golf champion, with Ch. Chesacroft Nippy Bob, well-known stud dog of the Grizzly Island Kennels located at Grizzly Island, California.

Dr. Miles Thomas, with his first field trial dog — AFC Aleutian Mike, who was a merry little soul.

FC & AFC Copper Topper Der Wunderbar, with his owner-trainer-handler, Greg McDaniels of Idaho. Copper is now retired, but he and Greg were a wonderful team.

CHESAPEAKE DOUBLE HEADERS

(A dog who wins both the Open and the Amateur stake
at the same trial is known as a "Double Header.")

Double Headers — All-Breed Competition

1961 FC & AFC Meg's Pattie O'Rourke   Dr. F. A. Dashnaw
1965 Dual Ch, AFC CFC Baron's Tule Tiger, CD   Eloise Heller
1966 FC & AFC Mount Joy's Louistoo   Mrs. E. C. Fleischmann
1976 FC Bay City Jake   Dr. M. E. Thomas and
      Pete Van Der Meulen

Double Headers — Chesapeake Specialty

1962 FC & AFC Meg's Pattie O'Rourke
1964 Dual Ch, AFC & CFC Baron's Tule Tiger, CD
1965 Dual Ch, AFC & CFC Baron's Tule Tiger,CD
1966 Dual Ch, AFC & CFC Baron's Tule Tiger, CD
1971 Dual Ch & AFC Tiger's Cub, CD   Eloise Heller

WINNERS OF THE CHESAPEAKE SPECIALTY FIELD TRIALS

Owner:

1932 (Nov. 27) Long Island, NY
Open All-Age 1st: KING OF MONTAUK   J. C. Hadder
1933 (Nov. 26) Long Island, NY
Open All-Age 1st: FC SKIPPER BOB   H. T. Conklin
1934 (Nov. 25) Long Island, NY
Open All-Age 1st: FC SKIPPER BOB   H. T. Conklin
1934 (Dec. 1) Benton, Maryland
Open All-Age 1st: FC SKIPPER BOB   H. T. Conklin
1935 (Nov. 15) Long Island, NY
Open All-Age 1st: FC SKIPPER BOB   H. T. Conklin
1936 (Mar. 28) Benton, Maryland
Open All-Age 1st: Dual Ch SODAK'S GYPSY
PRINCE   A.A. Bliss
1936 (Nov. 13, 14 & 15) Long Island, NY
Open All-Age 1st: Dual Ch SODAK'S GYPSY
PRINCE   Chesacroft Kennels
1937 (Apr. 1, 2 & 3) Benton, Maryland
Open All-Age 1st: FC DILWYNE MONTAUK
PILOT   Dilwyne Kennels
1937 (Nov. 12, 13 & 14) Long Island, NY ·
Open All-Age 1st: FC DILWYNE MONTAUK
PILOT   Dilwyne Kennels
1938 (Nov. 11, 13 & 13) Long Island, NY
Open All-Age 1st: SHAGWONG GYPSY   E. Monroe Osborne
1939 (Nov. 18-19) Long Island, NY
Open All-Age 1st: BOB OF MONTAUK   R. R. M. Carpenter, Jr.

1940 (Nov. 9-10) No awards made in Open All-Age
1941 (Nov. 8-9) Long Island, NY
    Open All-Age 1st: GUESS OF SHAGWONG   E. Monroe Osborne
There were no American Club Specialty Trials during 1942, 1943, 1944, 1945, 1946,
    1947, 1948 and 1949.
1950 (Apr. 22-23) Eagle, Wisconsin
    Open All-Age 1st: PINE RIDGE
    OF DEERWOOD   P. J. Gagnon
1951 (Apr. 28-29) Anoka, Minnesota
    Open All-Age 1st: FC & AFC NELGARD'S
    KING TUT   Mount Joy Kennels
1952 (May 3-4) Boise, Idaho
    Open All-Age 1st: BAYBERRY PETE   E. C. Fleischmann
1953 (Apr. 21-22) Long Island, NY
    Open All-Age 1st: AFC CHUCK'S RIP JOY   Mount Joy Kennels
    Amateur All-Age 1st: NATIVE SHORE
    PINK LADY   George Carmony
1954 (May 6-7) Wisconsin Rapids, Wisconsin
    Open All-Age 1st: FC & AFC RAINDROP OF
    DEERWOOD   P. J. Gagnon
    Amateur All-Age 1st: BAYBERRY PETE   E. C. Fleischmann
1955 (May 3-4) Elko, Nevada
    Open All-Age 1st: MOUNT JOY'S MALLARD   E. C. Fleischmann
    No Amateur Stake held
1956 (Mar. 6, 7 & 8) Watsonville, California
    Open All-Age 1st: CFC NELGARD'S BARON   C. N. Brignall
    Amateur All-Age 1st: FROSTY MILADY   E. C. Fleischmann
1957 (May 7-9) Hastings, Nebraska
    Open All-Age 1st: AFC MOUNT JOY'S
    MALLARD   E. C. Fleischmann
    Amateur All-Age 1st: AFC RIP   Frank Holliday
1958 (May 5, 6 & 7) Boise, Idaho
    Open All-Age 1st: AFC ATOM BOB   Dr. John Lundy
    Amateur All-Age 1st: CHESNOMA'S LOUIS   Winston Moore
1959 (Apr. 7, 8 & 9) Kansas City, Mo.
    Open All-Age 1st: FC & AFC ATOM BOB   Dr. John Lundy
    Amateur All-Age 1st: CAPTAIN RINGO KID Owen Compton
1960 (May 25, 26 & 27) Reno Nevada
    Open All-Age 1st: VC, AVC & CFC
    NELGARD'S BARON, CD   Mrs. Walter Heller
    Amateur All-Age 1st: FC & AFC ATOM BOB Dr. John Lundy
1961 (May 16, 17 & 18) Salt Lake City, Utah
    Open All-Age 1st: FC & AFC ATOM BOB   Dr. John Lundy
    Amateur All-Age 1st: FC & AFC MEG'S
    PATTIE O'ROURKE   Dr. F. A. Dashnaw
1962 (May 27, 28 & 29) Reno, Nevada
    Open All-Age 1st: FC & AFC MEG'S
    PATTIE O'ROURKE   Dr. F. A. Dashnaw
    Amateur All-Age 1st: FC & AFC MEG'S
    PATTIE O'ROURKE   Dr. F. A. Dashnaw

Some of the contestants in the 1953 Specialty Field Trial held on Long Island, N. Y.

1963 (May 6, 7 & 8) Boise, Idaho	
Open All-Age 1st: KO-KO'S	
SERGEANT RUSTY	Burt Ebaugh
Amateur All-Age 1st: AFC BOMARC OF	
SOUTH BAY, CD	August Belmont
1964 (May 12-13) Salt Lake City, Utah	
Open All-Age 1st: Dual Ch & AFC BARON'S	
TULE TIGER, CD	Mrs. Walter Heller
Amateur All-Age 1st: Dual Ch & AFC	
BARON'S TULE TIGER, CD	Mrs. Walter Heller
1965 (May 25, 26 & 27) Santa Rosa, California	
Open All-Age 1st: Dual Ch & AFC BARON'S	
TULE TIGER, CD	Mrs. Walter Heller
Amateur All-Age 1st: Dual Ch & AFC	
BARON'S TULE TIGER, CD	Mrs. Walter Heller
1966 (Aug. 9, 10 & 11) McCall, Idaho	
Open All-Age 1st: Dual Ch & AFC BARON'S	
TULE TIGER, CD	Mrs. Walter Heller
Amateur All-Age 1st: Dual Ch & AFC	
BARON'S TULE TIGER, CD	Mrs. Walter Heller
1967 (July 17-19) Santa Rosa, California	
Open All-Age 1st: FC & AFC MOUNT JOY'S	
LOUISTOO	E. C. Fleischmann
Amateur All-Age 1st: MOUNT JOY'S BIT	
O'GINGER	E. C. Fleischmann
1968 (July 30-Aug. 1) Park City, Utah	
Open All-Age 1st: MEG'S TAMI O'HARA	Dr. Miles Thomas
Amateur All-Age 1st: TIGER'S CUB, CD	Mrs. Walter Heller
1969 (July 29-31) Park City, Utah	
Open All-Age 1st: FC & AFC MOUNT JOY'S	
BIT O'GINGER	E. C. Fleischmann
Amateur All-Age 1st: KOOLWATER COLT OF	
TRICROWN	Michael Paterno
1970 (Aug. 11-13) McCall, Idaho	
Open All-Age 1st: MOUNT JOY'S	
MICKEY FINN	Harry Cosner
Amateur All-Age 1st: MOUNT JOY'S	
DILWYNE JEZ O'MEG	J. J. Mitchell and
	R. R. M. Carpenter, Jr.

FC & AFC Aleutian Surf Breaker with John McRoberts, who co-owns him with Dr. Miles Thomas. Surf is our most recent Field Champion and ran in the 1979 Amateur National Championship Stake.

```
                                Ch. Nelgard's Riptide
                        FC/AFC Atom Bob
                                Aleutian Keeko
              The Big Fellow
                                Wisconong Trigger II
                        Wisconong Champagne Lady
                                Wisconong Sadie
FC/AFC ALEUTIAN SURF BREAKER (OFA-291)
                                FC/AFC Atom Bob
                        Aleutian Chopper
                                Meg's Tami O'Hara
              Chopper's Bobbie
                                Sir Catalina Speed
                        Atomalina Myrtle
                                Gypsy's Atoma Bobbie
```

1971 (July 19-21) Santa Rosa, California
    Open All-Age 1st: Dual Ch & AFC
    TIGER'S CUB, CD   Mrs. Walter Heller
    Amateur All-Age 1st: Dual Ch & AFC TIGER'S
    CUB, CD   Mrs. Walter Heller

1972 (Aug. 8-10) McCall, Idaho
    Open All-Age 1st: Dual Ch & AFC TIGER'S
    CUB, CD   Mrs. Walter Heller
    Amateur All-Age 1st: COPPER TOPPER DER
    WUNDERBAR   Greg & Jan McDaniel

1973 (July 6-8) Knightsen, California
    Open All-Age 1st: FC CUB'S KOBI KING   Dan Hartley
    Amateur All-Age 1st: CFC NANUK OF
    CHESLANG   Hans Kuck

1974 (July 30-Aug. 1) Oakley, Utah
    Open All-Age 1st: Dual Ch & AFC TIGER'S
    CUB, CD   Mrs. Walter Heller
    Amateur All-Age 1st: KODI'S BOOMERANG Dr. W. E. Peltzer

1975 (Aug. 5-7) Sun Valley, Idaho
    Open All-Age 1st: FC CUB'S KOBI KING   Charles Sambrailo
    Amateur All-Age 1st: BAY CITY JAKE   Dr. Miles Thomas and
                                   Pete Van Der Meulen

1976 (July 12-14) Pescadero, California
    Open All-Age 1st: FC & AFC COPPER
    TOPPER DER WUNDERBAR   Greg McDaniel
    Amateur All-Age 1st: FC & AFC BAY CITY
    JAKE   Dr. Miles Thomas and
                                   Pete Van Der Meulen

1977 (Aug. 9-11) Burlington, Wisconsin
    Open All-Age 1st: JASPER T CUBS   Dennis Ludington
    Amateur All-Age 1st: CHESSIE COCOANUT J. J. Mitchell and
                                   R. R. M. Carpenter, Jr.

1978 (Aug. 15-17) Picabo, Idaho
    Open All-Age 1st: FC & AFC
    BAY CITY JAKE   Dr. Miles Thomas and
                                   Pete Van Der Meulen
    Amateur All-Age 1st: ALEUTIAN SURF
    BREAKER   Dr. Miles Thomas and
                                   John McRoberts

1979 (Aug. 21-23) Mason, Michigan
    Open All-Age 1st: FC & AFC BAY CITY JAKE Dr. Miles Thomas and
                                   Pete Van Der Meulen
    Amateur All-Age 1st: FC, AFC, CFC & CAFC
    CHESDEL CHIPPEWA CHIEF   Alex Spear

1980 (July 4-6) Half Moon Bay, California
    Open All-Age 1st: FIREWOOD'S ALEUTIAN
    WIDGEON   Linda P. Harger
    Amateur All-Age 1st: CUB'S TERRIFIC THOR Eloise Cherry

The Chesapeake Field Trial specialty of 1978 was by far the best we ever had. The quality of the work was excellent, and this event was supported by Chesapeake owners from all parts of the United States. There was an entry of 30 Open, 31 Amateur, 32 Qualifying, and 35 Derbies.

At this Specialty, there were quite a few new and promising dogs who deserve to be mentioned:

Atom Bob's Kodiak from Wisconsin, belonging to Ted Homes, who is a devoted and hardworking Chesapeake owner.

Auror's Indian Bear, whose Derby record was 24 points. He belongs to Dr. Miles Thomas and is a fine prospect.

Baltz Kandimans Bay, George Balthazar's dog from Texas, who already has won a licensed Qualifying stake.

Berteleda Bandit, fast and stylish, marks and handles well. Co-owned by Les Lowenthal and Steve Limas.

Berteleda Magothy, a bitch with promise, trained by Chuck Crook, and belonging to Alexandra Starr.

Ch. Briarmoor's Waterchief, is owned by John Cargal of Indiana. Chief broke in the first test — but with great speed, class and style. He is handsome besides!

Capital City Jake, now owned by Jane Kelso-Ballou. "Cappy" won 23 Derby points, and has a lot of ability.

Chemin De Fer of Chesdel, Dr. Marston Jones' flashy little female is being trained by John Dahl, and looks like a "comer."

Dakota Luke, hard-going and a good marker, is owned, trained, and run by John Moisan of South Dakota. Luke has quite a potential.

Dale's Cinnamon Chip, a fine sedge specimen with ability, is owned and trained by Charles Coleman of Southern California.

Fireweed's Aleutian Widgeon has placed in several major stakes. He is owned and trained by Linda Harger of Oregon, who is a fine handler.

Go Major Go is Harvey Hackney's Canadian prospect who certainly looked good to me.

Gross Schlect Bark Von Berg is an exceptionally large dog with good natural abilities.

Ch. Hi-Ho's Guns of Canton, CD, physically sound, good looking and a dog with a fine temperament. He is Stephen Loftsgaard's able challenger.

Ch. Kobi's California Quail, CD, belongs to John Smart of Oregon and usually gives a good account of himself.

Mount Joy's E.C. Bay, CD, has been entirely amateur trained by Jim Nicholes of California. "E.C." has already won an All-Breed Amateur stake.

Pralina's Nicholas, belonging to Dr. and Mrs. I. M. Pralina of Minnesota, is a very large dog of their breeding, who always runs well for Vivian Pralina.

12

Chesapeake Bench History and Records

THE FIRST American dog show was held in 1874, but it was 1876 before Chesapeake Bay Dogs were shown as a separate breed. Even in the first part of the twentieth century very few bench shows were held and even fewer Chesapeakes shown in the ring.

Our first bench championship title was made in 1910 by Jupiter, who was owned by M. R. Stewart. Only three more dogs of the breed attained this honor up to 1922. In that year Chesacroft Kennels made its first bench championship with Chesacroft Tobe, and then was very active for a number of years.

As the number of shows increased from 1940 on, so did the number of Chesapeake fanciers who became interested in showing their dogs. Almost without exception, Chesapeakes have been handled in bench competition by their owners. Only a few have been professionally handled over a period of time. Perhaps it is another phase of the breed's character to only do its best for its owners.

At start of the 1980s, the all-time list of Chesapeake bench champions numbered over 800.

Going to dog shows has often been made into a family enterprise. A surprising number of Junior Handlers has been developed, and they have had astonishing success. Starting, I believe with Terrie Urben, juvenile members of the Eller, Horn, Di Vaccaro and Lowman families became extremely adept at exhibiting their dogs. More recently, Charlene Coleman, John Smart's three daughters, Scott and Jamie Jones, Judy Berg, Karrie Dollar, Jennifer Cone, Beth and Kathie Kinney, and Laura Humer have all consistently won Junior Showmanship ribbons. Watching a large, powerful Chesapeake being shown by a youngster is yet another way of having our dogs presented to the public in a proper light — as dogs who are tractable and gentle, and who make ideal children's companions.

Ch. Crispin Roderick, CD, pictured winning the first Best in Show for a Chesapeake at an AKC all-breed event, at Lexington Kennel Club 1975 show under judge Len Carey. Cris, owned by the John Woods, has a pace-setting total of 115 Bests of Breed, 9 Group firsts and 22 other Group placements.

<pre>
                                        Ch. Duke of Boone
                          Boone of Coco
                                        Coco Queen II
              Wabash Country Jake
                                        Dead Eye Dick
                          Dyna of Cocoa's
                                        Cocoa's Cleo
CH CRISPIN RODERICK, CD
                                        Delaney's Cannon-Ball
                          Duke Bohn
                                        Nickie
              Chapel Jene CD
                                        Bullet of Atom Bob
                          Skippy
                                        Valerie Queen
</pre>

Our annual National Bench Specialty was inaugurated in 1937 and continued through 1941. With the onset of World War II, most canine activities throughout the country were discontinued for some time. It was 1954 before the National Bench Specialty was resumed. It has been held every year since. (A list of the Specialty winners is included at end of this chapter.)

A few years ago, it was decided by the Board of Directors of the American Chesapeake Club that the annual National Specialty should be rotated between the Eastern, Midwestern and Western sections of the country. Also, over the past few years, allowance has been granted for a second Specialty each year, held in a different section from that of the year's National.

In addition, there are now ten American Chesapeake Club "supported shows" each year. In these, the Club supports the entry by giving a cash contribution, and by furnishing bronze medallions to the winners of Best of Breed, Best of Opposite Sex, and to the highest scoring Chesapeake in the Obedience trial.

I feel that bench shows are very important because the awarding of a championship title in almost all instances guarantees a sound dog. It certainly establishes that the dog has no flaws that are considered disqualifications, such as a poor mouth, black color, or a curly coat. It means, as well, that the dog is well-adjusted and not shy, able to perform in front of a crowd. Permitting the judge to touch and inspect him, means that the dog has a friendly nature. He must also behave well in the presence of other dogs, for if he did not, any conscientious judge would dismiss him from the ring for bad conduct.

We are fortunate, in the Chesapeake breed, that we do not have two distinct types — a show dog and a working dog. This separation is found in many of the other Sporting breeds. Perhaps we are fortunate that Chesapeakes are not pretty or beautiful dogs. However, they can be quite handsome, and they give one a sense of their strength and power. In addition, they give the impression of dogs who can do the work it was intended they do. Happily, today, very few of our breeders overlook this requirement.

Another factor which has contributed to the improvement of the breed is that the Working Dog Certificate, issued by the American Chesapeake Club to those who have passed land and water tests in retrieving, is now regarded as a minimum requirement for any dog that is going to be bred, male or female. If a dog does not have one, the owner is often bluntly asked why he doesn't. And the majority of serious breeders would not consider breeding to such an individual. Good conformation no longer is enough — it must be seriously viewed in relation to soundness and to performance.

Am-Can Ch. Queen Cocoa, owned by Mrs. Lynn Lowe, winning Best in Show at the St. John's Newfoundland Club in July, 1974, under judge Winnie Heckmann. Cocoa's handler was Jeff Brucker.

                             Ch. Duke of Boone

                     Boone of Coco

                             Coco Queen II

            Byrd's Choctaw Tiger

                             Gay Lord of Grason

                     Gay Bell

                             Young's Bell Pure

AM. & CAN. CH. QUEEN COCOA

                             Native Shore Dusty Roads

                     Gay Lord of Grason

                             Ch. Native Shore Winona CD

            Mitsie Dew of Gay Lord

                           Randy's Ringo

                   Vinton Queen

                           Courrege's Sand

OFA (Orthopedic Foundation for Animals) and CERF (Canine Eye Registration Foundation) certificates are now commonly acquired among the bench dogs, as well as those who participate in Obedience and field trials.

The Best in Show Chesapeakes

To date, eight of our breed have won Best in Show at an all-breeds event — six at American Kennel Club shows and two in Canada.

Am-Can Ch. Queen Cocoa, belonging to Mrs. Lynn Lowe of Alabama, was the first, scoring in 1974 under judge Winnie Heckmann at the St. John's Newfoundland Kennel Club in Canada. Although Queen was shown only one year, she won 32 Bests of Breed and 3 Group placements, and was rated as the No. 6 Chessie in 1974. She was then retired. Bred to Ch. Crispin Roderick, she produced an excellent litter of which two are already champions: Burt's Bama Cocoa Bear and Shugar of Cocoa Bear. Shugar had the high score (195) in Novice A at the Maryland Specialty in October 1978.

Queen Cocoa is by Byrd's Choctaw Tiger ex Mitsie Dew of Gaylord. She is a rich, golden brown color and obviously a fine specimen of our breed.

Ch. Crispin Roderick, CD was the first Chesapeake to win an AKC Best in Show, scoring under judge Len Carey at Lexington, Kentucky in 1975. "Cris" belongs to the John Woods of the Blustrywood Kennels, now located in Kalamazoo, Michigan. Mr. Woods writes: "Chris has a soundness going and coming, seldom seen in the breed. He has such solid coupling and topline in sidegait that he seems to be one muscle from his nose to the tip of his tail. However, that wouldn't win for him if it were not coupled with his intense personality. When he really sparkles is when he is bordering on going out of control.

"Cris looks as good nearing eight years old as he ever has. I never remember showing him in a Group that he didn't draw a gathering to see, touch and question. He loved it! He is a pleasure in the hunting field and last year retrieved 87 ducks and 32 geese during our hunting season." Cris is OFA-167.

Am-Can Ch. Pond View Bolt, owned by Ruth Ann and William Eller and shown by Mrs. Eller, went Best in Show under judge Mrs. Maynard Drury at the Kanadasaga Kennel Club show at Canandaigua, NY in June 1975. Bolt, by Ch. Breakwater Dirk of Quickstep, CD ex Chesarab's Little Kara, was bred by Sheila Di Vaccaro. Purchased by the Ellers, and always handled by his owners, he won 65 Bests of Breed and 2 Group placements in the United States and 18 Bests of Breed and 8 Group placements in Canada.

Ch. Ashby's Chocolate Chip, owned by the John DeVries and handled by Glenn Butler, won Best in Show at Wilmington Kennel Club

Am-Can. Ch. Pond View Bolt, owned by the William Ellers and shown by Ruth Ann Ellers, won the Sporting Group under judge Kurt Mueller, and went on to win Best in Show under Mrs. Maynard Drury at Kanadasaga Kennel Club (NY) on June 5, 1975.

Native Shore Dusty Roads
Ch. Native Shore Jock of Wooltop
Imp of Bullskin
Ch. Breakwater Dirk of Quickstep, CD/WD
Garland's Cocoa-Moe
Ch. Cocoa's Teal WD
Mocha Rusty
AM. & CAN. POND VIEW BOLT, CD/WD (OFA CB-170)
FC/AFC/CFC Nelgard's Baron CD
Eastern Waters' Silver Baron
Ch. Eastern Waters' Silver Star CD
Chesarab's Little Kara
Ike's Hannibal
Ch. Linden's Kara
The Tide of Windy Bay

in followup of his win of the National Specialty held in conjunction with the show on April 24, 1976. Both wins were under Mrs. James Clark. Whelped August 1, 1968, Chip was sired by Ch. The Queen's Jester ex Ch. Ashby's High Tide. Lorraine Berg describes him for me: "Chip is a dark brown dog, well-boned and muscled, showing excellent power and balance in his conformation. The day he won Best in Show he had a beautiful coat and was in absolutely top form. He never, even once, put a foot down wrong and he really deserved to win."

Ch. Teal's Tiger, WD, owned by Susan Steuben, has been a recent sensation among Chesapeake bench fanciers. He became the fifth of the breed to go Best in Show, scoring at the Chintimini Kennel Club show at Corvallis, Oregon on March 11, 1978, with Edith Hanson handling. Whelped in August 1974, Teal is by Ch. Cinnamon Teal ex Ch. Susie Q. He is dark brown in color, 26 inches tall and weighs 90 pounds. Mrs. Hanson tells us: "Teal is very sound and is definitely up when showing. He is a very happy, friendly dog who loves everybody. So much so that his owners, who live out in the country, came home one night to find burglars in their house and Teal contentedly keeping them company." Teal (OFA-418, CERF 225/79-56) was trained and handled to his Working Dog title by Doug Hanson.

Am-Can Ch. Chesrite's Justin Tyme, CD, WD was awarded Best in Show at the Wampanoag Kennel Club show at Làkeville, Massachusetts on August 5, 1979, by judge Irene Schlintz. Justin, owned and handled by Jan and Jody Thomas of the Chesrite Kennels in Massachusetts, was whelped in July 1973 and is by Am-Can Ch. Donwen's Boo of Tricrown ex Ch. Seamaster's Ginger, CD. Reddish-brown in color, standing 24½ inches, and weighing 85 pounds, Justin is certified OFA-427 and CERF 187/78-14.

At this writing his great record includes 104 Bests of Breed, 2 Group Firsts and 14 other Group placements. He also has two legs toward his CDX title and is in training for Utility.

Mrs. Thomas reports: "I wish you could know him as we do, as he really is quite a character. He is our family pet and house dog. We now have six Chesapeakes in a six-room house, so are looking for a place with more land."

Can. Ch. Mossbank Model Chef became the first Canadian-bred dog to win a Best in Show, scoring at Club Canin de Montreal show, April 8, 1979 under judge Robert Nutbeem. "Chet", a big rugged dark-red dog, is owned by his breeders, the James McKinlays of Morpeth, Canada, and is handled by Martha Thorne. Only 1½ years old at time of the win, he is by Bold Chet of Morpeth ex Anjamar's Trash of Morpeth.

In addition to the Best in Show, "Chet" scored 6 Group placings (including 2 Firsts) in his first four weeks of showing. His handler reports that he is a dog with "a very positive, outgoing personality. A natural retriever, he hits the water like a Mack truck!"

Ch. Ashby's Chocolate Chip scored an all-breed Best in Show in followup of his win of National Specialty at Wilmington (Del.) Kennel Club on April 24, 1976, under judge Mrs. James Clark. Owned by John DeVries, and handled by expert Glenn Butler.

Cocoa King Tugboat

Can/Am Native Shore Dan

Jill of Greenwood

Ch. The Queen's Jester

Lawyer's Pride

Ch. Blakeford Queen

Missy's Baroness Lou

CH.ASHBY'S CHOCOLATE CHIP

Ashby's Wings II

Ashby's Dynamite

Mecklingburg's Queen Cocoa

Ch. Ashby's High Tide

Can/Am Ch. Native Shore Dan

Holly of Holly Hill

Can/Am Ch. Dyna of the Willows CD

Ch. Teal's Tiger WD, owned by Susan Steuben and handled by Edith Hanson, was Best in Show at the all-breed show of the Chintimini Kennel Club (Oregon) in 1978. Teal has a strong record in spite of being seldom shown outside of California.

```
                                   Dual Ch/AFC Tiger's Cub CD
                      Mott's Oley
                                   O'Timothy's Red Robin
             Cinnamon Teal
                                   Charlie's Chesapeake Too
                      Mott's Sugar
                                   Sindy Lue
CH. TEAL'S TIGER
                                   Nel's Bing
                      Rusty of Pepperwood
                                   Tika
             Ch. Suzie-Q
                                   Old Red
                      Sally Lynn
                                   Molly Lynn
```

Am-Can Ch. Chesrite's Justin Tyme, CD/WD, was Best in Show over an all-breed entry of 790 at Wampanoag kennel Club, Lakeville, Massachusetts on August 5, 1979 under judge Irene Schlintz. Handled by his owner, Jan Thomas.

Native Shore Vagabond Jerry

Ch. Kent Island Cocoa Daddy

Native Shore Susan of Kent

Am/Can Ch. Donwen's Boo of Tricrown WD

Dual Ch. Koolwaters' Colt of Tricrown

Tricrown Mota Cimba

Ch. Welcome of the Willows

AM. & CAN. CH. CHESRITE'S JUSTIN TYME, CD/WD (OFA-CB 427; CERF 135/78-57)

Missiquoi Wild root

Sean's Missisquoi Wild Root (11-71)

Richard's Storm Tide

Ch. Seamaster's Ginger CD

Ch. J. & J's Lot's of Luke CD

Donwen's Twinkle Toes (11-71)

Ch. Donwen's Romcroft Timber Queen

Ch. Eastern Waters' Chargn Knight became the sixth Chesapeake to win an AKC Best in Show at New Castle Kennel Club show (Pennsylvania on September 15, 1979 under judge Mrs. Peggy Adamson. Chargn Knight, bred and owned by Nathaniel and Susan Horn, is one of four champions in a litter whelped February 10, 1976 by Ch. Eastern Waters' Oak, CD, TD, WD ex Ch. Eastern Waters' Ever Amber, TD.

Winner of 16 Group placings at age of 3½ years, Chargn' Knight is light brown, stands 24½ inches and weighs 78 pounds. He is certified OFA-649 and CERF 185/78-57. Nat Horn writes: "Chargn is very enthusiastic about anything we do together. If he sees me preparing to go jogging, he can hardly wait and his facial expression says 'Let's go, let's go! He has the same attitude when we pack to go to a show. He is a happy, fun-loving dog."

Ch. Eastern Waters' Oak, CD, TD & WD, sire of Best in Show winner Ch. Eastern Waters' Chargn Knight, made history on his own. Cited by *Kennel Review* as the top producing Chesapeake of 1977 and 1978, he stands as sire of at least 24 champions, 6 with Group placements. In addition, 15 of his get have their CDs, 4 their CDXs, and two are Tracking title-holders.

By Am-Can Ch. Chesareid Amber Hue ex Ch. Eastern Waters' Baronessa, TD, Oak was whelped in August 1965 and lived until September 1978.

He was Rupert Humer's first dog and became an accomplished hunter who was used on ducks, geese, brandt, pheasant and grouse. In the blind, his thumping tail eagerly announced the arrival of a flight of ducks. The Humers say, "Neither chest-deep mud nor ice-clogged water deterred him from a retrieve."

Oak was twice Best of Breed at the National Specialty — in 1968 and then again seven years later in 1975 — at age of ten. Betsy Humer writes, "When he won the second time he gaited around like a four year old." He also finished his Tracking title at ten years.

Top Show Dogs

With this chapter, you will find a listing of the Chesapeakes that have won 20 or more Bests of Breed. Those on the list that have won all-breed Bests in Show have already been described. Here we will try to give you a picture of the others. Many of them I have seen. However, for some of them I have been dependent upon information supplied by the owners. I sent a questionnaire to all the owners, asking for information on the dog's size, height, weight, color, titles, OFA and CERF numbers, and comment on their ability in the hunting field. I also asked them to give me a vignette of their dog's personality.

Ch. Eastern Waters' Chargn Knight, who became the sixth Chesapeake to win an AKC all-breed Best in Show in September 1979 (at New Castle KC under Mrs. Peggy Adamson) is pictured in an earlier win of the Sporting Group under judge Howard Tyler. Handled by his owner, Nathaniel Horn.

Am-Bda. Ch. Eastern Waters' Brown Charger, CD, with owner-handler Dan Horn, winning Best of Breed under judge Bede Maxwell in 1972. "Charlie" won his first BOB when 1½ years old, his last when 8½.

CHART OF CHESAPEAKES WITH 20 OR MORE BEST OF BREED WINS, GROUP WINS and GROUP PLACEMENTS

Name	Best of Breed	Group Wins	Group Places	Owner(s)
Crispin Roderick	130	9	35	John Woods
Eastern Waters' Brown Charger	126		30	Daniel Horn
Ashby's Chocolate Chip	105	2	23	John & Christine De Vries
Chesrite's Justin Tyme	104	2	14	Jody & Jan Thomas
Hi-Ho Guns of Canton	100	1	10	Stephen & Ellen Loftsgaard
Rigby's Rosemount Dancer	90	2	16	Clyde Rigby
Chestnut Hills Pontiac	75			Karen Anderson
Eastern Waters' Chargn Knight	69	2	15	Nathaniel Horn
Teal's Tiger	67	5	27	Susan Steuben
Briarmoor's Bearpaw	65			Patricia Leakey
Pond View Bolt	65		2	William & Ruth Eller
Eastern Waters' Dark Knight	54			Daniel Horn
Eastern Waters' Big Gunpowder	51		2	William Boyson
Longcove's Golden Gemini	50	2	9	Alfred Kinney
Eastern Waters' Baronessa	46			Janet Horn
Eastern Waters' Silver Star	44			Janet Horn
Eastern Waters' Blazing Star	43			Wyn Gordon
Mallard of Mount Joy	43			Mrs. Charles Garthwright
Ray's Drake of the Pines	43		3	Ray & Lorraine Berg
Native Shore Jumbo Belle	42		1	Kenneth Krueger
Cub's Marin Echo	32		2	Les & Nancy Lowenthal
Queen Cocoa	32		3	Lynn Lowe
Cherokee Tanya	31		3	John & Pat Urben
Donwen's Boo of Tricrown	28		2	Wendy Trottier
Ches' True Grit	27		1	Drs. James & Brenda Stewart
Chesachobee's Tradition	27		2	Mildred Buchholz
Chesaford's Chestnut Newfy	25		1	Charles & Judy Cranford
Chesareid Amber Hue	25		2	William & Sybil Reid
Eastern Waters' Supercharger	25		1	Daniel Horn
Chesachobee's Gemson	24		2	Mildred Buchholz
Melody's Spun Smoke of Blabro	22		2	Dianna Blakey
Hi-Ho's Iron Eyes Cody O' Snocree	20			Stephen & Ellen Loftsgaard

Am-Bda Ch. Eastern Waters' Brown Charger, Am-Bda CD, was whelped July 13, 1965 and died at the age of nine in 1974. Bred by Janet Horn, and owned and handled by her husband Dan, "Charlie" was one of the most impressive Chesapeakes I have ever seen. He had a real field trial potential, I thought, when I saw him work in the field. It was too bad that Dan could not run him in field trials. Sired by Am-Can Ch. Chesareid Amber Hue ex Ch. Eastern Waters' Chobee Belle, CD, Charlie had an enthusiastic personality and was one of the nicest moving dogs I have ever seen.

Ch. Hi-Ho's Guns of Canton, CD/WDX, who is a terrific show dog, leaps in the water after a duck shot by his co-owner, Stephen Loftsgaard.

```
                              Abbie's Fargo
                    Fargo
                              Abbie's Dinah
            Gunther Brutis
                              Mallard's Echo Springs
                 Schafer's My Gal Sal
                    Frosty Joch's Jill
CH. HIHO'S GUNS OF CANTON, CD/WDX
                         Meg's O'Malley II
               Baronland's Creamy
                         Baronland's Lindaloo
            Echo's Goldie
                              Dual Ch/AFC Tiger's Cub CD
                 Cub's Fremont Echo
                              Ch. Chesareid April Echo
```

Ch. Hi-Ho's Guns of Canton, CD, WD is an exceedingly good-looking large male with a fine temperament. By Gunther Brutus ex Echo's Goldie, he is owned by Ellen and Stephen Loftsgaard of Northern California.

"Gunner" was the first Chessie to win a Sporting Group in the West. Now 6½ years of age, his national ratings have been excellent over a period of five years. He was declared a "top producer" for 1978, and carries OFA and CERF certification.

Ellen trained him and always handles him in ring competition, and he works beautifully for her. But he is Stephen's shooting dog, and also his field trial dog. He has three points toward his Canadian Field Championship and qualified for the Canadian National Championship Stake of 1977.

I consider him a real credit to the breed.

Ch. Chestnut Hills Pontiac, born October 1, 1972, was sired by Ch. Tuffy Anderson, CD, WD ex Ch. Cub's Lady Belle, CD, TD. He is a large dog, standing 26 inches high, weighs 95 pounds, and is a beautiful sedge color. (CERF 240/79). Karen Anderson writes: "Pontiac is gentle and very easy to live with. He is rather protective and quite reserved with strangers."

Ch. Briarmoor's Bearpaw is from the Briarmoor Kennels of Wisconsin — bred, trained and handled by his owner, Patricia Leakey. Sired by Tule Bob ex Ch. Lady Rebecca, CD, WD, he is 25 inches high and weighs 85 pounds. (OFA-494 and CERF 105/77-20). Mrs. Leakey tells us that, "Bear is a big, handsome dog with a happy-go-lucky temperament and he excels in showmanship because he really enjoys it so much. He loves the water and is such a strong swimmer he is currently being taught life-saving to capitalize on his ability to pull tired swimmers back to shore."

Ch. Eastern Waters' Baronessa, TD, born July 11, 1961, was bred by Janet Horn. By FC, AFC & CFC Nelgard's Baron, CD ex Ch. Eastern Waters' Silver Star, CD, Baronessa was light brown in color, 24 inches high and weighed 80 pounds. She scored 46 Bests of Breed and produced 8 bench champions. Her conformation was so good that her picture has often been used as the model for the standard of the breed. Her disposition was excellent, too. Janet writes, "She was a joy to show at all times, and was as lovely in character as she was in looks."

Ch. Eastern Waters' Dark Knight, TD, was a full brother to Ch. Eastern Water's Baronessa and fared almost as well as she did at the shows. "Darky" won 54 Bests of Breed. Trained and handled by his owner, Daniel Horn, Darky performed the unusual feat of winning his Tracking title at the age of 12. He was a brown, tall, slender dog.

Ch. Eastern Waters' Big Gunpowder, born in January 1967, was

**Karen Anderson showing Ch. Chestnut Hills Pontiac
to one his many Best of Breed wins.**

```
                              Native Shore Caesar
                        Native Shore Pal of Roedown
                           Farley Vale's Pearl
              Ch. Tuffy Anderson CD/WD
                              South Bay King Cole
                        Native Shore Belle of Roedown
                           Jill of Greenwood
CH. CHESTNUT HILLS PONTIAC
                              Dual Ch/AFC/CFC Baron's Tule Tiger CD
                        Dual Ch/AFC Tiger's Cub CD
                           Napolitano's Ladybug
              Ch. Cub's Lady Belle CD/TD
                              Shawnee Nip
                        De Fir's Nettie
                           Brinemixer Lucky
```

Ch. Briarmoor's Bearpaw, bred, trained and handled by his owner, Patricia Leakey of Wisconsin. A large brown dog, 25½ inches high and weighing 85 pounds, Bearpaw has won 65 Bests of Breed.

FC/AFC/CFC Nelgard's Baron CD

Dual Ch/FC/ASFC/CFC Baron's Tule Tiger CD

Joanie Teal

Tule Bob (OFA CB-114)

FC/AFC Atom Bob

Atom Bob's Tina

Sedge Queen

CH. BRIARMOOR'S BEARPAW

Jack of Country View

Brown Deer Jackson

Cocoa King Antoinette

Ch. Tesmer's Lady Rebecca CD/WDX (OFA-338)

Rough Water Otter

Brown Deer Gypsy

Van Nassau's Bay Cindy

Ch. Eastern Waters' Dark Knight, CD, with owner-handler Dan Horn, pictured winning Best of Breed at the 1964 Westminister. He also won a Sporting Group in September of that year.

Ch. Eastern Waters' Baronessa, TD, winning Best of Breed under judge James Trullinger at the American Chesapeake Club's Specialty in 1966. Shown by breeder-owner, Janet Horn.

bred by Janet Horn and sold to the William Boysons. He became Bill's gundog, which is what he liked best. Bill writes, "He also was extremely fond of puppies, of any breed. He road-worked at 16 miles per hour, which is quite a pace for a dog to make. He seemed to enjoy going to dog shows, completed his championship at the age of two, and won 51 Bests of Breed. He was friendly and sweet to all who came up to admire him." Gunpowder had a long and happy life on the marshes with Bill, whose Webfoot Kennels mostly bred gundogs.

Ch. Longcove's Golden Gemini, CD, WD, is one of the best dogs being shown in the ring today. A home-bred owned by Jeannie and Alfred Kinney, Gemini was born June 16, 1970 and is by Ch. Eastern Waters' Tallyman, CD ex Ch. Eastern Waters' Gold Honey, CDX, WD. The Kinneys are very proud of his outstanding record, which at time of this report included 49 Bests of Breed, 2 Group Firsts and 9 other Group placings. Gemini is a large dog, with good bone and substance, and I hear, is a fine mover. His progeny are doing well and he has produced seven champions, one of whom is the breed's only champion with UDT and WD titles.

Ch. Eastern Waters' Silver Star, CD, at the age of 10 months was Winners Bitch at the 1962 Specialty, then at 22 months was Best of Opposite Sex at the 1963 Specialty, and climaxed with Best of Breed wins of the 1964, 1965 and 1966 Specialties. Included in her total of 44 Bests of Breed was a win at Westminster. She was owned by Janet Horn.

Ch. Ray's Drake of the Pines, WD (OFA-57), bred and owned by Ray and Lorraine Berg, was born in April 1969. Sired by Ch. Eastern Waters' Oak, CD, TD, WD ex Ch. Ray's Miss Cocoa, CDX (who produced three other champions), Drake was medium brown in color, 25 inches and weighed around 90 pounds. The Bergs pride themselves on producing sound, all-round dogs. Lorraine writes, "Drake never cared too much for showing — his great joy was hunting. When he was about six months old, Ray took him for the first time. That year we had a one mallard limit per day. Drake kept finding crippled ducks faster than Ray could throw them back or hide them. Ray never got to fire a shot all day."

Ch. Eastern Waters Blazing Star, UDT established the excellent record of 43 Bests of Breed and a Group placement, and won both her Tracking and Utility dog titles in 1962. Bred by Janet Horn, she was by Ch. Eastern Waters' Sachem CDX ex Ch. Eastern Waters' Tallapossa, CD. Owner "Wyn" Gordon was greatly admired in the early days, as no woman before had trained and handled a dog to both Tracking and Utility titles.

Ch. Native Shore Jumbo Belle, CD was born on January 24, 1963. For Dot and Ken Krueger it was the classic case of the dog owning the master. The Kruegers knew she was special at first sight, and at 15 months Belle started proving it to everyone else. At that age she was judged Best of Sweepstakes at the 1964 American Chesapeake Club Specialty. She then went on to finish her championship at 17 months, undefeated in any classes. Belle was declared the Chesapeake Dam of the Year in 1969, and altogether she won 42 Bests of Breed. Her record, as well as that of her offspring, has been instrumental in creating a great many new Chessie enthusiasts.

Ch. Cub's Marin Echo, UD, WD (OFA CB-42), is owned by the Leslie Lowenthals of Mill Valley, California. She was trained by Nancy Lowenthal and handled by her in Derby and Qualifying stakes, as well as in her bench and Obedience work. She was called "Heller" because of being a determined and self-willed pup. Bright sedge in color, 22 inches high and weighing 70 pounds, Heller was the first California dog to win a Group placement. The daughter of Dual Ch. & AFC Tiger's Cub, CD and the sister of Dual Ch. Cub's Kobi King, Heller is mother of Field Trial Champion Bay City Jake.

Ch. Cherokee Tanya, CD belonged to the John Urbens of Wisconsin. She was sired by Alpine Chukkar ex Su Su Sal. Whelped in 1959, she made both her championship and CD title in 1962. She ran in licensed field trials, taking a fourth in a Derby stake of 30. She was extremely versatile — John Urben used her for hunting and little Terrie Urben, when only nine, took a first with her in Junior Showmanship. Tanya was brown, stood 23½ inches and weighed about 60 pounds. She was always bred to AFC Bomarc of South Bay, CD and they produced six bench champions. Cherokee Kennels is proud of Tanya's record of 31 Bests of Breed and 3 Group placements.

Am-Can Ch. Donwen's Boo of Tricrown, WD, owned by Wendy Trottier (formerly of Massachusetts), established the enviable record of 28 Bests of Breed and 2 Group placements. Wendy Trottier, who was a terrific handler, suffered a permanent severe back injury. She writes that she is no longer raising Chesapeakes; since she must limit herself to a smaller breed, she is now raising Papillons. Wendy tells us that Boo was a large, well-built dog with a strong, wide chest. He had a square head, a singular coat, powerful rear drive and fit the Chesapeake standard nicely. He was always a happy, eager dog, was friendly to all and loved swimming and retrieving.

Am-Bda Ch. Ches' True Grit, CD, WD, Am-Bda TD, is a really beautiful dead-grass male, belonging to the Doctors James and Brenda Stewart. In addition to his 27 Bests of Breed, and an AKC and a Bermuda Group placement, True Grit made the excellent average score of 193 in the three legs of his Obedience title. By Ch. Eastern Waters' Oak, CD, TX ex Chesarab's Turkish Taffy, he was bred by Sheila Di Vaccaro. He is often shown in Brace classes with Ch. Oak N' Thistle's Albatross, WD. They make a stunning pair and have seldom been defeated.

Handsome Ch. Native Shore Jumbo Belle, CD, being shown by her owner, Kenneth Krueger. Belle was Best of Breed over a large entry at the 1967 American Chesapeake Club Specialty.

William Boyson's Ch. Eastern Waters' Big Gunpowder was Best of Breed at the 1971 American Chesapeake Club Specialty.

Ch. Eastern Waters Oak, CD/TD/WD, bred by Janet Horn, owned by Betsy and Rupert Humer, pictured going Best of Breed for Mr. Humer. Oak — 25″, 85 pounds, dead-grass in color — was twice Best of Breed at the National Specialty, in 1968 and in 1975 (at age of ten!).

Duke of Kamiakin

Ch. Chief of Kamiakin

Blondie III

Can. & Am. Ch. Chesareid Amber Hue

FC/AFC CFC Nelgard's Baron CD

Can. Ch. Heather of Carnmoney

Can. Ch. Skipper Baptie's Joanne

CH. EASTERN WATERS' OAK, CD, TD, WD

Rex of Rapids

FC AFC/CFC Nelgard's Baron, CD

FC Tiger of Clipper City

Ch. Eastern Waters' Baronessa, TD

Ch. Eastern Waters' Sachem, CDX

Ch. Eastern Waters' Silver Star, CD

Ch. Eastern Waters' Tallapoosa, CD

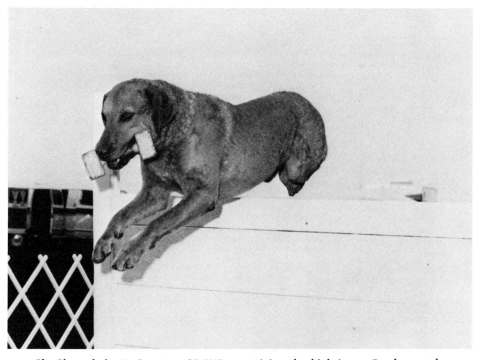

Ch. Chesachobee's Gemson, CD/WD, practicing the high jump. Bred, owned and handled by Mildred Buchholz.

<pre>
                        Ch. Easter Waters' Brown Charger CD
              Ch. Eastern Waters' Tallyman CD
                        Ch. Eastern Waters' Baronessa TD
      Ch. Longcove's Golden Gemini CD
                        South Bay Spider
              Ch. Eastern Waters' Gold Honey CDX/WD
                        Ch. Eastern Waters' Canton CD
CH. CHESACHOBEE'S GEMSON, CD/WD
                        Ch. Eastern Waters' Bronze Rex CD
              Ch. Chesachobee's Tradition CD/WD
                        Ch. Eastern Waters' Canton CD
      Ch. Chesachobee's White Wave
                        Ch. Eastern Waters' Neptune
              Chesachobee's Heloise
                        Ch. Eastern Waters' Surfer Girl
</pre>

Ch. Eastern Waters' Supercharger, owned by Dan Horn, has been doing well in the shows of 1977, '78 and '79. As this book goes to press, he is six years old and is on way to his CD. He has won 25 Bests of Breed and a Group placement.

Am-Can Ch. Chesareid Amber Hue was 25 inches tall and weighed 80 pounds. He was a handful for tiny Sybil Reid, his owner, who only weighed 110 pounds herself.

Amber was extensively used at stud and sired 81 pups, of which 10 became champions and many earned CD, CDX, TD and/or WD titles. His bloodlines are now carried by many Eastern dogs and he has definitely been a factor in improvement of the breed.

The Reids' home is on the shores of a lake in Bellingham, Washington, and Amber spent hours in the water retrieving anything movable and stacking these objects in a pile on their porch. He was hunted with and also ran in a few field trials. Sybil trained and always ran him herself.

Ch. Chesaford's Chestnut Newfy, TD (OFA-664 and CERF 199/79-29) was bred and is owned by the Charles Cranfords. I am pleased to note that all of the Cranford dogs have *both* OFA and CERF certifications.

Newfy was sired by Chestnut Hill's Pontiac ex Ch. Chesaford's Oak 'N Honey, CD. Judy Cranford writes, "Newfy has a most attractive personality, and his goal in life seems to be to please. He is a nicely-put-together, muscular dog, who swims every day of his life, whether we want him to or not. In his spare time he fishes for rocks in our little pond. Newfy loves the show ring and is a real pleasure to exhibit."

Ch. Chesachobee's Gemson, CD, WD was bred and has been trained and shown by Mildred Buchholz. He is by Ch. Longcove's Golden Gemini, CD ex Chesachobee's White Wave. One of Millie's current contenders, he has already won 24 Bests of Breed and 2 Group placements, and is now doing most of his CDX and WDX work. Gemson is also being trained for Tracking and has located several pet dogs who were lost.

Ch. Hi-Ho's Iron Eyes Cody O'Snocree belongs to Ellen and Stephen Loftsgaard. By Ch. Hi-Ho's Guns of Canton, CD, WDX ex Ch. Kaste's Cristie of Snocree, he is a large and powerful young dog of rich brown color. Cody has barely started his show career, but is doing exceedingly well. He was Best of Breed at the American Chesapeake Club's supported show at the Orange Empire Kennel Club in January, 1979.

Ch. Melody's Spun Smoke of Blabro, CDX, TD & WD, owned and trained by Dianna Blakey of Florida, is the foundation brood matron of Dianna's Chesavieda Kennels. At this writing, "Smokie" has 21 Bests of Breed and has produced 3 champions. Dianna writes, "Considering the fact that she didn't come to live with me until she was 2½ years old. we've done rather well in such a short time."

Mrs. Dana Gordon, with her well-known Ch. Eastern Waters' Blazing Star, UDT. Wyn Gordon did all the training herself—no small feat!

Ch. Chesaford's Chestnut Newfy, TD, owned by the Gene Cranfords of North Carolina. Newfy is a rich brown color, 25″ high and weighs 87 pounds, and has a most pleasing personality.

Ch. Chesachobee's Tradition, CD/WD, being shown to Best of Breed by his owner-trainer-handler, Mildred Buchholz of Florida.

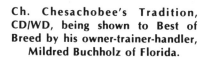

Ch. Chesarab's Little Acorn, CD, one of the many good dogs shown by Sheila Di Vaccaro. Acorn took Best of Breed at the American Chesapeake Club's 1972 Specialty, when only 18 months old.

Am-Can Ch. Chesareid Amber Hue, a sturdy, deadgrass dog, was from the first litter (whelped in 1960) raised by the William Reids. He was always shown by Sybil Reid, who made a fine record with him.

AMERICAN CHESAPEAKE CLUB
NATIONAL SPECIALTY SHOW TROPHY WINNERS

BEST OF BREED

Ch. Eastern Waters' Baronessa, TD Challenge Trophy
given by Dr. and Mrs. Daniel Horn

1969   Ch. Lady Ginger of Hampton Court
1970   Ch. Eastern Waters' Brown Charger, CD
1971   Ch. Eastern Waters' Big Gunpowder
1972   Chesarab's Little Acorn
1973   Colewood's The Innkeeper
1974   Ch. Salty Bomarc, WD
1975   Eastern Waters' Oak, CD, TD & WD
1976   Ch. Ashby's Chocolate Chip
1977   Ch. Teals Tiger
1978   Ch. Longcove's Golden Gemini, CD
1979   Ch. Redlions J J Sampler, WD
1980   Ch. Wyndham's Algonquin

BEST OF OPPOSITE SEX

Dual Ch. & AFC Baron's Tule Tiger, CD Challenge Trophy
given by Eloise Heller Cherry

1969   Ch. Native Shore Mighty Sultan, CD
1970   Ch. Koolwaters Ange Knu, CD
1971   Ch. Ray's Miss Cocoa, CDX
1972   Ch. Eastern Waters' Brown Charger, CD
1973   Sheba of Burning Tree
1974   Ch. Longcove's Autumn Haze, CD, WD
1975   Cub's Lady Belle, TD
1976   Ch. Chesarab's Little Acorn, CD
1977   Ch. Penny Ante
1978   Ch. Blustrywood's Great Lakes Gal
1979   Ch. Windown Aelwif of Wyndham
1980   Ch. Windown Aelwif of Wyndham

Am-Can Ch. Donwen's Boo of Tricrown, WD, owned by Wendy Trottier. "Boo", by Ch. Kent Island's Cocoa Daddy ex Tricrown Moto Cimba, stands 26″ high and weighs 95 pounds.

William Matheson with his Ch. Birkenhead De Nemours, CD, scoring Best of Breed.—*Gilbert.*

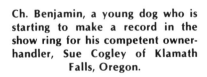

Ch. Benjamin, a young dog who is starting to make a record in the show ring for his competent owner-handler, Sue Cogley of Klamath Falls, Oregon.

Ch. Ray's Drake of the Pines, WD, owned by Ray and Lorraine Berg, has the fine record of 43 Bests of Breed and 3 Group placements. Drake has sired 9 champions, and he is Ray's hunting dog.

Ch. Cub's Lady Belle, CD/TD, with owner Karen Anderson, showing under judge Ed Squires. By Dual & AFC Tiger's Cub, CD ex De Fir's Nettie, Belle was bred by author Eloise Heller.

Ch. Longcove's Golden Gemini, CD/WD, bred and owned by the Alfred Kinneys of New Jersey, is pictured being shown by Jeannie Kinney to Best of Breed at the 1978 American Chesapeake Club Specialty.

Ch. Hi-Ho's Iron Eyes Cody O'Snocree winning Best of Breed for owner-handler Ellen Loftsgaard in January, 1979, at the Orange Empire KC show (California) under judge Walt Shellenbarger.

Cʜ. Kaste's Christie of Snocree, CD, going Best of Breed for owner Dr. John Schmidt. Christie was Top Producing Dam for 1978.

Well-known Eastern handler, Peggy Long, showing Lorraine Weremeichek's pretty Calbak Acorn to a Winners Bitch win.

ELLEN LOFTSGAARD is young, pretty and an extremely competent handler who has had phenomenal success in the show ring with many different breeds. Chesapeakes are her favorites and she has bred quite a few.

Ellen is pictured here with Ch. Hi-Ho's Guns of Canton, CD, WDX. Since 1973 "Gunner" has been in the Top Ten bracket of nationally known Chesapeakes, and has won over 100 Bests of Breed.

Ellen's husband, Stephen, runs "Gunner" in field trials. He has made points toward his Canadian Amateur Championship, and in 1976 qualified for the Canadian National Open Championship Stake.

Although she is a very busy lady, Ellen is always generous in helping others. I feel we are fortunate to have her prepare this article for us.

13

Showing Your Chesapeake

by Ellen Loftsgaard

SHOWING YOUR CHESAPEAKE on the bench can be lots of fun. Many fanciers really enjoy it, though like all competitive sports, it is more fun if you win—at least part of the time.

Showing is something you and your dog can do together, and it develops a very close relationship between you.

Fundamentally, exhibiting at a bench show is almost like competing in a beauty contest. But along with good looks, your dog's personality and attitude are factors in the final decision.

It's a good idea to first have your dog's appearance evaluated by someone who is knowledgeable about the breed. An officer of your local kennel club could probably steer you to a person who is competently familiar with the Chesapeake. Or you could get in touch with the American Chesapeake Club's Regional Director for your area. If you are assured that your dog is a good specimen of the breed, then by all means go ahead and show him. Just how good he is can only be proven in the ring.

Exhibiting in show rings brings the breed before the public and you will find yourself answering many questions about Chesapeakes. People will want to know if Chesapeakes are good with children, if they are a good house dog, or if they are protective. They will surely also want to know how they are as hunting dogs, and if they can be used on upland game as well as retrieving ducks.

A fine looking and well-behaved dog does a lot for the breed and many new Chesapeake homes are obtained when the public sees our dogs on the bench.

Four-weeks-old litter belonging to the R. Van Dorens of New Jersey.

If you decide you want to show your Chesapeake, you should write to the American Kennel Club, 51 Madison Avenue, New York, NY 10010. Ask for the booklet of Rules and Regulations pertaining to dog shows (free when ordered singly) and familiarize yourself with these rules. They will make clear to you the classes for which your dog is eligible and what you need do to enter him (or her) in competition. Upon request, the AKC will give you the name and address of local dog show superintendents from whom you can receive entry forms. The American Chesapeake Club's Regional Directors in your area will also help you to get started showing your Chesapeake.

To start training your dog for the show ring you should enroll him in a local conformation class. You can find out about these through the kennel club in your area. It's a good idea to "socialize" with your dog, to help get him used to strange noises and a lot of people. A good place to do this is at a local shopping center, or downtown where a lot of people gather. Accustom him to having strange people come up and pet him, for this is what he faces when the judge approaches to go over him in the show ring. Ask your friends to approach the dog from the front, run their hands over his back, and look at his teeth.

Entries for dog shows usually close about three weeks before the date of the show itself. The superintendent will mail you a confirmation of your entry, which usually informs you as to what time your breed will be judged, as well as the number of the ring.

Get to the show early and walk your dog around so that he will become accustomed to the crowd and to the noise of the loudspeakers. This allows time for him to relax before you take him into the ring to compete. It also gives you time to watch the judging in the other rings so that you can get an idea of the procedures of showing.

A handsome pair: Am-Bda CH. Ches' True Grit, CD/WD on right, with Ch. Oak 'N Thistle's Albatross, WD, winning Best Brace under judge Maxwell Riddle. They are owned by Drs. James and Brenda Stewart.

Ch. Chesaford Yankee Phoebe, owned by the David Rosenbaums, scoring Best of Breed at the 1977 Old Dominion KC show under judge Dan Horn.

The attractively decorated American Chesapeake Club bench at the Golden Gate Kennel Club show in San Francisco. — *Carter*

Nine of the fourteen Chesapeakes entered in the Anchorage Kennel Club show, April 1975, which was supported by the American Chesapeake Club.

CARE AND GROOMING

The Coat

A Chesapeake's coat is very important, not only as a judging consideration in the show ring, but also in hunting situations. To properly care for the coat, you should brush your dog daily, or at least every other day. The brushing will stimulate the natural oil in the coat, which is part of the breed's protection for adverse conditions while hunting. Use the type of brush that will not pull the undercoat out of the coat — that is, do not use a slicker or wire type brush. The brush should remove the dead hair, but leave the healthy undercoat intact.

It will be easier on your back if you stand your dog on top of a crate, or an old kitchen table, while you groom him.

Bathing

The Chesapeake should be bathed as seldom as possible. Frequent bathing removes the natural oils and causes the coat to become dry. When you do have to bathe your Chesapeake for a dog show, it should be done several days before the show to give the natural oils a chance to come back into the coat. Use a mild shampoo and be sure to get *all* of the soap out of the coat when rinsing the dog, for if you don't it can dry the dog's skin and cause dandruff. After the dog is dry, give him a good brushing to help stimulate the return of the natural oil.

Nails and Ears

Part of the grooming routine includes the care of the nails and ears. If your dog's nails are allowed to grow long, they may cause the foot to splay, or spread, or they may even grow in a circle and back into the dog's skin. This is most common with dewclaws because they are not in use. Cutting nails is easy with a special nail trimmer that can be purchased at most pet stores. The place of the cut is determined by noting the curvature of the underside of the nail; the hook-like projection is removed. Frequency of cutting depends upon the type and amount of exercise your dog receives. As an alternative, you can use a rough file and do it quite frequently, and you won't have to cut.

Ear trouble can cause pain and suffering and prove a distraction in the show ring, with your dog constantly shaking his head. The ear is a delicate area and trouble usually starts from an irritation of the lining inside the ear. With a breed like ours, which is worked in different terrains and often in water, it is very common for foreign matter to get into the dog's ears. A few signs of ear problems are shaking of the head, scratching the ear, and/or an offensive smelling ear with a dark-colored discharge. If the dog is beginning to show these symptoms, put warm mineral oil in the ear and massage the base to loosen dirt and wax particles. Then wipe out as much of the oil and dirt as possible with cotton held in your fingers. This treatment should be continued daily. Never wash the ears with alcohol, water or peroxide. If any of these symptoms continue for over a week, check with your veterinarian. If you routinely take proper care of the ears and keep them clean and dry, you will avoid ear troubles. But do seek professional advice before any infection becomes deep-seated, as most ear troubles can be easily remedied.

Grooming for the Show Ring

All of the routine care we have cited above—brushing, bathing, trimming nails and keeping the ears clean—are part of grooming your Chesapeake for the show ring. The breed does not require any trimming of body, feet, or ears. The only trimming that will be needed are of the whiskers around the muzzle and above the eyes. When trimming these whiskers, *always* use blunt-end scissors for the protection of your dog's eyes.

Attire for the Show Ring

When you are showing your dog you always want him well-groomed, but you too should always look neat in the ring. Your attire should be plain and not distract from your dog. Remember, you are showing *the dog*, not yourself. A tailored pantsuit, or simple skirt and blouse, or plain dress, look nice for the female handler. I am not saying that you can't win dressed in Levi's and a sweatshirt, but keep in mind that you are trying to make a pleasing team for the judge. Your shoes are very important, too, because you will have to run with your dog. You should be able to move freely, so select shoes that will be comfortable and safe on different surfaces such as wet grass, slick cement, hardwood floors, etc.

Training for Show

When teaching your dog to show, two commands will be very helpful. The first is "STAND-STAY" and the second is "HEEL." When you order "STAND-STAY", it lets your dog know that when you place his legs, he is to leave them as you place them and hold the stance until you tell him he can move. The "HEEL" command is used when you gait the dog in the ring for the judge's examination. This command tells the dog to move at your side at the pace you set for him.

A few helpful hints in training you and your dog for the ring:

1. Practice setting up your dog before a full-length mirror, and look at him from the side, from the front, and from the rear. In this way, you will see what the judge sees and you can decide how and where to place the dog's legs. In the show ring, you must never get between the dog and the judge.

2. When practicing moving your dog, have someone who knows about dog shows watch to tell if you are moving the dog at the proper speed. Some dogs need to be moved slower, some faster, than others, to have them look their best.

3. When you start showing, always listen carefully to what the judge says to you; if you don't understand, don't be afraid to ask him to repeat it. Also, always try to know where the judge is in the ring so as not to get caught with your dog not looking his best.

Showing a dog is really very little work and lots of fun. Try it — I'm sure you'll enjoy it. The majority of Chesapeakes are shown by their owners, so you will meet quite a few fine people who have the same interests as you.

Ribbons galore for four of Hi-Ho's Guns of Canton's get: (l. to r.) Hi-Ho's Iron Eyes Cody O'Snocree, Kaste's Christie of Snocree, CD, Hi-Ho's Guns of Canton, CD/WDX, Snocree's Daisy Clover and Snocree's In the Spirit.

Ch. Berteleda Maggie, UD/WDX and Ch. Cub's Marin Echo, UD/WD, two handsome specimens owned by Les and Nancy Lowenthal, and trained by Nancy. Maggie and Echo also serve as Les's hunting dogs.

Shown at the start of the 1978 Tracking Test held by the American Chesapeake Club is Ch. Chesachobee's Gemson, CD/WD, and breeder-owner-trainer, Mildred Buchholz.

14

Obedience History
and Records

WAY BACK in 1937, Allein Owens Jr.'s Bay Rum became the first Chesapeake to receive an Obedience title when he passed the Companion Dog requirements. In 1938, Mrs. Allein Owens, Jr. and her Daybreak accomplished the same feat. It was 1941 before three made their CD title.

Then the war came along and Obedience, like most dog activities, gave way to the war effort. Only a few dogs competed. But once the country returned to normal, Chesapeake Obedience fanciers resumed their activity. Many owners felt that besides being fun, Obedience work is also a necessary part of properly bringing up a young dog.

To date, as we go into the 1980s, 512 Chesapeakes have won their CD title.

The first two Chesapeakes to win the more advanced title of Companion Dog Excellent, both in 1943, were: Chessie, owned by Julia Griffith and Ch. Water Witch, owned by Mrs. Allein Owens, Jr. Only a few dogs each subsequent year passed these difficult requirements. By end of 1979, the total of Chesapeakes who have earned CDX stood at 118. We list them, showing the year in which each won the title.

COMPANION DOG EXCELLENT TITLE-HOLDERS

Year:	Dog:	Owner:
1943	Chessie	Julia Griffith
	Ch. Water Witch	Mrs. Allein Owens, Jr.
1947	Gladsted C	Gladys Clough
1952	Wisconong Jodri	Mrs. W. H. Drisko
1953	Ch. Wil-da's Drake	L. Wilson Davis
1954	Captain Corky	Melvin Lund
	Happy	Drew Ellis

Year:	Dog:	Owner:
1955	Cocoa King's Molly	Charles Davis
	Eastern Waters' Papoose	Mildred Buchholz
	Ch. Jodri's Catamaran	Mrs. Carl Underwood
1956	Ch. Jodri's Corvet	Mr. & Mrs. W. H. Drisko
	Powhatan Ted	Mrs. K. K. Wallace
1957	Roscoe	Joseph Simpson
	Ch. Eastern Waters' Nugget	Mildred Buchholz
1958	Ch. Eastern Waters' Sachem	Mrs. Daniel Horn
	Ch. Marengo's Jacob	Karl Haselman
	Ginger Thyme	Ted & Erna Zyss
1959	Cocoa King Sallee	Harlan F. Saug
	Ch. Marengo's Jacob	Ruth Haselman
	Otto von Yanz of Country Oaks	P.D. & R.R. Yanz
	Tengri's Papago	Mary Pantzer
1961	Ch. Eastern Waters' Blazing Star	Wyn Gordon
	Mike of the Lazy Three C	E. Schlattmann & C.F. White
1962	Duchess of Hi Point	R. C. Little
1963	Conroy's Bird	W. K. Boyson
1964	Cherokee's Calamity Jane	R. F. Bosnack
	Chesachobee's Gold Nugget	Mildred Buchholz
	Randi Cocoa of Sir Brandi	J. W. Watkins
	Ch. Kensington Big Brown	Nathaniel Hurwitz
1965	Dual Am. Fld. Ch. Meg's O'Timothy	Dr. & Mrs. F. A. Dashnaw
1968	Oppo-Arko Raunchy Paragon	F. & E. Knoll
	Ch. Ray's Nimrod Precaution	R. & L. Berg
1969	Ch. Eastern Waters' Gold Honey	Jeannie K. Kinney
	Ch. Ray's Marshland Stormy	R. & L. Berg
	Ch. Ray's Miss Cocoa	R. & L. Berg
1970	Chesachobee's Lone Star	D. O'Brien & M. Buchholz
	Rio Grande Duke	Al Dan Russo
	Z's Becky	A. & M.E. Mazzola
1971	Autumn Mist	D. & S. Diess
	Brown's Taffy Apple	Flo Ann Brown
1972	Ch. Berteleda Maggie	L. & N. Lowenthal
	Black Brant's Honey Bear	Lorraine Weremeichik
	Calbak Dark Cloud of Bo-Jib	Ilsa Sternberg
	Ch. Cub's Marin Echo	L. & N. Lowenthal
	Cub's Queen of Sheba	L. R. Schwartz
	Golden Boy's Titian Eve	Eve Keeler
	Patrick's Amber Chess	L. & E. Patrick
1973	Breakwater's Smiling Jack	C. & E. Morris
	Brown Baron II	Ilse Fass
	Warden Chief	Don Gillmore
1974	Chesachobee's Cocoanut	D. & B. Blakey
	Ch. Chesachobee's Magic	Janet Horn
	Eastern Waters' Independence	Susan Horn
	Eastern Waters' Ladyslipper	Diane Lehman
	Ch. Eastern Waters' Marmora	Elizabeth Humer
	Wendy's Miss Dusty Dawn	Herbert L. Swinney
	Ch. Wildwood's Song of Spring	Dorothy Beck

Year:	Dog:	Owner:
1975	Cub's Minnesota Patsy	D., G. & S. Iverson
	Koolwaters Little Beaver	G. Herberg
	Ch. Vonmarc's Guide	K. & J. Wood &
1976	Berteleda Kobi	Carl Larkin & Alice Lyon
	Ch. Chesachobee's Bold Baron	Micky Tellander &
		Mildred Buchholz
	Chesachobee's Ovedio Millie B	Dianna Blakey
	Ch. Chesachobee's Papoose	Marguerite Willis
	Ch. Chesachobee's Stuff 'N' Stuff	Lydia & Dianna Blakey
	Crosswinds Flying Orion	Eunice Wynne &
		Walter Stahl, Jr.
	Evansland Firecracker Belle	Steven & Gayle &
		Donald Iverson
	Ch. Longcove's Autumn Haze	Jeannie & Alfred Kinney
	Mount Joy's Winkle	Alexandra Starr,
	Tess	David Warren & Stephanie
		Beach
	Tuolumne's Coriander	David & Carol Deckman
1977	Ch. Baron's Sandy Bay	David & Kathleen Miller
	Ch. Beaver's Misty Reef	Robert & Cary Kelly
	Berteleda Binavere	Nancy & Leslie Lowenthal
	Ch. Chesachobee's Gemson	Mildred Buchholz
	Chesarab Bolta of Eagle Isle	Mary & Sheila Di Vaccaro
	Ch. Chesarab's Little Acorn	Sheila Di Vaccaro
	Ch. Chesareid Precious Gem	Scott Ansley & Sybil Reid
	Chesavieda's Ornamental Buoy	Dianna Blakey
	Cherokee Blue Chip	James Deschane
	Chesie of Barkley Lake	Richard Laplant
	Ch. Crosswinds Flying Explorer	Herbert Swinney &
		D. A. Culp
	Deschane's Chocolate Delight	James & Leigh Deschane
	Duke of Garth	Dominic & Diane Pelino
	Eastern Waters' Betsy Ross	E. Christopher &
		Susan Cone
	Ch. Eastern Waters' Chese V Zybura	Jere Zybura
	Eastern Waters' Harvest Gal	S. Jean Simpson
	Eastern Waters' Yankee	Rupert & Elizabeth Humer
	Frisco Valley Rain Drop	Rosemary Parsons
	Ima Sandy Too	David & Kathleen Miller
	Kobi's California Quail	John Smart &
		Frank Garrett
	Magellan's Dutchman, T.D.	E. J. Frinkman
	Misty Morn's Cinnamon Cinder	Julia & Lorne Cole
	Neshaminy Creek Petunia	Mary Jane Pappler
	Shari's Baron of Grey Cloud	Mrs. Patrick Gannaway
	Snocre's Sophie Tucker	John Schmidt
	Tallizar Sayzar	Mary Teresa Brown
	Triumphant Azure Dee	Erin Davidson
	Ch. Tuck-A-Hoe's Breezy Widgeon	Ruth & James Tucker
	Willow Winds Wild Kally	Mrs. Allan Stang
	Z's Holly Echo	John & Laur McAulay

Year:	*Dog:*	*Owner:*
1978	Chesavieda's Ornamental Buoy	Dianna Blakey
	Cogley's P. R. Betsy Ross	Abill Coryell
	Duke of Garth	Dominic & Diane Pelino
	Kara Allan	Sherri & David A. Derr
	Ch. Eastern Waters' Chesaford Sun	Mr. & Mrs. Charles E. Cranford
	Ch. Melody's Spun Smoke of Blabro	Dianna Blakey
	Slingshot's Boomerang	B. W. & Beverly Hirsig
	Ch. Z's Danny Canuk	Arthur & Mary Mazzola
1979	Chesnick's Beirdneau Lucias	Janis & Jim Nicholes
	Chestnut Hill's Coke	Karen W. Anderson
	Jessica Lamb CD	Toby Rae Carnine
	Ch. Misty Morn's Cinnamon Cinder CD, TD	Julia Lorne Cole
	Ch. Mitsu-Kuma's Rum Bun	Dyane M. Baldwin & Barbara Mullen
	Ch. Mitsu-Kuma's Saxon Pond	Wm. C. Dyane Baldwin
	Montauk Waters' Genie	Jennifer L. Cone
	Mount Joy's Sara C	Gerald & Roberta Sundrud
	Summer Winds Topaz	Doris Hodges

Utility Dog titles are much harder to obtain, and through the end of the 1970s only 17 Chesapeakes had passed these rigorous tests.

A recent star has arisen in this field. She is Dianna Blakey, of Florida, a most adept young handler whom we all admire. Dianna, a Mildred Buchholz protege, has finished three dogs to UD titles.

Togetherness — at the Christopher Cone home.

Ch. Wisconong Jodri, UDT, taking the high jump for her owner and trainer, Mrs. W. H. Drisko of Wayzata, Minnesota. Jodri was the first Chesapeake to win the Utility title (in 1954).

UTILITY DOG TITLE-HOLDERS

Year	Dog	Owner:
1954	Ch. Wisconong Jodri	Mrs. W. H. Drisko
1956	Ch. Jodri's Catamaran	Mrs. Carl Underwood
1958	Ch. Eastern Waters' Nugget	Mildred Buchholz
1962	Ch. Eastern Waters' Blazing Star	Wyn Gordon
1971	Oppo-Arko Raunchy Paragon	F. & E. Knoll
1972	Brown's Taffy Apple	Flo Ann Brown
1973	Ch. Berteleda Maggie	L. & N. Lowenthal
	Ch. Cub's Marin Echo	L. & N. Lowenthal
	Z's Becky	A. & M. E. Mazzola
1974	Brown Baron II	Ilse Fass
1975	Autumn Mist	D. & S. Diess
1976	Chesachobee's Cocoanut	Dianna Blakey
1978	Ch. Chesachobee's Ovedio Millie B	Dianna Blakey
	Crosswind's Flying Orion	Eunice Wynne & Walter Stahl, Jr.
1979	Ch. Chesavieda's Ornamental Buoy, TD	Dianna Blakey
	Slingshot's Boomerang	B.W. & Beverly A. Hirsig
	Wendy's Miss Dusty Dawn	Herbert L. Swinney

Montauk Water's Genie, CDX, doing the catwalk exercise for her Junior handler, Jennifer Cone, as an exhibit at an Eastern dog show.

Ch. Eastern Waters' Betsy Ross, CDX, racing in the scent hurdle relay team of the K-9 Obedience Trial Club's competition. Owned and trained by Susan Cone.

Laura Humer, daughter of the Rupert Humers of New Jersey, going Best Junior Handler with Eastern Waters' Yankee, CD. Laura is an exceedingly talented young lady in this competition.

Best Junior Handler

Winners of the Miss Lou's Brown Cluny Trophy, donated by Alfred B. Kinney.

1970	Kathy Kinney of Buena, New Jersey
1971	Kathy Kinney of Buena, New Jersey
1972	Kathy Kinney of Buena, New Jersey
1973	Kathy Kinney of Buena, New Jersey
1974	Jamie Jones of West Palm Beach, Florida
1975	Christine Eller of Leesburg, New Jersey
1976	Christine Eller of Leesburg, New Jersey
1977	Laura Humer of Rumson, New Jersey
1978	Laura Humer of Rumson, New Jersey
1979	Laura Humer of Rumson, New Jersey

The long "Sit" at an Obedience match, put on at a Chesapeake Club Day.

Highest Obedience score to Beth Morris and Breakwater's Flagon Dragon; Highest Jr. to Lydia Blakey and Chesachobee's Ruff 'n Ready; Second Highest, Dianna Blakey and Chesachobee's Cocoanut. Highest scoring Champion was Elizabeth Humer's Eastern Waters' Mamora.

15

Teaching Formal Obedience

by Eve Keeler

PERHAPS you have been thinking that you might like to compete in formal Obedience work—presuming, of course, that your Chesapeake is now ready for the demanding commands and precision training required in this field.

You should start by writing the American Kennel Club, 51 Madison Avenue, New York, N.Y. 10010, requesting a copy of their booklet, *Obedience Regulations*, most recently published in February 1979. Single copies are available without charge.

Read the booklet thoroughly. It will provide you with all the rules and regulations, and will familiarize you with the commands and what is expected of your dog.

You can train your dog by using one of the methods prescribed in two very fine books: *The Pearsall Guide to Successful Dog Training (Obedience from the Dog's Point of View)*, by Margaret and Milo Pearsall, published in 1976 by Howell Book House Inc., and *The Complete Dog Book,* the offical publication of The American Kennel Club, the newest edition of which was published in 1979, also by Howell Book House Inc.

Much valuable information is also contained in *Understanding Your Dog*, by Dr. Michael Fox, published by Coward, McCann & Geoghegan, Inc.. in 1972.

However, attending a class has the advantage of affording you a knowledgeable instructor, who can not only train you to train your dog, but can also tell you when your timing, correction procedure, or method of praise is not working for you.

Six champions from the Chesavieda Kennels, all owned by Dianna Blakey. From l to r.: Chesavieda's Ornamental Buoy, UDT/WDX; Chesachobee's Stuff-N-Stuff; Chesachobee's Ovedio Millie B, UDT/WD; Chesachobee's Cocoanut; Chesachobee's Chesavieda; and Melody's Spun Smoke of Blabro. CDX/WD.

Montauk Water's Genie, CDX, doing scent discrimination. Owner Jennifer Cone trained and handled Genie to her CD when she (Jennifer) was only ten years old.

Philosophy of Training

Obedience training is a continuation of the communication that we sought during Kindergarten Puppy Training (KPT), *see Chapter 6.* However, now your demands will require more precise responses from your dog. The commands that he now learns will be used throughout his life; some of them may even save his life. Again, the basic form of communication is a correction followed by praise. The correction, never punishment, is used to correct your dog into the proper position corresponding to the command. As soon as he is in that position, he *must receive your verbal praise.* He will accept the correction for what it is, a means of telling him that he must be in the command-dictated position, and there will be no hard feelings on his part. This means that praise must follow *every* correction—it's what makes a happy, eager, top-scoring worker. A *properly* given correction usually will not have to be repeated; "properly" means the right method at the right time.

As you commence formal training with your dog, you'll be perfecting his KPT in many respects. Remember that it is easier to avoid a problem than to correct it. Don't be in a hurry to remove the leash. If your dog really knows the exercise, switch to a lighter weight leash to test him. When he really knows an exercise, stop giving many little corrections, which only act as an annoyance to turn your dog off; give one that makes it count. Change your tone of voice constantly; whisper the commands (when showing in the ring, your nervous tension will change your tone of voice). As in socialization, you must work in different areas with different sounds and surfaces. If you train outdoors, try the training indoors. As your dog learns a command, apply that command to his home environment. Almost all formal obedience training will help your Chesapeake in his gun dog work. Inversely, any trained field dog can easily earn a CD degree with very little additional training.

The CD, CDX and UD Degrees

The Companion Dog (CD), Companion Dog Excellent (CDX), and Utility Dog (UD) are degrees earned in Obedience showing. Each degree requires three passing scores under three different judges at AKC-licensed Obedience trials. A passing score is 170 points or more, out of a possible 200 points, and must include at least one half of the points specified for each exercise in the following schedules:

CD (Novice)

Heel on Leash and Figure Eight	40
Stand for Examination	30
Heel Free	40
Recall	30
Long Sit	30
Long Down	30
TOTAL	200

CDX (Open)

Heel Free and Figure Eight 40
Drop on Recall 30
Retrieve on Flat 20
Retrieve over High Jump 30
Broad Jump 20
Long Sit 30
Long Down 30

                            TOTAL 200

UD (Utility)

Signal Exercise (Heel, Figure
    Eight and Recall) 40
Scent Discrimination
    Article No. 1 30
    Article No. 2 30
Directed Retrieve 30
Directed Jumping 40
Group Examination (Stand) 30

                            TOTAL 200

Upon notification by the AKC that you have completed the requirements, the respective suffix (CD, CDX, or UD) is added to your Chesapeake's official title. The following descriptions present the exercises that you must perform with your dog and their practical application:

The *heel on leash* (CD and CDX) demonstrates the ability of the dog and handler to work as a team. The *figure eight* (on leash for CD, off leash for CDX) again demonstrates working as a team to maneuver in and out of traffic and terrain. The *heel off leash* (CD and CDX) and the *signal exercise* (hand signals for UD) demonstrate the ultimate of you and your Chesapeake working together without physical restraint. The *stand for examination* (CD and in a group for UD) proves the dog's temperament, showing neither shyness nor resentment during a physical examination by a stranger, such as a veterinary or judge.

The *recall* (CD, with down for CDX, and part of the signal exercise for UD) shows that the dog stays where left, responds promptly to the come command, and then returns to the heel position (for calling the dog in from the field). The *retrieve on flat* and *retrieve over high jump* (CDX) prove not only that the dog promptly retrieves in a straight path (taking a line), even over an obstacle, but, that the dog delivers to hand. The *directed retrieve* (UD) demonstrates the dog's ability to work to man's hand signals (taking a line on a bird). The *broad jump* (CDX) shows that the dog will clear an obstacle in his path on command.

Ch. Eastern Waters' Nugget, Int &
Am UD/ AM UDT, clearing a fence.
Owned, trained and always handled
by Mildred Buchholz.

Chesachobee's Gold Nugget,
CDX/TD, taking the high hurdle for
owner Mildred Buchholz.

Owner Mildred Buchholz plans to
take Ch. Chesachobee's Gemson,
CD/WD, through the full Obedience
routine, including Tracking.

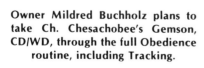

The *scent discrimination* (UD), where the dog selects the handler's article by scent alone and delivers that article to the handler, demonstrates man's ability to use the dog's natural ability (great for finding lost articles in the brush). The *group exercises* of *sit* and *down* (handler in sight for CD and out of sight for CDX) demonstrate the dog's stability on a stay command (steady to shot.)

Champion in Obedience

A new degree has recently been instituted by the AKC which will permit the use of the letters O.T.Ch. (Obedience Trial Champion) preceding the names of qualifying dogs. Only dogs that have earned the Utility Dog title can earn points toward an Obedience Trial Championship. Points are recorded for dogs earning a First or Second place in Open B or Utility class (or Utility B, if divided) according to a schedule of points established by the AKC Board of Directors. To become an OTCh. a dog must win 100 points that include: a First place in Utility (or Utility B, if divided), with at least three dogs in competition; a First place in Open B with at least six dogs in competition; and a third First place in either of these competitions. The three First places must be won under different judges.

The first Chesapeake to earn this degree is still in the future. However, with the proper KPT, socialization, and formal Obedience training, this degree is well within the realm of the Chesapeake intelligence and trainability.

Ch. Autumn Mist, UD/WD, shown with her owner Sally Diess, taking first place in Group Obedience at the Portland KC show in October 1971.

Ch. Chesavieda's Ornamental Buoy, UDT/WDX, the first male Chesapeake to become a Ch. UDT.

Ch. Chesachobee's Ovedio Millie B, UDT/WD, another of Dianna Blakey's well-trained and handled Obedience contestants.

MILDRED BUCHHOLZ, affectionately known as "Millie" to hundreds of Chesapeake owners, is shown here with one of the many champions she has bred—Chesachobee's Smokey Glenn's Chesa BB, litter sister to Chesachobee Gemson. Millie has the extraordinary record of having personally made 35 bench champions, 48 Obedience titles and 5 WDs. She is a deeply respected authority on Tracking and her suggestions and comments will be extremely helpful to anyone wishing to teach his dog to track.

Three generations of Tracking title-holders, all from Mildred Buchholz's Chesachobee Kennels: Nugget; Ty-Dee, CD; Great Guns, CD; and Nipdeteat.

16

Tracking with Your Chesapeake

by Mildred Buchholz

IF YOU ARE a person who will accept the fact that when a dog is tracking, he has an ability very unique to him, one that he alone understands—then welcome aboard!

No one trains a dog to track in the sense we generally think of as training—the dog already knows very well how to track. Rather, you must consider that you are teaching him to use his gifted nose on command, with control, and dedication. The two of you must learn to work together—the foundation for the most important ingredient, *a trust in each other.*

It is absolute fact that any dog can track regardless of conditions and circumstances if he is fortunate to have a handler who believes in him and will let him work in his own way.

If you are a person that doesn't use common sense in teaching a dog to work for you, regardless of the type of work—control training, field work, etc.—save yourself some time. Don't read on, as tracking will defeat you. It will take work on your part to teach the dog to follow a specific trail, to work on command, and under control. He *can*, and you will learn to believe in his ability as this happens; then comes *trust*. This trust is a two-way deal; it is equally important that he trusts you to believe in him. This factor cannot be over-emphasized. A lack of it will lead to a million excuses and reasonings as to why the dog failed to be successful on track!

Remember he *can* track, you don't have to teach him how. But you do have to initiate the idea and desire in him *to want to track* that trail, now, and *"stay on track."* This is where you must have the ability to get across to him what it is you want him to do.

239

Tracking is the most enjoyable and rewarding experience you will ever share with your dog—"a poor man's hobby," but how impressive it is to watch a trusting handler and dog team. The dog simulates a picture of drive and purpose; the handler, confidence, and assurance. Chesapeakes are extremely natural in tracking. This is in their breeding, but it is possible to motivate any dog of sound temperament to want to work for you if your approach is "common sense in teaching." Teaching is understanding, which is the only proper approach to the teaching of anything.

Fact number two, and this may be my farewell to some of you. You cannot *force* a dog to track. Those of you who depend on this approach in training your dog, now will realize why I state you are not training your dog to track, you are teaching him. No dog has ever been succesfully force-trained to track.

You can accomplish the tracking title, in many cases, almost entirely by yourself with your dog. You don't need assistants or intricate, expensive equipment.

The dog will work in a harness and in a very short time, associate tracking with his harness. The harness, usually made of leather, should be comfortable and non-restricting. You can often find a suitable harness in a pet section of a drug store or department store, or have one custom made for your dog at a leather or harness shop.

You will need a six-foot lead and a twenty-to-thirty foot lead. Your long lead should be of nylon webbing, heavy enough not to blow easily in the wind and smooth enough to slide through brush and high cover. You will find it wise to select your "long-lead" carefully, as it will improve your handling 100 percent. Add to your collection, eight to ten stakes or markers. These again you must select with some foresight. You want them to be about three feet high, visible to you and of a material that will slide into the ground easily and be durable for many years of tracking.

Chesapeakes are naturally quick to spot anything flapping (such as a flag) in the distance and I would advise not using any material at the top of your markers. Some suggestions are: ¾ inch wooden dowels with one end pointed and the top end painted a bright color, or P.V.C. pipe cut in lengths of three feet is excellent. Garden stakes or archery arrows with metal tips can also be used. Test the ground where you live and see which type of stake seems suitable; you want to be able to walk along and place the marker securely without having to stand there pounding it in the ground. They should be visible to you at about 100 yards and not too obvious to the dog. When you have selected the best type for your ground conditions make up a set of eight or ten and have them with you on all training sessions. You will also need a leather glove or similar leather article, and you will soon be adding various different items to your collection. Equipment now assembled and ready, it's time to learn to "lay a track."

In tracking the dog, a main factor is to keep him directly on the ground scent put down as you walked. You cannot do this unless you know exactly where the track is yourself. I would suggest you take yourself out for a few lessons without the dog. Place a marker in a field, indicating your start, walk ahead in a straight line for about 50 to 60 paces and drop a dime; turn and come back directly to the marker. Drive off and come back in ten minutes, start at your marker and see if you can walk out and find your dime! You will find yourself quickly learning to select landmarks you will remember and to walk a straight line. A field that looks fairly nondescript soon has many landmarks to a trained eye. An excellent track-layer is basic for training a good dog and handler team. This cannot be over-emphasized in your foundation work with the dog. If you plan to work with a friend as a track-layer, safeguard your friendship by seeing that both of you learn to be good track-layers.

Scent, as we think of it, is not necessarily the way it is for the dog. However, if you understand and believe a few basic facts, you can eliminate a great many of what appear to *you* to be problems, but which are *not* to him.

1. Each and every human has a different "scent," just as we all have different fingerprints. The dog has the ability to instantly discriminate and sort these out.

2. No other strong odor can cover scent to the degree that he cannot follow the underlying scent. Eliminating misconceptions, you will find yourself gaining confidence as you realize that he truly is remarkable. If I could keep you feeling this way, tracking would be a breeze. The very first time you announce you are about to teach your dog tracking you will find an expert at your elbow just dying to send you into deep depression with theories of wind velocity, ground temperature versus air temperature at various ratios, etc., etc. Their theories will range from the most scientific to the absolutely ridiculous, and make you feel you have to enroll for a Ph. D. in science before taking the first step in harness. My advice to you is quite simple—tune them out, remain steady "on course," believe in your dog, have patience and faith, and you will find he has the ability also.

3. He is able to handle all that scientific stuff all by himself! In the first stages of training it is not necessary to work with another person; you can do all his foundation work yourself. Remember, he can discriminate different human scents, so switching to a stranger is no problem once he understands what he is out there to do and responds eagerly to your commands.

Your voice and commands, as in all training, must convey your sincere feelings. His starting command should be a phrase such as "GO FIND IT," or "HUNT FOR IT" in a low, excitable tone. In the actual American Kennel Club tracking test you are allowed to give verbal encouragement as often as you like. You can also *verbally* correct or reprimand the dog in a quiet manner. These things you will develop during your practice sessions. An example of a verbal reprimand: if the dog becomes intrigued with some foreign matter during the track to the point of interfering with his concentration, you would say, "NO, LEAVE IT," in a firm tone, and he should know exactly what you mean and respond. If a dog is going too fast and hard on the track, you must teach him the word "EASY" to slow his pace. "FIND IT" or "TRACK" will always mean keep your concentration, keep your nose down and work close. Encouragement, even in very difficult situations, can often be the deciding factor in a *pass* or *fail*. Learn this well and be very careful not to show a hint of impatience in your voice. He may be face-to-face with one of those scientific horrors and on the brink of solving the whole mess. He needs your calm voice saying "THAT'S IT, GOOD" - "WORK IT OUT, GOOD." There is no time limit in an AKC tracking test, as long as the dog is working. Remember that no judge can fail you if your dog is on track and working. Learn to *drive* him to keep him working when it looks like he's about to quit and learn to *shut up* and not break his concentration with constant chatter.

This communication will come easily between you if you start it from the beginning and are constantly teaching him to associate with the phrase and tone followed by praise. The nicest part of competing for your Tracking degree is the complete naturalness you are allowed to have with your dog, compared to the single commands of the Obedience ring. Do not use his name during tracking as it will divert his attention back to you. Do not use the word "COME," as again you do not want him coming back to you, or to put his concentration on you. In this type of work you must be oblivious to him; you should be able to switch handlers, and not have him care.

It's time now to head for the fields. You do not need virgin acreage, but do use guidelines for *starting* the beginner dog: 1) Choose a cool time of day, either early morning or evening, before dark; 2) dampness is in your favor; 3) select a quiet area with short, plush grass, such as a lawn; 4) a very windy day is not the best for a newcomer; 5) always bring fresh water for your dog's comfort.

Your first few lessons will only require an area 75 yards by 75 yards. A golf course just before dark is ideal, or a school yard after the kids have gone home, or a large corporation front lawn after closing.

Select something your dog enjoys and will get excited to "GO FIND." This could be a toy or anything that will make him want to go

Pulling towards the second flag. Shown is Ch. Chesaford's Newfy, TD, with his breeder-owner-handler, Judy Cranford, at the 1978 American Chesapeake Club's Specialty Tracking Test.

Ch. Chesachobee's Bronze Atlas, CD/TD/WD, picks up speed on this track with his owner-handler, Robert McCann.

out and hunt and find. Use your imagination and spend some time at home getting him very keen about this item. Having found your location, and arriving in a confident frame of mind, park the car and get your six-foot lead, two markers, and the selected item together. Put your dog in harness, hook his lead to the plain collar and tie him securely to something close to where you will start the track and he can watch what you are doing. Walk away to your start and put your marker in. Stand there and talk to your dog, show him the article, enthusiastically trying to keep his interest on you and what you are doing. Carrying the article and the second marker, walk slowly out about 30 paces. Place the second marker and continue five to ten more steps, turn and face the dog. Wave the article and talk to him—put the article down and sit on it for a count of ten, walk back to the start, using your markers to keep you *on course.*

Go over to the dog and hook his lead to the harness, holding him by the collar, head up, and take him to within a foot of the marker and begin to let him sniff around. If he gets interested and heads out down the track, you're off to a very good start. If he is more interested in jumping on you or bouncing around, you must be patient as you try to get his interest in the ground where you stood at the start; you may have to literally go for a walk down the path to the article, feeling like you have accomplished nothing. Your first lesson is simply to get into his head that there is something out there. When he comes to the article, either by tracking like a champ or because the two of you came upon it on your walk through the markers, you must give him a great deal of *genuine* praise. Throw it for him, or play tug with it, anything that is exuberant and makes it fun to have found it.

Leave your markers in place and come back to the start with the dog and the article. Again, tie him up, stand at the start, talk to him and walk the same course again. If he did well the first time, go 20 steps beyond your last drop and place the article, sit on it, talk to him, and walk back through the markers. Take him, same as before. If he is eager to move on down the track and is out in front and pulling, restrain him slightly so he is not pulling so hard. Every time his head comes up (to visually try and find it) stand still and verbally caution him to "TRACK," refusing to go with him, until his head goes down to the ground scent, praise quietly and begin to move again with him, saying "GOOD, THAT'S RIGHT."

During your first three days of teaching, lay three to four tracks in this same manner each day. If he is eager to do the work, start immediately to restrain him, making him pull and refusing to go with him unless the head is down. Remember, the article at the end is the pot of gold, the finale of the track, and you must strongly make him feel he has been a super dog to find this thing.

At the end of three days, having followed instructions to a "T," even the most unsure dog should be moving on down the track in front of you. Maybe he will not be pulling, and still is easily distracted and look-ing to you for reassurance, but indicating to you a definite improvement from the first day on the first track. Do not be discouraged for you have accomplished a great deal and are well on your way. But do not go on to anything but a straight track until this dog *is* moving out front, concen-trating and responding to your encouragement to "TRACK."

Soon after the third day you will be up to 100 yards on a fresh track. Your progress from here out will be determined solely by his attitude. You will see, and must determine this for yourself; you should know your own dog's personality, and his enthusiasm or lack of enthusiasm should be obvious to you. AS IN ALL TRAINING, DO NOT PRO-CEED TO THE NEXT PLATEAU UNLESS THE DOG IS CONFI-DENT AT THE PHASE HE IS IN NOW. A new dog starting in tracking will usually weave back and forth across the actual track; this is quite natural and will diminish as he becomes more experienced. Eventually he will be driving hard and true on the actual track. Very often a dog will stop and study something, the significance of which is not obvious to you. Let him check and study for a few seconds, stay quiet, then remind him to "LEAVE IT" and "TRACK CLOSE."

This is an important part of communication—you *do not* know for sure what went on there and on a blind track you *absolutely do not* know; the track-layer could have dropped something out of his pocket or a mouse in season may have left her calling card there. Do not be quick to take verbal action. Let him know you trust him, and he certainly would not take you acourting Miss Mouse; give him the benefit of the doubt always, but quietly remind him of his responsibilities. You will soon find him appreciating your understanding and he *will* continue his work. You must realize on a blind track that when he stops and studies and appears to be hung up, he *could* be working a turn and he should not be worried that you are going to pressure him to "GET TO WORK," when he *is* working a possibly difficult situation. Naturally, if he stops on a track and is obviously sniffing animal droppings, or poking his head down a gopher hole or staring off at something going down the road, he is not concentrating on his tracking and your tone would firmly say "LEAVE IT ALONE," and "GET BACK TO WORK." All these things begin in your first few days of tracking and will continue all through your training; he will soon respond quickly and you will learn the fine art of working with him.

Chesapeakes are very quick to enjoy tracking and soon are trying to take you out for a drag; you must hold them back, slow their pace, and teach them the word "EASY." This is for their own good as they will also outrun their nose by 30 to 40 yards before they realize the track stopped going straight and took a turn. Once an eager tracker, a

Ch. Melody's Spun Smoke of Blabro, CDX/WD, practicing her Tracking work with Dianna Blakey.

Ch. Count Chocula, CD, working for his owner and trainer, Elizabeth Gough. Count had an excellent Tracking record.

Chesapeake very seldom needs to be reminded to "TRACK" or "GO FIND IT"—his enthusiasm is very often his difficulty. Help from the beginning, don't wait until he has started developing problems; slowing him down is all that he needs.

When your dog is doing 100 yards with great drive and concentration (usually within a few days) it is time to put in a turn. Place your marker at the start, walk out about 50 yards and put another marker; walk five more steps and turn 135 degrees to the right or left, continue another 30 paces, and place a third marker. Go another five to ten paces and place the article. Walk your track exactly back to the start. By this time your dog will not be watching you lay the track; he will well understand what the harness and the starting marker means. He will begin as usual, and you will now see if he has already begun the habit of just driving in a straight line. If so, he will shoot past the turn without so much as a nod. If this happens don't let him go more than 20 paces from your second marker; back up so you are before the marker and he is just ahead of it (you know the turn is a few feet from him), and remind him to "TRACK CLOSE" firmly. Again see if he gives an indication that something happened there. It is very important that he discovers this himself *and* makes the commitment of the direction of the turn without your guidance. Verbally encourage him, but make him actually *take* you on that first turn. When he does, pour on the praise, as he has truly committed himself and shown you where to go.

It is quite natural for a dog in the beginning stages to circle a great deal at the point of a turn, checking thoroughly both sides before deciding on the direction. You must be patient as he does this—and he must believe that you will be patient; these are the things that you are subtly doing to build the trust in each other. If the dog stops or circles, be very conscious that you are remaining in the straight-ahead position. Do not find yourself facing in the various directions he is going, or he will begin to take it as a cue that you will follow in behind him. If you do this you are subconsciously guiding him. The first time you run a blind track you will not know where the turn is and won't dare turn in any direction and he may be relying on that cue which you have subconsciously given him in your practice sessions.

From here on you will increase the length of your tracks—the amount of 90 degree turns, and the age of the track. You will also be using the long lead around 12 to 15 feet and learning to handle the lead without becoming hopelessly entangled. Hold the lead at waist level; this is the most comfortable position for you and gives you strong communication from him. You must feel through the lead what he is telling you, which is why a tracking dog must be pulling and keeping the line tight. The minute it goes slack stop; stay straight, and wait for the pull again, either straight ahead or in the direction of the turn. A well-trained dog will leave no doubt in your mind when he is telling you where to go next. Increase all your steps sensibly, remembering that you are building a mutual confidence. There is no doubt that he could do 500 yards with three turns in a very short time, but you will have lost the communication between you if you rush your schedule.

Once he is thoroughly eager to track, switch to the leather glove for the article, and insist that he indicate it to you in some way. He does not have to retrieve it and bring it to you, but you do want a positive indication from him. There is absolutely no sense in doing an entire difficult track with ease and having to worry frantically if he will pass over the glove at the end. This would fail your entire performance: he *must* indicate the article.

At various points in your training have someone lay a one-turn blind track. Go back on your own for awhile again, then a two-turn blind track. These blind tracks will be the best confidence builder for *you* and it's best to do them in easy stages as you progress in your schedule. Once the dog is tracking with vigor (only work him about twice a week), it should always be a highlight of the week for both of you. Once he is doing full 500 to 600 yard tracks, aged over an hour, once a week is enough, as it will keep his drive at a peak. Be sure you test your dog's ability in many different areas, different cover, changes of cover, different terrain, under many weather conditions, and at different times of the day or night. Use different track-layers (make sure they know what they are doing) and have many distractions.

In a test, one or both of the judges will follow right behind you during parts of the track, or during the entire track. Your dog must be at ease with people around you or close to him when he is working. As in all training, have your dog completely reliable and very well prepared for his test situation.

There will be a time when he settles into tremendous reliability and your confidence is 100 percent. Then you will go out one day and have him *appear* to completely blow it, something you simply cannot justify in your mind. Don't try to, and don't worry about it. There are times when it will simply be something you cannot understand. Can you put nose to the ground and track? Don't worry about that isolated incident to the degree that it will lessen your confidence in his ability.

There is no possible way I can tell you how long it will be before you are ready for a test. But you will have walked many, many miles of tracks in practice, and only *you* will know when you have thoroughly prepared yourselves for any situation. Tracking is not an easy title and should be well deserved. Most tests have a maximum of 10 to 12 dogs and it is totally unfair to enter one in hopes of lucking through it. I strongly recommend your reading and having in your personal library for constant reference the book, *GO FIND*, by L. Wilson Davis, published by Howell Book House, Inc., 230 Park Avenue, New York, N.Y. 10169. Also, send for a copy of the AKC's "Obedience Rules and Regulations," which you can request free from The American Kennel Club, 51 Madison Avenue, New York, N.Y. 10010.

Now that you are on the way to becoming an expert, it's time you learned the lingo for your new-found sport:

First and Thirty. Means the starting flag and thirty yards in the direction of the track. First and Thirty is telling you actually where the track is for thirty yards, after that you are on your own.

Cover. Vegetation: some sites have sparse or light cover, while others are dense and plush.

Change of cover. Means the track goes from a clover field to a thicket type cover.

Leg. Means the distance between one turn on the track and the next turn.

The drop. Article left at the end of the track.

Blind Track. A track which the handler and dog have not seen laid and they will run the track with no knowledge of its layout other than the First and Thirty.

Plotting. One or both of the judges must personally lay out each track a day or more before the test with the help of the Club members holding the test. This plot then is charted on a map showing yardage of each leg, turns and drop with landmarks for the judges to use in their reference.

Laying tracks or Track-layer. On the day of the test, the person called the track-layer will walk each track, using the map and removing all markers except the First and Thirty; he will leave the article (THE DROP).

Cross Track. Something (animal or person) other than track-layer that crossed over the laid track.

Flags. Same as a Marker; used in giving direction of the plotted track.

Fresh Track. The dog runs the track soon after the track-layer walks the course.

Aged Track. Time lapse after the track has been laid. Example: Aged 30 minutes, aged two hours, etc.

Passed. Both judges must agree that the dog worked out the course of the track-layer and indicated the article to the handler, who in turn shows it to the judges.

TD title. That's the one we're after! This title may be earned at anytime after six months of age, either before, in the middle of, or after any other titles awarded by the American Kennel Club.

Certify or Certification. A statement dated within six months of the Tracking Test, which is signed by a licensed American Kennel Club judge that has seen the dog work to his satisfaction and he feels is ready to enter a test. This statement must accompany your entry to, the test.

Tracking Judges. Deemed by the American Kennel club as qualified to understand various conditions that exist when a dog is working a scent trail such as weather, lay of land, cover and wind. They must have a thorough knowledge of dogs working under various conditions.

Whistle. Left to the end, in hopes that you will never have to know what it is. The judge will blow the whistle if the dog is too far off track or has lost interest; meaning "back to the drawing board" or that you have *failed.*

To round out your expertise, some things about the weather that might help you out while you are tracking:

1. Dew on the grass at night or in early morning is a sign of fair weather (dew forms only when air is dry, skies are clear.
2. When distant sounds are loud and hollow, look for rain.
3. Birds perch more before a storm because low pressure air is less dense, making it harder to fly.
4. Smells are stronger before rain.
5. High clouds won't rain on you no matter how threatening they look.
6. Rising smoke foretells fair weather.
7. Face the wind and the storm will always be on your right.

Tracking is a great deal of work, time-consuming, great fun (it *must* be), and very rewarding. It would have to be compared to the confidence and trust the blind have in their guide dogs. When a dog is taught to track in this manner—in harness, on lead, disciplined and under control, taught to follow the ground scent—he cannot possibly confuse his tracking with any other type of work you might wish to do with him.

TRACKING TITLE-HOLDERS

Issued	Dog:	Owner:
1955	Ch. Wisconong Jodri, UD	Mrs. W. H. Drisko
1958	Tengri's Munkatars, CD	Eugene Pantzer
	Tengri's Papago, CD	Mary Pantzer
1959	Tengri's Maia	Mary Pantzer
	Wings Tertius	Bernadette Foster
1960	Ch. Eastern Waters' Nugget	Mildred Buchholz
	Tengri's Mariska	Mary Pantzer
1962	Chesachobee's Kris Kringle	P. Leavy & M. Buchholz
	Ch. Eastern Waters' Blazing Star	Wyn Gordon
	Tengri's Bogomil	Eugene Pantzer
	Tengri's Nor	Mary Pantzer
1963	Chesachobee's Gold Nugget	Mildred Buchholz
	Chesachobee's Ty-Dee	Mrs. O. T. Smith
1966	Chesachobee's Great Guns	Mildred Buchholz
	Chesachobee's Nipdeteat	Mildred Buchholz
1967	Chesachobee's Gale	Jill Jones & M. Buchholz
1969	Enid's Chesbay Candy	Enid Towart
1970	Ch. Eastern Waters' Baronessa	Janet Horn
1972	Ch. Eastern Waters' Thunderchief, CD	Nathaniel Horn
	Longcove's Peniles Aftermath	Janet Rosenblum
1973	Ch. Ches' True Grit	Drs. J. & B. Stewart
	Chesachobee's Cocoanut, CDX	D. and B. R. Blakey
	Chesachobee's Donner	Carole Borthwick
	Eastern Waters' Lady Slipper, CD	Diane Lehman
	Eastern Waters' Independence, CD	Susan Horn

Am-Bda. Ch. Ches' True Grit, CD/TD, has earned both American and Bermudian Tracking titles for his owner, Dr. James Stewart of Woodbine, Maryland.

1974	Calbak Dark Cloud of Bo-Jib, CDX	Ilsa Sternberg
	Chesachobee's Snorkel, CD	George Jones
	Ch. Chesacroft Eastern Waters' GG	Janet Horn
	Ch. Eastern Waters' Dark Knight, CD	Janet Horn
1975	Chesachobee's Golden Sand	M. Buchholz & Scott Jones
	Ch. Cub's Lady Belle	Mrs. Ronald Anderson
	Eastern Waters' Ever Amber	Susan Horn
	Ch. Eastern Waters' Oak, CD	R. & E. Humer
	Ch. Eastern Waters' Patronessa	Drs. J. & B. Stewart
	Magellan's Dutchman	E. Frinkman
1977	Ch. Carolina's Cub, CD	Charles Cranford
	Ch. Chesachobee's Fantastic, CD	Mr. & Mrs. Charles Cranford
	Ch. Chesachobee's Ovedio Millie B, UD	Mildred Buchholz
	Ch. Chesavieda's Ornamental Buoy, CDX	Dianna Blakey
1978	Ch. Chesachobee's Bronze Atlas, CD	Robert McCann & M. Buchholz
	Ch. Chesaford's Chestnut Newfy	Mr. & Mrs. Charles Cranford
	Ch. Oak N'Thistle's Albatross	Drs. James V. & Brenda Stewart
1979	Chestnut Hill's Bruiser	Ronald B. Anderson
	Chestnut Hill's Dusty	Christine Anderson
	Ch. Melody's Spun Smoke of Blabro, CDX	Dianna D. Blakey
	Ch. Misty Morn's Cinnamon Cinder, CD	Julia & Lorne M. Cole

A Guide Dog leads his blind master past the gates of the school in San Rafael, California. Most of the Chesapeakes trained for this work were sired by Ch. Storm Cloud II or FC/AFC/CFC Nelgard's Baron. CD

Note the alert, intelligent and pleasant expression on this Chesapeake Guide Dog's face.

17

Chesapeakes as Guide Dogs

SHORTLY AFTER WORLD WAR I, the first attempt to use a dog to lead blind people was made in Germany. Because the German Shepherd was one of the best breeds available in Germany, they were the only breed trained for this work for quite some time. An excellent technique was developed and blinded German veterans were the first in the world to have a Guide Dog.

In 1929 the Seeing Eye was established in Morristown, New Jersey. Here again the German Shepherd was, for some time, the first choice among breeds.

In 1942, at the outbreak of World War II, Guide Dogs for the Blind, Inc., was established on the West Coast. It started in rented quarters south of San Francisco, but in a few years bought and established its present plant at San Rafael, California.

Shortly after World War II was over, William Johns, formerly of Seeing Eye, was hired to head this new organization. Describing the work required of a Guide Dog, Mr. Johns wrote:

> Temperament is of primary importance in all Guide Dog work. The qualities that we look for are willingness and a sense of responsibility. A dog that is high in body sensitivity and fairly high in ear sensitivity is most desirable. To explain this a little further, Guide Dogs must be willing to do whatever is wanted of them for a blind person cannot force his Guide Dog to do its work. These dogs must have a tremendous sense of responsibility and must actually realize that the blind person is in their care. A sound temperament is essential because the dog must work through heavy traffic, with its attendant noises and confusion, and through crowds of people. A dog that is at all shy cannot do this.
>
> The beginning or foundation of Guide Dog work is basic obedience. The first five commands that a Guide Dog learns are "Come," "Sit," "Down," "Stay," and "Fetch." Until these are letter perfect the work in the harness does not begin. Elementary harness commands are "Forward,"

"Right," "Left," "Halt," and "Easy." "Forward" is not really a command in the true sense of the word, but is more of a request. The blind person desires to go "Forward" but this is where the dog's sense of responsibility comes into play. The dog must determine whether or not it is safe for the blind person to go forward. If there is a car approaching, the dog will not immediately obey this forward command, but will wait until the car has passed and then automatically start forward without a second command.

Every Guide Dog learns to lead his blind master around obstacles that may be in the path, overhanging obstacles, and through the heaviest of traffic. At the end of each block the Guide Dog automatically stops at the curb. The blind person reaches out with his foot, finds the curb, and thus realizes he is at the end of the block. The blind person then gives one of three requests: "Forward" which means go straight ahead, "Right" to turn right, or "Left" to go left. It is up to the dog to determine if these requests are safe, and when they are to follow them. In the event that a car is blocking the sidewalk or driveway, the dog automatically takes the blind person around the car without any command, because of course the blind person cannot determine his surroundings or his conditions.

Guide Dogs are trained to ride in elevators, buses and streetcars. They must work in the very heaviest traffic where there are traffic signals. They must also be able to lead their masters through country or residential sections. Their work demands the highest degree of intelligence.

Johns had owned and hunted Chesapeakes for many years. He approached some of us who had been breeding West Coast Chesapeakes and said he would like to try one as a Guide Dog. So I gave him a puppy from my husband's duck club.

She worked so well that several other Chesapeakes were tried, and all were successfully trained to do this blind-leading work. From 1953 to 1959, 25 Chesapeakes went out with blind people as their Guide Dogs. The vocations of these people were quite varied: some were teachers, some students, some salesmen. Two ladies were switchboard operators, several men were musicians, others operated vending stands.

Chesapeake Guide Dogs were intelligent and their sense of responsibility was outstanding. They were quiet and they made excellent house dogs. The blind people really liked them.

The one flaw that many of them seemed to develop was that they became too protective. When they left the school with their blind masters they were working perfectly. But as the weeks and months passed, the Chesapeakes became so devoted to their masters that they became *overprotective* of them. Often they would not let other people come near them, in some instances even wives or husbands. This, obviously, created an impossible situation in the family, on streetcars or buses, as well as in their job situations. Because of this fault of over-possessiveness, Guide Dogs for the Blind was obliged to discontinue training Chesapeakes for this work.

Three more Chesapeakes who passed the difficult Guide Dog training course. The highest degree of intelligence, alertness and willingness is required of each dog.

This young lady supports herself working as a switchboard operator. Each day her Guide Dog, Della, takes her back and forth from her home to her job.

Bud Noon and CFC/National Can FC of 1956, Baker's King. Sired by CFC Conroy's Golden Arrow ex Chesaseal Happy Princess. King did a lot to popularize the breed.

Can Ch. Mossbank Model Chet, by Bold Chet of Morpeth ex Anjamar's Trish of Morpeth, is the first Canadian-bred Chesapeake to go Best in Show. Shown by Martha Thorne, he is pictured winning this honor under judge Robert Nutbeem, at the Club Canin de Montreal on April 8, 1979. Bred and owned by the James McKinlay family of Morpeth, Ontario, Canada.

18

Chesapeakes in Canada

NOTE: The information for this chapter has been supplied through the kind cooperation of officers and members of the Chesapeake Bay Retriever Club of Canada. Bob Wheelan, its president, has been most solicitous. Elizabeth Lavoy, an old time breeder and owner of the Conroy Marsh Kennels has been extremely helpful, as have Jim and Mary Anne Kilgannon. Mr. Kilgannon is a popular Canadian bench show judge and his wife, formerly Mary Anne Sherman, is a well-known Obedience exhibitor. Phyllis and David Rankin are interested in field trials and in seeing top American bloodlines come into Canada. Hans Kuck, who has had spectacular success in Canadian and American field trials, has supplied a resume of the current field trial situation. I am extremely grateful to all.

RECORDS INDICATE, writes David Rankin of Porcupine Plain, Saskatchewan, "that Chesapeakes have been in Western Canada since before the railroad's completion in 1885. At times, Canadians have even exported Chesapeakes back to the United States, notably George Fairburn in the 1930s with his Bud Parker dogs from Neepawa, Manitoba. I think that most progressive Canadian breeders have always realized that they had to measure their dogs against the best they could find, rather than remain secure in their own backyard. Consequently, I believe there will always be a steady traffic of brown dogs back and forth across the border between the United States and Canada. That is a necessary and good thing if we are to progress."

Elizabeth Lavoy, who has been a well-known and highly respected Chesapeake breeder for over 30 years, tells us, "When I started my Conroy Marsh kennels in 1945, I was told there were only nine breeders or kennels in our country. I recall that these were:

Kennels:	Owner:
Copper City	William Brennan, Moranda, Quebec
Ducklore of Cocoa King	Leverne Wright, Picton, Ontario
Oil City	Frank Cockerel, Edmonton, Ontario
Gilroy	Bob Gilroy, Coquitlan, BC
Baker's	Archie Baker, Edmonton, Ontario
Conroy Kennels	Ed Bolander
Carmoney Kennels	Munro Coleman, Edmonton, Ontario
Midnapore	Peg Des Roches, Vancouver, BC

"Since that time, quite a few new breeders have started. Among them:

Garjo	Gary & Joan Brown, Slittsville
Waterlord	Don Crompton, Carleton Place
Watermaster	Bill Levigne, Weston, Ontario
Cheslang	Hans Kuck, Half Moon Bay, BC
Jojak	J & J. Babcock, Sydenham, Ontario
Westpeake	Brian West, Sylvan Lake, Alberta
Timberview	Aldergrove, BC
Chessyland	Massey, Ontario, Canada

Mary Anne Kilgannon is a prominent Obedience contestant of great ability. She has made the fine scores of 198 in Open A with her Ch. Ever Amber, CDX and 197 in Novice B with Amber's son, Ever Amber Joy of Mallards, CD. A third Kilgannon Obedience titlist is Amber's daughter, Ch. Ever Amber of Redwood, CD.

Mrs. Kilgannon writes that there is Tracking competition in Canada now, but she does not know of any Chesapeakes that have thus far earned their Tracking titles. She has been kind enough to compile a list of the 24 Canadian Chesapeakes that have earned CD's, and the five that have made CDX.

Canadian Chesapeakes who have earned Companion Dog titles:

1959	Alpine Bonnie Chips	1974	Copper River Current of Bowena
1961	Heather's Peter of Chesgord		Ch. Pritchard's Queen of Sheba
	Jade's Marty of Aintree	1975	Noralfob's Chester-Do-Good
	Juno Moneta Mist		Rusty's Autumn Splendor
	Kip Knob Key for Clebuds		Ch. Count Chocula
	Sunpoke Bronze Duke	1976	Eastern Waters' Little Acoma
1963	Ch. Koko Queen		Garjo's Copper King
	Shah-Zada of Shad-dron		Redwood's Buckley of Amber
1966	Ch. Ever Amber		Conroy's Dark Rebelle
	Kerno's Mariner Moe	1978	Bracan's Skipaleaut Brigette
1967	Chesareid Evening Star	1979	Pelikana Firefly
1971	Ever Amber's Joy of Mallard		
1972	Ch. Ever Amber of Redwood		

imberton Mick, the first Canadian Chesapeake
win a Field Trial championship (1946). Owned
by Oscar Krogg.

Can FC Oil City Ted, owned, trained
and run by Frank Cockrall, in 1955 became the fifth Chesapeake to win this
coveted title.

Veteran handler, Alex Spear of Pennsylvania, with Can FC/CAFC and
Am FC/AFC Chesdel Chippewa
Chief. A fine marker and excellent
handling dog, Chief is a real credit
to the breed.

Canadian Chesapeakes who have earned Companion Dog Excellent titles:

1966   Chum of Rambling Willows
1968   Ch. Ever Amber, CD
1974   Ch. Donedin Cannabis
1975   Ch. Pritchard's Queen of Sheba
1976   Koolwater's Little Beaver

Our picture of the Canadian field trial situation is quite complete, as both David Rankin and Hans Kuck are vitally interested in trials, as is Bob Wheelan.

Bob Wheelan writes, "Last year there were four good Chesapeake Open dogs in Canada: Hans Kuck's Nanuk of Cheslang, now retired; Go Major Go, owned by Harvey Hackney; Cocoa's Tiger Cub, belonging to Bunny Stevens, and Dual Ch. Marmaduke of Havelock, owned by Bill Furr." Besides these, Wheelan mentions several that he feels will do well in the major stakes of 1979: Bill Furr's dog, Barry, (Budweiser ex Cub's Magothy), Frank De Grow's Hawk, (Cub's Canadian Cub ex Lady Dormedatoo), Bill Little's Cappy (Capital City Jake ex Ginger of Humboldt). Wheelan hopes, of course, that he will do well with his own Cub's Berteleda Tiger. He tells us that John Hudson, David Rankin and Bunny Stevens all have good, young prospects.

Hans Kuck has owned and trained one of the most outstanding field trial dogs in Canada. As I have seen Nanuk run, since his Junior Stake days, I feel well qualified to describe him. Nanuk is extremely stylish, an excellent marker, and has always had a spectacular water entry—which attributes made him a favorite among both judges and spectators. Nanuk was less than three years old when he completed both his Canadian Field Championship and Canadian Amateur Field Championship. He also finished his American Amateur Field Championship in 1975. He is one of the few Canadian retrievers who has earned an American title. He qualified for the 1974 and 1976 U.S. Amateur National Championship Stakes, as well as the 1973-'74-'75-'76-'77 and '78 Canadian Nationals. Nanuk was retired in 1978, finishing with the outstanding record of 73 Canadian and 34 American All-Age points—a total of 107. We all admire the amazing record made by Hans and Nanuk.

David Rankin tells us that, "Canadian field trial competition is so much stiffer today and the game has become so highly specialized that the ordinary person like myself needs a lot of help simply to get to line with a dog which won't embarrass Chesapeake people. I think in the last few years the quality of Chesapeake pups being taken to trials in Canada has improved substantially and they have needed to. People who are serious about being competitive have had to realize that just any brown dog will not do. They have had to get their pups from field trial blood and nothing

CFC/Am FC & AFC Nelgard's Baron, CD, made his Canadian Field Championship for owner-trainer Munro Coleman in 1953, and was subsequently sold to author Eloise Heller (Cherry.)

Can Dual Ch. Baron's Skipper Bob with owner-trainer Alf Guns, for whom he won his championship in 1957. Bob closely resembled his sire, Nelgard's Baron.

Jim Kilgannon going Best of Breed with his Ch. Ever Amber, CDX. Shown by co-owner, Mary Anne Kilgannon, Amber was 2nd highest scoring Chesapeake in Obedience in 1966. She made her CDX title in 1968.

Bunny Stevens and her CFC & CAFC Cocoa's Tiger Cub have been a great combination in the trials. Sired by CFC Prince Cocoa of Kent ex Miss T Starr, Bunny's Tiger Cub has won many points for her.

Am AFC/ Can FC and CAFC Nanuk of Cheslang, with owner Hans Kuck of British Columbia. Nanuk was a stylish, exciting dog to watch—a fine marker and a good handling dog.—D. Carter

CFC Ce-Pine Sandy Duke with owner Cyril Hicks.

Marshal Willis and Can FC Gypsy's Mallard of Vigloma, who was American bred. Mallard was quite prominent in the field trials of the 1960s.

less. They have had to look at the strength and the weakness of the various lines, whether Baronland, Mount Joy, Atom Bob, Beewacker's Chester, or the Deerwood line.''

I asked Hans Kuck to give me a report on the Canadian field trials of today. He writes, "Since the time I became actively involved in running dogs in field trials, there has been a steady increase in the number of Chesapeakes entered, and in their quality.

"Can. FC and Can. AFC Rocky of Calpeake, belonging to Carolyn and Vic Lacusta, is a dog that I particularly admire, as he was so consistent. He won his share of trials, had many placings and acquired a point total in the high 70s.

"In the same period, Tiger of Abelina was run by Bob Kierstead of Kingston, Ontario, in the Eastern Canadian circuit. He won a trial early in his life, and also earned several placings. He usually finished most of the trials in which he was entered. Unfortunately, he was unable to earn the last half point he needed to complete his Field Trial Championship.

"Bunny Stevens has trained and handled her good male, Can. FC and Can. AFC Cocoa's Tiger Cub. Her Cub has often done excellent work and has qualified for numerous Canadian Nationals. He was a finalist in the 1975 National, held at Williams Lake, B.C.

"Canadian Dual Ch. Marmaduke of Havelock, a good marker and fine handling dog, does well in the very stiff competition of the Prairie Circuit for his owner, Bill Furr of Winnipeg, Manitoba. Bill also owns a Junior dog that is one of the best youngsters I have seen in a long time. My prediction is this young dog will go on to become a competitive Open dog.

"Al Gladu had great success with his Kodiak Zane in Junior and Qualifying Stakes, and was Top Junior dog of the Winnipeg Retriever Club '75-'76.

"In Ontario, a great many new Chesapeake fanciers are competing in field trials today: Lionel Adair with Lady's Tiffany Tonya, Bob Wheelan with Cub's Berteleda Tiger. Both had good Junior seasons. Marty Pinder and Dana and Frank Degrow placed their Cub's Shadow of the Hawk in almost every Minor Stake, and we expect great things from Hawk in the near future.

"Go Major Go and Harvey Hackney from Estevan, Saskatchewan, were very close, last year, to completing his Field Championship. I have no doubt that he will finish the job this year. He was the winner of the Amateur Stake at the 1978 Chesapeake Bay Retriever Club of Canada's Specialty Field Trial.

"Chabasco of Cheslang, owned by Ted Kennedy and Hans Kuck, and jointly trained by Francis Kennedy and myself, was also a good Junior and Qualifying dog and was very successful on the Canadian West Coast. Chabasco and Nanuk, his sire, achieved a very rare feat at the Upper Vancouver Island licensed All-Breed Trial of July '75. They were the only two Chesapeakes entered in a field of 160 Labradors. Nanuk, the father, won the Open All-Age Stake and Chabasco, his son, won the Junior Stake.

"We must not overlook Bob Cambell of Richmond, B.C., whose Chuck of Cowchin Bay ran with a high rate of success in Junior and Qualifying Stakes, placing and winning in both.

"Our Chesapeakes successfully compete against a vast field of Labradors and Goldens, and, percentage-wise, our record of wins is most impressive."

CANADIAN FIELD TRIAL CHAMPIONS
*Indicates American bred

Dog:	Owner:
1946 Timbertown Mick	Oscar Krogg
1952 Conroy's Golden Arrow	Pat St. Peter
1953 Nelgard's Baron*	Monroe Coleman
1954 Midnapore's Copper Mountain Chum	Peg DesRoches
1955 Oil City Ted	Frank Cockrall
1956 Dual Ch. Baker's King	Bud Noon
1957 Dual Ch. Baron's Skipper Bob	Alf Gunns
1959 Ce-Pine Sandy Duke	Cyril Hicks
1960 Gypsy's Mallard of Vigloma*	Marshal Willis
1962 Rockyview's Radar Duke*	Ron Davidge
1964 Prince Cocoa of Kent	Murray Sim
1965 Dual Ch. Baron's Tule Tiger*	Eloise Heller
1968 Rocky of Cal-Peake	Vic Lakusta
1973 Nanuk of Cheslang*	Hans Kuck
1974 Cocoa's Tiger Cub	Bunny Stevens
1975 Chesdel Chippewa Chief*	Alex Spear
1978 Dual Ch. Marmaduke of Haveloch	Bill Furr

The Chesapeake Bay Retriever Club of Canada, which started just a few years ago, has become a terrific organization and has provided real impetus to all phases of breed activity. It is doing a top job of promoting interest in the breed in Canada.

Their newsletter, published five times a year, is sent to all their members. It contains a wealth of information. There are articles on field training, for both hunting and field trial dogs, as well as articles on Obedience and show techniques. They list the current results of what dogs have won and placed in the shows, Obedience and field trials. They feature hunting dog tales, humorous stories, and veterinarian articles on current health problems. They also list Pups for Sale and Dogs at Stud.

Can FC & CAFC Rocky of Cal
Peake, winner of over 70
Open points. Trained and
handled by Victor and
Carolyn Lacusta of Calgary,
Alberta. Rocky finished the
1972 Canadian National
Championship Stake.

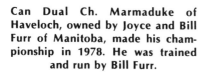

Can FC Prince Cocoa of Kent, owned by
Murray Sim, won his Canadian Field
Championship in 1964. He was an alert
dog with excellent marking ability.

Can Dual Ch. Marmaduke of
Haveloch, owned by Joyce and Bill
Furr of Manitoba, made his championship in 1978. He was trained
and run by Bill Furr.

Can FC Midnapore's Copper Mountain Chum,
owned by Peg Des Roches of British Columbia,
made his Field Championship when he was only
28 months old. Chum was sired by Midnapore
Pat ex Ch.Mick's Buffalo Jean.

JANET HORN with her Am-Can. Ch. Eastern Waters' Skipjack, CD. He was sired by Ch. Eastern Waters' Neptune out of Janet's favorite dog, Ch. Eastern Waters' Baronessa, TD.

In 1975-76 Skipjack won nine CACIBs (Certificate of Aptitude for International Championship, four of which must be won in three different countries, plus a field qualification). Skipjack won these in France, Italy, Germany and Switzerland.

No one could be better qualified to write about Chesapeakes in Europe than Janet Horn. Residing in Switzerland and using it as a home base, she and her husband Dan, traveled extensively and attended many of the bench shows and field trials held in Central Europe, as well as in the Scandinavian countries.

19

Chesapeakes Abroad

by Janet Horn

THE CHESAPEAKE breed is not known to have crossed the Atlantic before 1936. The first Chesapeakes to be exported were introduced into England by the Earl of Sefton, to improve his Labradors. At that time the kennel club would register Interbred retrievers, which could be bred into one or another of its recognized retriever breeds, and the existence of common ancestry for the Chesapeake Bay Retriever and the English Retriever is well documented.

These first Chesapeakes in England were Ch. Chesacroft Dark Hazard, and some puppies from Chesacroft Kennels owned by Anthony A. Bliss. The quarantine was disastrous to the puppies but the adult dog came through it well. It is not known that he was bred to Chesapeake bitches in England.

Dr. Helen Ingleby, an English breeder working as a pathologist in a Philadelphia hospital and residing in the United States for many years, took a bred bitch into England to whelp a litter, and the puppies were permitted to leave the quarantine as soon as they were weaned. The bitch could then be shipped back to the states. Dr. Ingleby told of her sister and herself loading the puppies into a car and driving through Scotland selling puppies as they went. One of the purchasers was W. Somerset Maugham. In spite of Dr. Ingleby's attempts to bring the breed she loved into her native land, the dearth of breeding stock remained such that the Chesapeakes she left there were bred to Labradors, and so these early importations failed to establish the breed as a separate one in Britain.

World War II further delayed the exportation of Chesapeakes to Europe, but American servicemen stationed in England brought their dogs with them, and the next introductions of the breed were in this random fashion. It was in the early '60s that Captain Robert Conlin put his Alpine Abi through quarantine, later bringing the dog home when his tour of duty was ended. Abi sired at least one litter out of a bitch who appears to have been bred in Britain. At about this time, Bruce Kennedy, who bred cattle in Scotland, had sent a man to look at cattle on the Eastern Shore of Maryland, and this emissary's reports of the Chesapeake dogs of that area so intrigued Mr. Kennedy that he commissioned the purchase of a bitch, and named her Doonholme Dusty. Doonholme Dusty flourished in Scotland, and was several times bred to a dog owned by a gamekeeper, Brandy of Cowal by Alpine Abi.

This was the only Chesapeake breeding in Britain when Mrs. Margaret Izzard of Ryshot Kennels, best known for excellent Flat-Coated Retrievers, and also for breeding and training Labradors and Goldens, became interested in learning about the Chesapeake firsthand. In 1967 she acquired a puppy from Mr. Kennedy, which she named Ryshot Welcome Yank. She trained him for the field and worked him with her other retrievers. Mrs. Izzard worked her dogs hard, picking up at the shoots on estates, and Yank was always asked for by estates where coastal waters had to be worked. Mrs. Izzard was active in showing her retrievers which were truly of "dual" character, and her showing of Yank did much to make the Chesapeake known in England. When Yank was approaching the age of five it was agreed that it was time to seek a suitable mate for him, and Mrs. Izzard imported Eastern Waters' Ryshot Rose, who in 1974 produced a litter. This bitch died not long after, and in the summer of 1975 the British dog fancy mourned the passing of Margaret Izzard. Her death was also a great loss to the Chesapeake breed.

Mr. J. H. A. Allen, who farms and breeds cattle in Devonshire, remembered that when he was a small boy he lived near an American Army base and one of the officers had a Chesapeake of which he and his mother became very fond. Many years later, his love of shooting and dissatisfaction with available Labradors prompted him to obtain a Chesapeake bitch from Mr. Kennedy. Her character and ability so confirmed his feeling for the breed, that when illness prevented her being bred, he imported a bitch from America, Eastern Waters' Morag, who in 1975 produced the second litter sired by Ryshot Welcome Yank. Some of the puppies from this and from the Izzard's litter were exported to France, Denmark, Sweden and Finland.

In England, Mrs. Joyce Munday carries on with Chesapeakes from the Yank-Morag breeding, and Mrs. Christine Parris' foundation bitch, Ryshot Yank's Sea Star, is the one that Mrs. Izzard had chosen from her litter for herself. These breeders work and show their dogs and are doing much to stimulate interest in the breed. Understandably, the English retriever breeds are strongly entrenched in their country of origin, but the greatest obstacle to the establishment and growth of the Chesapeake breed in England is the quarantine.

International and Nordic Ch. Ryshot Yank's Seacoral, retrieving in style for owner Marianne Nilsson of Sweden. His sire is Ryshot Welcome Yank; his dam, Eastern Waters' Ryshot Rose.

Vattlestugans Zeus, pack on back, will accompany his master, Thomas Brynils of Sweden, into some of the high country.

France is the next country into which comparative early importations of Chesapeakes are known to have been made. The Comte de Bonvouloir, a breeder of Golden Retrievers, and founder and first president of the Retriever Club de France, began to introduce Chesapeakes from the United States shortly after World War II. The first to be recorded were a bitch, Cinnamon of Whichway, bred by Mrs. W. Huntting Howell, and a dog, Lucky Boy of Tesuque, bred by Peter Beasley. There were other importations within the next few years, and this writer remembers that Mrs. A. W. Owens, Jr., was one of the breeders who sent Chesapeakes to France in the late 1940s. At this time the Comte had over 30 Goldens in his kennel, named Le Chenil de Saint-Jean-du-Bois (the Kennel of Saint John of the Wood) and he showed to their championships the first Goldens to attain that title in France. The Comte J. de Bonvouloir was the author of a delightful book, *Les Retrievers et Leur Dressage*, now many years out of print, but well worth a search to possess. It includes a chapter on the origin and description of the Chesapeake Bay Dog Retriever and is illustrated with charming line-drawings; the coy flirtation between the Chesapeake and her legendary suitor the otter, is a gem.

Although the Chenil de Saint-Jean-du-Bois is no more there are still a few Chesapeakes in France that carry on its bloodlines bred with more recent imports. M. Philippe Valette, an ardent duck hunter who has owned this breed for nearly 30 years, had his first one from the Comte de Bonvouloir's last litter. He imported in the late '50s and early '60s from Alpine Kennels and from Silverdart Kennels in the United States. In shoots on his estate, M. Valette and his friends bring down as many as 50 ducks in a day, and he reports that the other retrievers quit when they get tired, but the Chesapeake keeps on working until the last bird has been retrieved. The few Chesapeakes in France are used for hunting, highly prized by their owners, but little known to the general public. There are many fine hunting breeds of French origin.

This kind of hunting is limited to private estates, and the retriever interest in France is small, though its formal guardian, the Retriever Club de France, continues under the presidency of M. Le Carriere, designating its Specialty at the Paris show and holding one formal Field Trial a year. A win at Paris, and a "Mention Trés Honnorable" in a Field Trial, are among the requirements for a retriever to earn a French Championship, so it is essential that this trial be held to provide opportunity for retrievers to prove themselves in the field. Labradors, easily imported from England, now outnumber the Goldens in France, and few French retriever owners had ever seen a Chesapeake when in 1975 I was a temporary resident and exhibited my American Champions, Eastern Waters' Skipjack, CD, and Eastern Waters' Stardust in a number of dog shows, and attended field trials. My Chesapeakes attracted a great deal of atten-

Danish Ch. Doonholm Dandy (in foreground) with Clipper,
both owned by Ole Lind Peterson of Denmark.

Danish Ch. Doonholm Dandy delivers to his owner Ole Lind Peterson of Denmark.

tion and interest. From the litter produced by them while overseas, one bitch remained in France to be trained and hunted by her owner.

Importations into Holland and Denmark have been more recent but the breed has found such favor in these watery countries that Denmark now claims a population of about a hundred Chesapeakes, while Holland has reported forty to fifty. These figures reflect some breeding done within these countries, as well as importations. Meager information on Holland has been available; the man who first imported Chesapeakes into Holland thought that about nine of the breed had been imported from abroad, first from the United States in the early '50s, then from the Comte de Bonvouloir in France, from Bruce Kennedy in Scotland, and again from the states. Some of the American breeders known to the writer to have exported Chesapeakes to Holland in those early days are Dr. John Lundy, Richard and Sheila Di Vaccaro, and Ernest Wermerskirchen. Further American imports in the '70s were Eastern Waters' Magic Pearl, and a male puppy from Mrs. Robert G. Lee. Chesapeakes bred in Holland have been exported to other European countries including France and Denmark. In 1971 a Chesapeake Club was formed in Holland to promote and safeguard the interests of the breed, and some informal trials were held, but there appears to be little interest among Dutch Chesapeake owners in participation in field trials and shows.

It is said that the first Chesapeakes to reach Denmark were imported in the late 1930s; however, none of this breeding survived World War II, and no details are available at this writing. The Chesapeakes which formed the foundation of breeding stock for present-day Denmark were imported from the United States in the mid-60s: Baronland's Cub's Cary Grant, Sal of Wermerskirchen and some others not fully identified. More have been imported continuously since then, from Holland, Scotland, from Mount Joy Kennels and Smart's Kennels among others in the United States, and from neighboring Sweden. Mr. Ole Lind Pedersen, secretary of the County Planning Road division in Holstebro County, Jutland, serves in several capacities in the Danish Retriever Club, among them as breeding warden for Chesapeakes. The Danish Retriever Club holds Specialty shows and several field trials a year, and a field trial award is required for a retriever to earn the title of champion. Mr. Pedersen owns and works both Chesapeakes and Labradors, using them mostly for hunting and picking up; he is active in field show competition and has done some breeding.

Some breeding also has been done at the Dienesmindes Kennels of Dan Madsen. Denmark is typical wetland with a very long shoreline, located in the center of the flyway of different ducks and geese, and the hunting is very good, and sometimes great. Upland game is good, too,

Judge Mildred Buchholz awarded Best Puppy to Vattlestugans Oden, owned and handled by Marianne Nilsson at the Swedish Dog Club in 1976. Oden is by Ch. Chewonski ex Ch. Ryshot Yank's Secoral.

Friedeborg av Komsalo, five-months old female by Finnish Champion Chutney ex Eastern Waters' Winnepesaukee. Bred and owned by Gun Holmstrom of Helsinki.

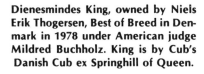

Dienesmindes King, owned by Niels Erik Thogersen, Best of Breed in Denmark in 1978 under American judge Mildred Buchholz. King is by Cub's Danish Cub ex Springhill of Queen.

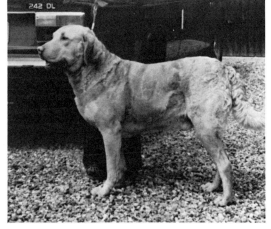

Viktoria Sundvall showing her Swedish Champion Vattlestugans Hera, who is a beauty. Hera is trained to retrieve badger, fox and rabbit. She is shown here with 40 pheasants she retrieved after a battue-hunt in which 805 pheasants were killed by 12 guns.

and there are no bag limits, but all hunting is on private lands which must be owned or leased by the hunter. The last quarter of this century is bringing the same changes that have been seen in North America; draining the wetlands deprives the waterfowl of natural habitat and breeding grounds, and this type of hunting may be a threatened sport in Denmark, too.

Regardless of changes in the sport that developed the breed, the Chesapeake continues to develop its special group of devotees in its own country and so it is in Denmark, where a nucleus of serious fanciers is working in its interests.

In the early '70s Chesapeakes began to find their way into Norway and Sweden, from Denmark, the United States, and England. The first Chesapeake in Sweden was Chesachobee's Echo, imported from Mildred Buchholz in 1973 by Josta Westerlund and Lars Andersson. Echo produced the first litter of Chesapeakes in Sweden, in October, 1975, sired by one of the first of the breed in Norway, Smarts Petter owned by Britt Eli Overeng. All dogs entering these two Scandinavian countries and Finland are required to spend several months in quarantine, with the exception of those coming from England, which has contributed two Ryshot-bred bitches, brought as puppies from Margaret Izzard's kennel by Marianne Nilsson and Klas Norrman at the New Year of 1975. Once inside one of these countries, a dog may not leave it without going through quarantine on its return. The ramifications surrounding an attempt to breed outside the country, by artificial insemination, are mind-boggling. Dogs may pass freely from one country to another within these three for breeding, shows and trials.

Early in 1976 the first Chesapeakes were imported into Finland, by Mrs. Ulla Axelsson and Gun Holmstrom, two puppies from the first litter, Eastern Waters'-bred, in Switzerland. From the quarantine in Finland, the male puppy, Eastern Waters' Jeremysquam, went to Sweden where, before his early death, he sired a litter out of Chesachobee's Echo. Eastern Waters' Winnepesaukee remained in Finland, others followed, and in 1978 she produced the first Chesapeake litter in Finland, sired by Chutney. Meanwhile Chewonski, from the first Swedish litter, has sired several litters, out of Ryshot's Sea Coral owned by Marianne Nilsson, registered in the Nilsson's "Vattlestugan" kennel name, and there are now about 60 to 75 Chesapeakes in the three countries.

Fanciers in Sweden, Norway, and Finland are working closely together to improve and establish the breed and to advance its interests. Their Specialty events are well and enthusiastically attended. The leading breeders have experience with other breeds, and know how to make use of shows and trials to balance emphases on type and working ability; they must overcome greater difficulties than are met in non-quarantine countries yet they are well qualified to do so, and the Chesapeake breed has made impressive progress in Scandinavia in its first five years there.

The breed is new in Switzerland, and the parents of the first Swiss registered litter, American and Canadian Champion Eastern Waters' Skipjack, Am. and Can. CD, and American Champion Eastern Waters' Stardust, returned with their owner to the United States while all the puppies went to other countries in Europe. These transients made friends for the breed during their sojourn abroad and importations of three Chesapeake puppies took place in the next three years. Eastern Waters' Jupiter went to J. Mauler in 1976, and later that year another male, Eastern Waters' Mountaineer, was delivered to Peter Winkler. Jupiter passed into the ownership of Maya Machler who is showing him to the first Swiss championship for this breed. In 1979 Miss Machler imported a bitch-puppy, Eastern Waters' Juno. Under the guardianship of Frau Leonie Bernhauser, the breeding warden, and other friends in the Swiss Springer Spaniel—Retriever Club, the breed is in good hands in Switzerland.

The foregoing reports on all the countries in Europe where the Chesapeake breed has been established and is making progress. A few Chesapeakes have been said to be in Germany but they have not been identified and in that country the retriever interest is very small. An American, Elliott Roosevelt, had two Chesapeakes while living in Portugal, and these accompanied him to England and later passed to other owners, one in Sweden.

The first champion Chesapeakes in Europe were Danish Ch. Doonholm Dandy owned by Ole Lind Pedersen, and Danish Ch. Dienesmindes Tjaika owned by Joergen Berthelsen; as in most European countries, these titles are conferred only when the dog has added a field award to its bench wins. Next in Europe was the first Norwegian champion, Dienesmindes Fenella, owned by Sverre Bilet, and Norwegian champions now include Glory, owned by Sverre Bilet; El Grengo, owned by Svend Age Moller; Smarts Mitra, owned by Sigmund Vasassen; Smarts Petter, Smarts Delta de Queen, and their son, Chesarengs Anton, all owned by Britt Eli Overeng; and Chewonki, owned by Charlott Adolfsson of Sweden. The first Finnish champion was Chutney owned by Gun Holmstrom, finished in 1978. Ryshot Yank's Sea Coral, owned by Marianne Nilsson, became the first Swedish champion Chesapeake in 1977. In 1978 Coral was the first to gain the title of Nordic Champion, which requires championship certificates won in Sweden, Norway and Finland. In this year, also, Coral became the first Chesapeake to win the title of International Champion, under the regulations of the F.C.I. Vattlestugans Hera, owned by Viktoria Sundvall, became the second Swedish champion Chesapeake in 1978.

Smart's Petter, owned by Britt Overing of Norway. He is Dual Ch. Cub's Kobi King ex Chesareid Cinnamon Teal, CD.

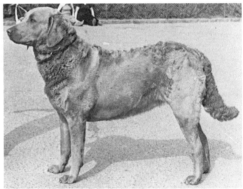

Left, Nuch Glory, an excellent female. Right, Nuch Dienesmindes Fenella. Both owned by Sverre Bilet of Oslo, Norway.

Eastern Waters' Winnepesaukee, the nice dead-grass female owned by Gun Holmstrom and Ulla Axelsson of Helsinki. By Ch. Eastern Waters' Skipjack ex Ch. Eastern Waters' Stardust, she was bred by Janet Horn.

Nuch Chewonki, Norwegian show champion, owned by Charlotte Adolfson of Sweden. By Ch. Smart's Petter ex Chesachobee's Echo, Chewonki has won 3 CACIBs, has gone Best of Breed several times and also has a Tracking prize.

Chesareng's Anna, one of Britt Overing's fine brood bitches.

Britt Overing of Norway owns this handsome bitch, Smart's Delta Queen. She is by FC & AFC Bay City Jake ex Cub's Cinnamon Teal.

In F.C.I. member countries, which includes the Continent of Europe, the Chesapeake is a recognized breed and may win championship titles by meeting the requirements which include: at least a one-year interval between first and last awards of the Certificate of Aptitude for International Championship; four CACIBs which must be won in three different countries, plus a field qualification. In 1975-76, American Ch. Eastern Waters' Skipjack, CD, won nine CACIBs in four countries and added the Canadian titles after his return to America; during this period Am. Ch. Eastern Waters' Stardust shown in fewer shows, won five CACIBs in three countries. In Britain the Chesapeake breed does not have championship status and the provision for showing it is in "Any Variety" classes; Chesapeakes are not eligible to compete in British field trials. Retriever field trials on the Continent are generally modeled closely after their English counterparts, and differ very much from American trials. They also vary from one country to another and while little or no water work may be required in western Europe, the water work in Scandinavian trials is often quite demanding. In all countries where the breed has championship status, the Chesapeake is eligible to participate in Retriever trials, and in Denmark and Sweden, Specialty trials for Chesapeakes are held.

As in its own country the fame of the Chesapeake has spread because of its prowess in the hunting field, and its popularity increases as it becomes more widely known for its unique breed character. The breed character and personality of the Chesapeake is the source of its ability to inspire the devotion and loyalty of its fanciers to a degree found in few other breeds. It is casting the same spell over its owners overseas and creating a coterie of devotees fully as ardent as those of its homeland. Most of the Europeans who acquire Chesapeakes and want to carry on with breeding them, have or have had other retriever breeds. Not all new owners are Nimrods; some with a love of the water and outdoor living have liked the idea of the Chesapeake as companion, guardian, and playmate for the family—another of the specialties at which this "specialist" breed excels. In every country the breeders and fanciers who are in a position to be most influential, recognize the special qualities of the Chesapeake, and while endeavoring to advance its interest they are alert to the dangers of overbreeding and overpopularity, and a primary aim is to ensure that it shall continue in good hands. The Chesapeake in Europe shares its owner's home and is regarded as a member of the family, much loved and highly prized.

Chesapeake Day at Clearfield, Utah in April, 1978.

A good turnout for the first Northern California Working Dog Stake, held near San Francisco.

An American Breed

20

The American Chesapeake Club

SEVERAL ineffectual attempts to form a Chesapeake breed club had been made in the last part of the nineteenth century.

One of these was the Chesapeake Bay Dog Club, organized on April 17, 1890. Major J. M. Taylor's classic book, *Bench Show and Field Trial Records and Standards of Dogs in America from 1884 to 1891,* lists the officers and members of this club. Taylor tells us that a breed standard was forwarded to the secretary of the American Kennel Club on September 26, 1885. However, no action was taken on this standard.

Finally, in 1918, the present club was organized and, along with an official standard for the breed, was recognized on September 17 of that year.

We have the distinction of being the very first breed club recognized by the American Kennel Club. Anthony Bliss' booklet of 1936 tells us more about this:

> When the present American Chesapeake Club was formed in 1918 (with a membership of only 14), it was with the idea of standardizing and encouraging the Chesapeake Bay dog, especially in regard to the working ability of the breed. Earl Henry, long known as the "Chesapeake King" was the first president.He also served as chairman of the "Standing Committee". The members were able to set up a standard to be used in the ring so that the types of Chesapeakes were at least restricted to two or three, rather than many different ones. Further than that, the formation of the Club and the standard encouraged the registration of the dogs with the Field Dog Stud Book and the American Kennel Club, thus keeping the strains purer than would otherwise have been the case. On the whole, the minutes of the annual meetings show a great interest until 1926, when the membership began to dwindle. In 1921 there had been 41 members, but this number fell as low as 18 within a few years. Unfortunately, the club was unable to hold any field trials and so a great part of the most popular side of the Chesapeake was lost to practical demonstration.

In 1932 Mr. Bliss was elected president of the American Chesapeake Club and headquarters were moved East. With Bliss in charge until 1937, the club enjoyed a regime of increased activity. He saw that the breed was given widespread publicity and he encouraged owners to participate in bench shows as a means of bringing the breed before the public.

He also arranged for the club to hold its first licensed field trial in November in 1932, the second such event ever held in the United States. This trial had a Puppy Stake and an Open All-Age Stake for Chesapeakes only, as well as the country's first Open All-Age for all breeds.

Following this, a Specialty Field Trial was held (for Chesapeakes only) every year until 1942, when it was interrupted by World War II and not resumed until 1950. From that date on, the Specialty Field Trial was usually held in conjunction with the club's annual meeting.

Records kept from 1937 through 1949 are very sketchy, and there was little stimulation from club officers and very little activity among the dog owners. It was not until 1950, when William Hoard of Wisconsin was elected president, that the club again became alive and active. Since that time, each year has seen an increase in membership and at the end of 1978 there were over 800 members, representing every state of the Union, as well as Canada and abroad.

The present organization of the club is very efficient. All of the members of the Board of Directors are expected to take a definite responsibility, and head the standing committees. One director heads the Bench Show Committee, another oversees field trials and another concentrates

American Chesapeake Club Training Day. Teaching the dogs to "Down."

New Jersey Chesapeake Day, with instruction in the proper way to pose your dog in shows. — *Courtesy of Susan Cone.*

The happy winners at a Chesapeake Day picnic trial: Dan Szechenyi and Cub's Lightning Bolt, Norene Szechenyi and Cappy's Lady Go-Diver, and Marianne Ivey with Cub's Shogun of Juanita Bay.

1979 American Chesapeake Club president Kent Lowman with Mrs. Lowman and their three brood bitches: Ch. Crosswinds Flying Gee Bee, WD, Ch. Crosswinds Flying Echo, WD, and Ch. Crosswinds Flying Beryl, CD/WDX.

on Obedience activities. In addition, a Board member serves as head of the Membership Committee, another is in charge of the Working Dog Certificate records, and another supervises the OFA and CERF records.

The Board of Directors of our club has taken the position that since most large breeds of dogs suffer from the incidence of hip dysplasia, the only way it can be prevented and eliminated from the Chesapeake breed is to have all Chesapeake owners have x-rays taken of their dog's hips. These x-rays are sent to The Orthopedic Foundation of America and they have three of their qualified veterinarians examine every x-ray. If the dog's hips are unsound they will not issue one of their certificates. Breeders are urged to only mate dogs where both have the OFA approval.

Another stand the club has taken is that CERF certification is equally important. A CERF certificate will only be given to a dog who has been examined by a registered veterinarian ophthalmologist and the finding is that the dog's eyes have no cataracts nor any evidence of progressive retinal atrophy. Unfortunately, this, too, is a hereditary weakness found in many of the retriever breeds.

A few years ago the club felt it was important for Chesapeakes to demonstrate the fact that they still were working dogs. Consequently, the titles of Working Dog, and Working Dog Excellent were created. The club issues a certificate (WD or WDX) to dogs who have passed simple retrieving tests on land and water. The Regional Directors of the club hold these Working Dog and Working Dog Excellent tests'in many areas of the country.

Our Regional Directors' program was inaugurated about ten years ago, and we now have one or two club members serving in this capacity in almost every state. Their function is to be a source of information for club members in their area. In addition to keeping track of all local Chesapeake owners, they keep informed on available stud dogs and on any litters that have been bred.

Another of their functions is to hold Chesapeake Days, or practice sessions for the Chesapeake owners in their area. Anyone who brings his dog can receive instruction in retrieving, in showing, and in Obedience work. A great many members participate and as these are strictly informal sessions, anyone owning a Chesapeake is welcome to attend. These events have resulted in more of our dogs running in field trials and being entered at bench shows and Obedience trials. There is a great value in bringing hunting dogs to these events, for they must perform in the presence of other dogs, as they often must in the hunting field. It teaches the dog manners for when he is around a group of people and a group of dogs.

For the past ten years, this program has been under the supervision of Nancy Lowenthal, who has worked terribly hard on it and made it an unmitigated success.

Watching the baby. Crosswind's Kellett guards little Charlie Andersen, son of Jon and Carol Andersen of Highland Park, Illinois.

Marge Thornley's Kodiak is happy to baby-sit.

Home at the William Hoards—FC & AFC Wisconong Deerwood Trigger, with his girl friend, Susie of Wisconong.

Beautiful blonde Melody Martiniuk and her favorite pup. Melody is the daughter of the John Martiniuks of Tok, Alaska.

Anyone interested in joining the American Chesapeake Club can write to the American Kennel Club, 51 Madison Avenue, New York, NY 10010, for the address of the current Secretary. Dues are now $15 per year. New members must be sponsored by two club members and the initiation fee is $5. A membership includes receipt of the club bulletin, which is published six times a year. This newsletter offers a vast amount of information of interest to Chesapeake owners. It lists bench show wins, field trial results and Obedience placements, and includes Dogs at Stud, Dogs for Sale, and Puppies for Sale. Lists of the dogs who have received their OFA and CERF certificates are printed. News stories are included as well as several hunting tales. Most members eagerly look forward to receiving their copy.

The American Chesapeake Club is probably one of the most active and helpful breed clubs of today. Because of its interest and efficiency, American Kennel Club registrations of the breed have gone up every year and more and more people now own and love Chesapeake Bay Retrievers.

BIBLIOGRAPHY

ALL OWNERS of pure-bred dogs will benefit themselves and their dogs by enriching their knowledge of breeds and of canine care, training, breeding, psychology and other important aspects of dog management. The following list of books covers further reading recommended by judges, veterinarians, breeders, trainers and other authorities. Books may be obtained at the finer book stores and pet shops, or through Howell Book House Inc., publishers, New York.

BREED BOOKS

AFGHAN HOUND, Complete	Miller & Gilbert
AIREDALE, New Complete	Edwards
AKITA, Complete	Linderman & Funk
ALASKAN MALAMUTE, Complete	Riddle & Seeley
BASSET HOUND, Complete	Braun
BLOODHOUND, Complete	Brey & Reed
BOXER, Complete	Denlinger
BRITTANY SPANIEL, Complete	Riddle
BULLDOG, New Complete	Hanes
BULL TERRIER, New Complete	Eberhard
CAIRN TERRIER, Complete	Marvin
CHESAPEAKE BAY RETRIEVER, Complete	Cherry
CHIHUAHUA, Complete	Noted Authorities
COCKER SPANIEL, New	Kraeuchi
COLLIE, New	Official Publication of the Collie Club of America
DACHSHUND, The New	Meistrell
DALMATIAN, The	Treen
DOBERMAN PINSCHER, New	Walker
ENGLISH SETTER, New Complete	Tuck, Howell & Graef
ENGLISH SPRINGER SPANIEL, New	Goodall & Gasow
FOX TERRIER, New	Nedell
GERMAN SHEPHERD DOG, New Complete	Bennett
GERMAN SHORTHAIRED POINTER, New	Maxwell
GOLDEN RETRIEVER, New Complete	Fischer
GORDON SETTER, Complete	Look
GREAT DANE, New Complete	Noted Authorities
GREAT DANE, The—Dogdom's Apollo	Draper
GREAT PYRENEES, Complete	Strang & Giffin
IRISH SETTER, New Complete	Eldredge & Vanacore
IRISH WOLFHOUND, Complete	Starbuck
JACK RUSSELL TERRIER, Complete	Plummer
KEESHOND, New Complete	Cash
LABRADOR RETRIEVER, Complete	Warwick
LHASA APSO, Complete	Herbel
MASTIFF, History and Management of the	Baxter & Hoffman
MINIATURE SCHNAUZER, Complete	Eskrigge
NEWFOUNDLAND, New Complete	Chern
NORWEGIAN ELKHOUND, New Complete	Wallo
OLD ENGLISH SHEEPDOG, Complete	Mandeville
PEKINGESE, Quigley Book of	Quigley
PEMBROKE WELSH CORGI, Complete	Sargent & Harper
POODLE, New	Irick
POODLE CLIPPING AND GROOMING BOOK, Complete	Kalstone
ROTTWEILER, Complete	Freeman
SAMOYED, New Complete	Ward
SCOTTISH TERRIER, New Complete	Marvin
SHETLAND SHEEPDOG, The New	Riddle
SHIH TZU, Joy of Owning	Seranne
SHIH TZU, The (English)	Dadds
SIBERIAN HUSKY, Complete	Demidoff
TERRIERS, The Book of All	Marvin
WEIMARANER, Guide to the	Burgoin
WEST HIGHLAND WHITE TERRIER, Complete	Marvin
WHIPPET, Complete	Pegram
YORKSHIRE TERRIER, Complete	Gordon & Bennett

BREEDING

ART OF BREEDING BETTER DOGS, New	Onstott
BREEDING YOUR OWN SHOW DOG	Seranne
HOW TO BREED DOGS	Whitney
HOW PUPPIES ARE BORN	Prine
INHERITANCE OF COAT COLOR IN DOGS	Little

CARE AND TRAINING

COUNSELING DOG OWNERS, Evans Guide for	Evans
DOG OBEDIENCE, Complete Book of	Saunders
NOVICE, OPEN AND UTILITY COURSES	Saunders
DOG CARE AND TRAINING FOR BOYS AND GIRLS	Saunders
DOG NUTRITION, Collins Guide to	Collins
DOG TRAINING FOR KIDS	Benjamin
DOG TRAINING, Koehler Method of	Koehler
DOG TRAINING Made Easy	Tucker
GO FIND! Training Your Dog to Track	Davis
GUARD DOG TRAINING, Koehler Method of	Koehler
MOTHER KNOWS BEST—The Natural Way to Train Your Dog	Benjamin
OPEN OBEDIENCE FOR RING, HOME AND FIELD, Koehler Method of	Koehler
STONE GUIDE TO DOG GROOMING FOR ALL BREEDS	Stone
SUCCESSFUL DOG TRAINING, The Pearsall Guide to	Pearsall
TEACHING DOG OBEDIENCE CLASSES—Manual for Instructors	Volhard & Fisher
TOY DOGS, Kalstone Guide to Grooming All	Kalstone
TRAINING THE RETRIEVER	Kersley
TRAINING TRACKING DOGS, Koehler Method of	Koehler
TRAINING YOUR DOG—Step by Step Manual	Volhard & Fisher
TRAINING YOUR DOG TO WIN OBEDIENCE TITLES	Morsell
TRAIN YOUR OWN GUN DOG, How to	Goodall
UTILITY DOG TRAINING, Koehler Method of	Koehler
VETERINARY HANDBOOK, Dog Owner's Home	Carlson & Giffin

GENERAL

AMERICAN KENNEL CLUB 1884-1984—A Source Book	American Kennel Club
CANINE TERMINOLOGY	Spira
COMPLETE DOG BOOK, The	Official Publication of American Kennel Club
DOG IN ACTION, The	Lyon
DOG BEHAVIOR, New Knowledge of	Pfaffenberger
DOG JUDGE'S HANDBOOK	Tietjen
DOG PEOPLE ARE CRAZY	Riddle
DOG PSYCHOLOGY	Whitney
DOGSTEPS, The New	Elliott
DOG TRICKS	Haggerty & Benjamin
EYES THAT LEAD—Story of Guide Dogs for the Blind	Tucker
FRIEND TO FRIEND—Dogs That Help Mankind	Schwartz
FROM RICHES TO BITCHES	Shattuck
HAPPY DOG/HAPPY OWNER	Siegal
IN STITCHES OVER BITCHES	Shattuck
JUNIOR SHOWMANSHIP HANDBOOK	Brown & Mason
OUR PUPPY'S BABY BOOK (blue or pink)	
SUCCESSFUL DOG SHOWING, Forsyth Guide to	Forsyth
TRIM, GROOM & SHOW YOUR DOG, How to	Saunders
WHY DOES YOUR DOG DO THAT?	Bergman
WILD DOGS in Life and Legend	Riddle
WORLD OF SLED DOGS, From Siberia to Sport Racing	Coppinger